Memories from a
Russian Kitchen

Memories

FROM A

Russian Kitchen

from shtetl to golden land

Compiled and edited by
ROSALIE SOGOLOW
Illustrated by
BONNIE STONE

FITHIAN PRESS / SANTA BARBARA / 1996

For our grandchildren—
that they may know us.

Published by Fithian Press
A division of Daniel and Daniel, Publishers, Inc.
Post Office Box 1525
Santa Barbara, CA 93102

Book design: Eric Larson

LIBRARY OF CONGRESS CATALOGING-IN-PUBLICATION DATA
Memories from a Russian kitchen : from shtetl to golden land / compiled and edited by
Rosalie Sogolow : illustrated by Bonnie Stone
    p.   cm.
    ISBN 1-56474-148-6 (cloth : alk. paper)
    1. Cookery, Russian. 2. Cookery, Jewish. 3. Former Soviet republics—Social life
and customs. 4. Short stories, Soviet. I. Sogolow, Rosalie, date.
TX 723.3.M45 1996
641.5947—dc20   95-23418
                                                                      CIP

And I am host to the invisible throngs
Who fill my reveries and build my songs.

—ALEXANDER PUSHKIN, 1833

CONTENTS

Zakooski (Appetizers)   24

RECIPES: Black Radish Appetizer, Stuffed Eggs, Ground Herring, Minced Herring (Farshmak), Gefilte Fish (Stuffed Fish), Pashlet (Poultry Liver Pâté), Marinated Cabbage Appetizer, Eggplant Caviar, Armenian Bean Appetizer, Stuffed Eggplant, Smoked Salmon Vinaigrette, Cucumber and Yogurt Dip

Pervoye Blyudo (Salads)   44

RECIPES: Salad Olivier (Sliced Cold Chicken with Potato), Carrot Salad, Carrot Salad II, Beet Salad, Beet Salad II, Chicken–Vegetable Layered Salad, Russian Salad (Vinaigrette), Tenderness Salad, Satsivi (Chicken Salad with Walnuts), Vegetable Salad (Vinaigrette), Salad Mimosa, Layered Potato Salad, Herring Under a Blanket, Salad Dressing for Fresh Fruit, Corn and Mushroom Salad, Cucumber Salad with Sour Cream, Meechdah (Dream Salad), Spinach and Yogurt Salad, Green Cabbage Salad

Vtoroye Blyudo (Soups)　　　68

RECIPES: Matvei's Chicken Soup, Solyanka (Soup with pickles and various meats), Tanov (Armenian Soup), Kharcho (Georgian Beef and Rice Soup), Sauerkraut Soup, Borscht (Cold Beet Soup), Borscht II, Green Borscht, Borscht III, Borscht IV, Mushroom and Barley Soup, Bean–Barley–Vegetable Soup, Vegetable–Split Pea Soup

Izdeliye iz Testa (Dumplings and Noodles)　　88

RECIPES: Vareniki, Lokshen Kugel (Noodle Pudding), Cottage Cheese Pudding (Kugel), Plum Kugel, Potato Kugel, Galushki (Dumplings), Apple Galushki, Pelmeni, Matzo Balls with Beef Filling, Potato Dumplings with Chicken or Meat, Soup Mandlen (Soup Nuts)

Pirogi and Piroshki (Filled Pies)　　112

RECIPES: Samsa (Piroshki with Pumpkin), Pirog (Large Pie), Grandma's Knishes, Meat Pie / Mushroom Pie, Beliashi (Tatar Meat Pies), Kulebiaka (A large flat pie), Cabbage Pie

Blini (And Other Russian Pancakes)   130

RECIPES: Carrot Pancakes, Blini (Russian Pancakes), Blinchiky (Blini or Blintzes), Potato Pancakes (Latkes), Cabbage Pancakes, Buttermilk Fritters (Oladushki), Apple Pancakes, Sour Cream Pancakes, Chremsel

Garneer (Side Dishes)   152

RECIPES: Pilaf with Almonds and Raisins, Eggplant Slices, Sonya's Vegetable Surprise, Eggplant and Sauce, Potato–Onion Casserole, Passover Carrot Pudding, Steamed Zucchini, Mamaliga, Vegetable Ragout, Baked Cabbage Casserole

Glavnoye Blyudo (Entrees) 168

RECIPES: Beef Stew in Sweet and Sour Sauce, Myeena (Liver and Potato
Pudding), Beef Stroganoff, Pomsteak (Fried Meat), Shashlik, Beetochkee
(Chicken Patties with Mushrooms), Dolma Golubsi (Grape Leaves
Stuffed with Meat), Combined Dolma, Golubtsi (Stuffed Cabbage), Fish
Fritters, Yazeek (Tongue in Aspic), Lamb Moussaka, Tongue with
Tomato Sauce and Vegetables, Pozharsky Rissoles (Chicken Cutlets),
Tabakah (Game Hens), Chicken with White Sauce, Braised Beef in a
Pot, Chicken Paprikas with Dumplings, Kartoffilnee Cutlyete (Potato
Cutlets) with Mushroom Sauce, Mushroom Sauce, Cousin Sarah's Sweet
and Sour Meatballs, Gutcha's Cholent, Kotlyete (Beef Patties)

Khleba, Napeetki, Kasha
(Breads, Beverages, Kasha
—and other good things) 196

RECIPES: Challah, Kasha (Buckwheat Groats), Baked Kasha with Wal-
nuts, Kasha Varnishkas (Kasha with Bows), Kasha with Mushrooms,
Japanese Tempura—Russian Oladee (Fritters), Barley and Mushroom
Casserole, Passover Bagels, Compote of Dried Fruits, Mikhail's Favorite
Topping for Waffles, Stawberry Kissel, Varenya (Radishes in Honey),
Kvass

RECIPES: Grandmother's Napoleon, Rugelah, Apple Cake, Mazurka (Raisin–Nut Cake), Lekhah (Honey Cake), Lekhah II, Sharlotka (Sponge Cake), Sharlotka with Apples, Torte "Maximka," Prague's Torte, Megobrik (Honey–Nut Cake with Raisins), Strawberry Fantasy, Fruit Coffee Cake, Flaky Torte, Mandelbreit (Almond Slices), Cousin Sarah's Mandel Bread (Almond Slices), Chocolate Torte, Lemony Apple Meringue Cake, Cranberry Fruit Roll, Black and White Sour Cream Torte, Pteetchnye Moloko (Bird Milk Torte), Hvorvest (Bows), Kartoshka (No-Bake Chocolate Cookies), Rozachki ("Roses"—Cream Puffs), Fruit and Nut Cake, Nuga (Nut Cake), Torte Annetchka (3 layers), Buttermilk Cake, Lemon Pastry, Strudel, Grandma's Strudel, Cookies with Condensed Milk, Russian Pastry Bites, Lilichka's Cake, Cherry Meringue Pie

Preface

THIS BOOK represents a journey into the past. It is a sampling of recollections and favorite ethnic dishes, preserved for posterity by students of the Senior English as a Second Language classes of Jewish Family Service of Santa Clara County, California. What began as an English project and collection of recipes soon took on a life of its own. Our students are unique. They are babushkas and dyedushkas (grandmothers and grandfathers), whose lives span nearly the entire twentieth century. Mostly from the former Soviet Union, ranging in age from sixty to ninety, their collective experience encompasses two world wars, and the remarkable transition from a shtetl existence and tsarist monarchy to a totalitarian regime. They have witnessed, first hand, the painful birth and establishment of communism, and seen with their own eyes the incredible dissolution of an entire country and way of life as they had known it for the preceding seventy-five years! They have had countless experiences that we can only read about with amazement and wonder.

Working as a volunteer teacher over the past eight years, I have been constantly amazed at their remarkable spirit and fortitude and have marveled at the stories they have shared. Coming to a new world and bringing with them only the few items which they were allowed to squeeze into two small suitcases, they were forced to leave behind so many of their lives' most meaningful possessions. What they did bring were their memories. I felt a very strong need to capture these valuable recollections and am thankful for the opportunity to have done so. Not only was this project a wonderful way to improve their language skills, but a productive vehicle for reporting and preserving their eyewitness accounts of a rich history.

We started by collecting favorite recipes, some handed down from their own mothers and grandmothers. But the personal stories that emerged from our class discussions gave us a glimpse of a life that was very different from our own—one that could have belonged to many of us, had our parents or grandparents not left their homeland when they did. Some of the stories are poignant, some humorous. But all of them are revealing and provocative in their own way. As our writers became accustomed to expressing some of these long forgotten memories, some very deeply personal and emotional accounts began to come forth. As Jews living in a country with a long history of anti-semitism, many of their stories understandably portray vivid descriptions of events involving the persecution and discrimination which they and their families suffered over their lifetimes. Even in their impoverishment, Eastern European Jews managed to create a remarkable culture. Under the tyranny of the tsars and in spite of persecution, their spirit and traditions somehow survived.

Happy memories of childhood often intertwine with other more frightening ones, such as the frequent pogroms by roving gangs of terrorists in which thousands were robbed, brutally murdered or seriously injured. These descriptions, together with the moving recollections of the trials endured during time of war, and the general hardships involved in the often frustrating process of everyday survival, present a panorama of emotions and revealing portraits of another world. For a while, I wondered if it was appropriate to combine these accounts with something as mundane as cooking and recipes. And yet, as bad as things sometimes got, life did go on. Even under the harshest conditions, young people still exhibited the exuberance of youth, people still fell in love, and the daily practices of their lives somehow went on. There was still music or theater or ballet to bring a breath of fresh air to their existence, and humor has always been a saving grace. Being able to poke fun at themselves and their troubles somehow made it all more tolerable. Holidays were observed, albeit often in secret, and people took pleasure in whatever ways they could. Special foods are a part of our memories, too.

Food has traditionally played such a big part in our lives. From the time we come together to celebrate the birth of a child, to the time we come together to honor the memory of those who have died, along with birthdays, holidays, weddings, bar mitzvahs and all the other lifetime events in between, we celebrate with food. Food is more than sustenance. It is a way to maintain and enjoy our heritage and the cultural diversity all around us. It is a way to come together and join the past to the future. Hopefully, our grandchildren will someday savor the legacy of our dishes and our remembrances and pass them down to future generations.

One of our challenges was to overcome the age-old "shutt-arein" ("so much of this," or "a little bit of that") method, so commonly used. We had to convert to a more conventional and precise form of measurement, preferred by those of us attempting to duplicate these delicacies without the benefit of their creator's presence. Also, the Russian preference for using terms like "a glass" of flour (but no conformity as to the size of the glass), and the use of their own metric system (i.e. 200g of butter, etc.), presented additional problems. Of course, we also had many a chuckle over instructions like "cut up the meat and beat it!" It certainly was a learning experience for all of us!

Although a number of recipes found in this book are quite old and have been included for the sake of preservation and interest rather than practicality, most of the dishes are commonly served and enjoyed in Russian homes today. Health-conscious cooks may wish to substitute some ingredients which are lower in fat content or cholesterol, but for the sake of authenticity, we have presented the recipes as originally recorded. Unfortunately, some of the ingredients that are commonly used in many Russian dishes are different than the ones available here. Certain berries, fish, types of flour, and especially things like sour cream and milk products simply are not the same here. But our cooks have been making modifications since their arrival on our shores, and assure us that it's still possible to prepare these delicious dishes, making a few necessary substitutions. Throughout the book you will find that most of the recipes where American cooks would normally use baking powder list a combination of baking soda and vinegar instead. Apparently, baking powder is not available in Russia, and so this combination serves the same purpose. (When mixed together, the vinegar activates the soda.) Also, in converting from metric measurement to our standard form, odd amounts have been rounded off: i.e., instead of 2 cups and 2 teaspoons of flour, we have simply listed "about 2 cups of flour." As in all recipes that have been handed down, some judgment is usually required. Good cooks all over the world have had to use their "eye" somewhat.

We should also point out that these are *Russian* recipes, some of which are also Jewish ones. Though we do not claim that this is a kosher book (the world our contributors lived in was not a kosher world), we have made every effort to follow traditional Jewish dietary laws and have suggested alternatives wherever possible: IMO or sour cream substitute, mocha mix or other non-dairy creamers, margarine instead of butter, and so on.

I have derived much personal satisfaction as a teacher working with such remarkable students. They, too, are my "family," and I continue to learn from them every day. We try to teach communication and survival skills, but this endeavor went beyond the usual curriculum. It was a labor of love...a gift to the community and to all those who will come after them. I thank them for sharing their feelings and experiences so we can all benefit from the wisdom of their years.

It is with great pride that we present our stories and favorite dishes. As you make your way through the sections, we hope you will begin to understand a little of the people and the places from whence they came and will take pleasure in sharing the memories from our Russian kitchens.

ROSALIE SOGOLOW
Teacher and Principal
Senior ESL Program
Jewish Family Service of Santa Clara County

Acknowledgements

"Spaseeba, Bolshoya!"—Thank you, thank you, thank you....

My extraordinary students have become my friends and *mishpochah* (extended family). They have enriched my life immeasurably, and by sharing their experiences, have allowed me a precious glimpse into their world. There would be no book without them.

Of course, we could not have succeeded without the hard work of all our volunteer teachers and assistants. Teachers Pat Markman, Raymond Kopp, Roberta Bernstein and Yeugenia Romm and teaching assistants Vivian Snyder, Ruth Schwartz, Bill Marlin, Tamara Fayner, Rita Gorlin, Lucy Kutikova, Mort Needle and Sonya Slutsker worked enthusiastically from start to finish. They spent many hours, along with me, in the compilation, translation, testing, tasting and all the details that went into its creation. I would also like to thank Mark Chyorny, Natalie Brodskaya, Inna Eydus, Vickie Epstein and Jenny Khorol-Sharal for their valuable assistance in the translation of some of our stories.

We are most grateful to artist Bonnie Stone for creating the wonderful images seen on these pages. Her beautiful drawings help us to present a visual, as well as gastronomical and emotional journey into our new emigrés' cultural heritage.

An extra big "thank you" goes to Vivian Snyder and Ruth Schwartz for their painstaking checking and typing of our recipes, a particularly challenging job. Thanks, also, to my friend, Michelle Gabriel, for her helpful advice in our efforts to get this manuscript published, and to my music consultant, Marilyn Handloff. And we are most appreciative of the legal advice and assistance so graciously given by Mr. Ronald Yin and the firm of Limbach & Limbach.

Most of the recipes in this book have been tested by members of Brandeis University National Women's Committee, Santa Clara Valley chapter, as their contribution to this project. We appreciate their generosity and perseverance in this undertaking. Their comments and suggestions proved extremely helpful.

The encouragement and enthusiasm of my children, Wendi Fast and Larry Sogolow, were more appreciated than they will ever know. I would like to dedicate my efforts to them and to my grandsons, Joseph and Jacob, and all of our grandchildren to come, for whom this historical treasure was intended. To my husband, Sid, goes my everlasting love and gratitude for his opinions and support, and for sharing his computer with me for the hundreds of hours this project required.

And finally we are greatly indebted to our many supporters—and especially our angels, Areta Stadler and David Lustig, whose gracious generosity enabled our dreams to become a reality. We are also grateful to Carol Gopin, Rosa Levit (who gets a big kiss and a hug "from the bottom of our Russian hearts"), Zoya Lazer, Vlada Gelfond, Galina Chyorny, Tamara Saidian, and all the J.F.S. staff for their guidance and support. We are hopeful that the proceeds from this book will help continue the vital assistance that this agency provides in so many ways to our newcomers and the community as a whole.

—R.S.

Introduction:
The Place that was Home....

RODINA—Russians call it "The Motherland." Through the centuries, the recurring struggles against foreign intrusion and homegrown tyranny formed the basis of a distinct "Russian" character. Americans usually refer to anyone or anything from the former Soviet Union as Russian. But today it is much more complex than that. For the purposes of our book, when we say "Russian," we are still talking about all of the former republics. However, they are now independent states and known presently as the Commonwealth of Independent States. In present-day terminology, all those former republics aligning themselves with the autonomous state of Russia are known as the Russian Federation. However, each region is distinctly different and striving to preserve its own identity. There are over fifty different languages spoken, though most children learn the Russian language in school.

A little historical background might prove useful in better understanding the diversity and turmoil surrounding the arrival and existence of Jews in this vast and fascinating land. (For a more detailed chronology, see "A Brief History" on page 261).

Jews had lived in Russia for hundreds of years, but when Catherine the Great took most of Poland in the 1700s, Russia gained a large Jewish community. Where did they come from? Though the history of the diaspora is uncertain, they probably arrived indirectly from Germany, the Mediterranean and the Turkish influx that had spread into many parts of southeastern Europe. In the nineteenth century the Russian empire contained, by far, the largest concentration of Jews in the world—over five million people. Since they were neither Slavs nor Christians, they were automatically distrusted. Like any other nonconformist element in the tsar's empire, they had to be contained. And so, in 1833, the tsar decreed that from that time on Jews must be confined within a specific area known as the "Pale of Settlement."

The notorious Pale was not really a ghetto. It was a vast territory encompassing a large part of the Ukraine, including all the Black Sea ports, the western provinces known as Byelorussia (or White Russia), Lithuania, and a large portion of what had once been Poland. In other words, the areas where most of the Jews already lived. The reason for this restriction was to keep them from migrating into traditional Orthodox northern Russia, although a good number had previously settled in both Moscow and St. Petersburg by this time. But Tsar Nicolas I decided that isolating the Jews was not enough. Even though he had the largest standing army in the world, he nevertheless insisted on drafting young Jewish boys for terms of twenty-five years or more. The purpose of this was not primarily military, but an attempt to wean them from their homes, their traditions, their religion, and their values, and to turn them into Russian Orthodox believers. It is estimated that approximately fifty thousand Jewish boys were lost to this policy in the middle of the nineteenth century.

Though most Jews were strictly forbidden to live in big cities, exceptions were made for those who had served in the tsar's army for the required twenty-five years. These privileged people were able to raise their families away from the confinement of the shtetl. But for the most part, Jews lived in their own towns and villages where their own Yiddish language was usually spoken. They were most often merchants or craftsmen such as tailors, shoemakers or blacksmiths, though some supported themselves by farming the land. They were given the "privilege" of paying higher taxes and encouraged to convert.

During the nineteenth century, Russia was ruled by five Romanov tsars. Their policy toward the Jews was difficult to fathom. They pushed them toward agriculture, but denied them the right to own land. They wanted to make them more "Russian," but restricted them to the Pale. How did Jews survive without a state of their own or a government to protect them? They invented their own form of government, known as *hevrat* or "societies." There was a society for orphans, for funerals, for marriage, for education, to settle disputes, and anything else that might be necessary. If there was a problem, people went to the proper society. Each had its own rules, and a rabbi or two could always be found to settle any dispute that happened to arise. From 1881 to 1923, two million Jews came to the United States from Poland, Russia, Romania and other Eastern European countries. That was the beginning of the first wave of immigration. They were running from oppression, poverty and discrimination. They were running to find a better life—in America, Palestine or other promising places.

After the October Revolution in 1917, everything changed completely. All private property was nationalized. A bloody civil war raged until 1921. The Red Army supported the revolutionary forces. The White Army wanted to restore the tsar's empire. The Ukrainians wanted independence and fought the Bolsheviks. (Petlura's gang of nationalists roamed the countryside terrorizing Jews and was part of this group.) The peasants revolted and wanted to take the land back from the landlords. The Germans came to occupy the Ukraine. And the Jews were caught in the middle of it all.

On the other side of the coin, giving the land to the peasants and "liberating" all the people was an appealing concept. The Bolshevik movement did, in effect, benefit Russian Jews enormously, too. The Bolsheviks removed all the restrictions imposed upon them by the tsars. The universities were opened to them, as was the Communist party. Jobs became available, and Jews took advantage of the situation. They poured out of the *shtetlach* en masse. They headed for the big cities, first in Byelorussia and the Ukraine and then to Moscow and Leningrad. In a way, what happened in the Soviet Union in the 1920s and 1930s paralleled what happened to those who had left earlier to cross the ocean. When they left the *shtetlach*, they changed their language from Yiddish to Russian, just as Jews coming to America changed from Yiddish to English. They changed their clothes, their education, their morals and their occupations. They wanted to become like everyone else.

Unfortunately, this more liberal atmosphere was destined to end. Groomed for leadership by Lenin, Joseph Stalin assumed control of the Communist party from 1922 to 1953. It became government policy during his regime to forbid Jews access to universities or advancement in their jobs. His repressive policies and reign of terror affected every aspect of their lives. Germany's invasion of Russia in 1941 caught Stalin by surprise. Hitler had promised non-aggression and trade in the 1939 German–Soviet Pact. The German army was eventually turned back—but at a cost of about twenty-five million Soviet lives. There wasn't a person alive in Russia who was not affected by that war, including Russian Jews. Besides displacement and extreme hardship, nearly every family experienced the loss of relatives and friends.

A fundamental dilemma of Russian Jews in the last decades has been that they have been identified legally and socially as Jews, even though they are culturally, by and large, Russians. Ironically, the Soviet state actually played a big part in preserving Jewish identity through their insistence that Jews be so identified on all legal documents. Socially they were regarded as Jews, no matter how Russianized they were in their culture.

After years of economic stagnation, Mikhail Gorbachev emerged in 1985 advocating *glasnost* (openness) and *perestroika* (restructuring.) These policies, plus the reduction of global tensions, won him the Nobel Peace Prize in 1990. But these same policies also had the effect of resurrecting long dormant feelings of ethnic pride and led to a rebirth of nationalism. They spelled the beginning of the end for the seventy-five-year reign of communism.

In the aftermath of the earth-shaking coup of 1991 that brought an astonishing end to the Communist era, the Motherland is left reeling in a sea of uncertainty. Boris Yeltsin enjoys the distinction of being the first democratically elected president of the new "Russia." The old USSR is no more. In its place is a loosely knit commonwealth, unsure of how to function in an unfamiliar world. It is a country struggling under the weight of a teetering political machine. The people want desperately to reap the benefits that independence and a market economy promise to provide, but they are inexperienced and just aren't sure how to go about it. The dream of a new democracy is fresh, but the unbounded optimism is gone.

With the end of the cold war came a loosening of restrictions on immigration. The window opened, and for the first time in decades Russia's Jews were allowed to leave. After years of waiting for permission and repeated refusals, during which time their jobs were automatically lost, the outpouring experienced nearly a century before again began to take place. But with the new-found freedoms of the new commonwealth, the specter of anti-Semitism has again reared its head. The transition to a new and unfamiliar market economy has been slow and painful. Whenever people are hungry and times are hard, it is convenient to find a scapegoat. Many fear that things will get worse before they get better and that the window, once again, will slam shut.

Our aging emigrés have watched the tides of change. They have made the journey that began in the *shtetlach* of the Pale and only recently ended in America, the place that their ancestors thought of as the *Goldena Medina* (the Golden Land). They came for the same reason that their predecessors came— to find a better life for their children and grandchildren. They are safe now. But they worry about family and friends still left behind and hope that history will not repeat itself. Meanwhile, there are the memories...of the *Rodina*...the Motherland...the place that was home.

This is a book about memories,
They tell of our lives and our times;
They're all about people and places
That continue to live in our minds;
It's also a book about cooking,
The foods we've enjoyed through the years;
Foods that have given us pleasure,
Through laughter and sorrow and tears.
So, what is this cookbook, exactly?
It's a book for your hearts and your hands;
We hope that you all will enjoy yourselves
With foods from our faraway lands.

A Jewish pike—*gefilte fish*,
A European omelette dish,
Dumplings, potatoes, a Russian meat jelly,
Our very own international deli!
Add to that...a piece of herring,
A glass of vodka—for laughter and sharing;
Our stories are old—our recipes are, too...
We wish good health and appetite
To every one of you!

—ESFIR DYNKINA
Translation by Inna Eydus and Rosalie Sogolow

Memories from a
Russian Kitchen

Zakooski

(Appetizers; literally, "little bites")

All things must have a beginning, and so, too, with our tales. They are presented here in random fashion—a smorgasbord of snapshots, intertwined with the dishes we wish to share.

Our meal begins with the first course…to whet the appetite, a precursor of that which is yet to come. Begin the journey with us, with our *zakooski*—our "little bites" of life.

Some Things Never Change

Esfir Dynkina
Technical designer, St. Petersburg

I was born in Latvia, in Dvinsk. It's called Daugavpils now. I don't remember anything about this town. I was only a little child when I lived there. In 1915, during the First World War, my parents moved to St. Petersburg. We went to my grandparents' home.

In Russia at that time, there was a monarchy with Tsar Nicolas II. I remember his birthday. Everything was perfectly illuminated on all the streets. There were beautiful fireworks, and many flags with the emperor's portraits. Steamers were also illuminated on the rivers. Everything sparkled. The tables were covered with drinks and food for all the people on the streets. The tsar knew that the Russian people liked to drink. I think it was the last birthday of the emperor.

I grew up, studied and worked in St. Petersburg/Leningrad. My favorite month was June. June days are long and nights are short. The long evenings are called "white nights." During the late evening or night when everyone was sleeping, my husband and I often took a ride on bicycles to the suburb of Pushkin. It's a wonderful town. Before the revolution, it was called "Tsar's Village." It was the emperor's residence. Nicolas II abdicated his throne in this town. The poet Pushkin and his friends studied there at Lycee. Close to this building stands a monument to him. He's sitting on a bench and reading. You enter this town through Egypt's gates. The town isn't large. There are beautiful palaces and houses. The house where Pushkin lived is there. Inside the house was a large portrait of his wife, Natalie. She was a beauty. The main palace, called "Kathrine's," is large, and there is a perfect park there. Most buildings which were ruined during the war were restored and are now museums.

Many things have changed since the days of the tsar, but some things never change. There are still white nights in June, and Russian people still like to drink vodka and read the poetry of Pushkin.

The Price of a Black Radish

ELENA TSYNMAN
Music teacher, St. Petersburg

It happened in 1942 in the time of World War II. I lived in Tashkent with the parents of my husband, my stepdaughter and baby son. One day, when I came to the conservatory where I worked, I received an unexpected allowance of 400 rubles. I was a postgraduate student, and it was a yearly stipend for books. But after the war started, we gave up hope of ever receiving it.

I went home joyfully. I dreamt of how I would pay my debts and buy food and coal for my family. On the way, I stopped at a bazaar. I saw a black radish and decided to buy it. I took out fifty rubles and paid ten rubles for the radish. But when I put the change in my bag, I saw that all the money had disappeared. 350 rubles had been stolen from me! The woman who was next to me disappeared also. I came home with a black radish which cost me 360 rubles. It was my budget for a month!

The Russian proverb says, "Horseradish is not sweeter than the black radish." But my black radish was more bitter than the horseradish!

Black Radish Appetizer

ELENA TSYNMAN

My grandmother used to serve this for Friday night dinner, but I make it any time. She and my aunts liked to use "grebbinis" (chicken fat), but these days I usually use vegetable oil for a healthier dish. It is good served with bread or crackers or as a garnish for potatoes.

Peel and grate coarsely 3 medium-sized black radishes.
Add a little salt to taste.
Chop 1 medium onion.
Fry the onion in vegetable oil or chicken fat.
Cool the onion and mix it with the black radish.
Serves 6–8.

The Parade *and*
The Train Robbery

Boris Altshuller
Plant director, Vilnius, Lithuania

My name is Boris Altshuller, and I am seventy-seven years old. I was born in a small city in the Ukraine near Kiev. There were a lot of events in my life that deserve to be told. But perhaps the present generation would have trouble believing that we lived and worked under such difficult conditions. Some of my memories are so bad and so tragic, that I would prefer not to talk about them. So, I will tell about two incidents that happened in my very early years.

The Parade

The first incident occurred when I was two years old, so I will tell you about it from my mother's words. It was in 1919, at the time of the Civil War, when changes of power in our cities happened all too often. (The White Army, the Red Army, Petlura's Ukrainian nationalists, etc.). And every time, when the power changed, there was a big battle, and then the victorious army entered the city.

After one such battle, the White troops (supporters of the tsar) marched into the city. The windows of our house faced the main street. There was a parade march of the winning soldiers, accompanied by a brass band. In front of the troops marched the Cossack Cavalry Unit of General Shcuro. This general was known as an organizer of Jewish pogroms and murderer of Jews. The Cossacks passed through the street, dressed in felt cloaks with special fur hats on their heads. There were daggers with silver handles on the belts. They were riding horses and looked very brave.

My mother was a young woman, and she was curious to see such entertainment. She was holding me in her arms, when a Cossack officer riding on our side of the street saw the typical Jewish face of my mother, with her child. He pulled out a gun and shot twice. The first bullet flew by, only an inch from my head. When he fired again, the second bullet also barely missed my mother. As the parade continued on, she stood frozen to the spot, hardly daring to breathe. Luck was with us that day. My mother could only think of how relieved she was that by some miracle we were still alive.

The Train Robbery

The second episode occurred in 1924. I was seven years old, and I remember very clearly what happened. My parents went to Moscow to visit their relatives, and took me with them. We had a good time there. I was taken to the Jewish theatre for the first time, and I still remember that the play was *King Lear* by Shakespeare—in Yiddish.

With good feelings from the time we spent in Moscow, we were returning home. We traveled by train, which passed through the deep forest on its way. At that time, there were a lot of bandit gangs, based in the forest. They called themselves "Greens," and their plan was to attack the passing trains and rob the passengers. As we crossed the wooded area, the people inside the train suddenly became very nervous. My parents pushed me to the floor and covered me with their bodies. Other people put themselves on top of us, and I couldn't understand why they pressed me so hard. But then, the windows exploded, and bullets began to fly through the car. The train was being fired on from both sides.

The attackers killed the locomotive engineer and his assistant and began boarding the train. Before the train stopped, one of the passengers, a Red Army officer, pulled out his gun and began to shoot back, but soon realized that it was useless. He quickly hid his weapon under the seat and tore away the shoulder straps from his uniform. When the train came to a stop, the doors opened and the armed bandits appeared. They had sacks fastened to their belts in which to throw the valuables they would take from the passengers.

The first thing they wanted to know was, "Who was shooting?" and "Where is the gun?" They threatened to kill everyone if they didn't find out. Well, the defender turned out to be a very brave man. He pulled out his gun, and told them that he was the one. Then, in front of my eyes, he was shot instantly. And then they started to rob the people. They took off all the earrings, rings, coins, cigarette cases—even the gold teeth they knocked out from people's jaws. We carried a lot of things that we had bought in Moscow. There were gifts our relatives had given us, and also things for my school. All these things were taken out and loaded on carts, with horses harnessed and ready to go.

By this time, somehow, the officials at the next big station were informed about the attack. A cavalry unit was sent to crush the bandits. They jumped out from the forest and fired at the departing men with machine guns. In a short time, their job was done, and the "Greens" were defeated. Our baggage remained on the carts, and we were told to drag our things back into the railway cars. A new crew was sent, and eventually, in two to three hours, we continued on our way. One more interesting thing I remember from this story is that when the bandits were taking our things (rings, money, etc.), my father kept silent. But when they tried to take his cigarettes, he told them, "No! I won't give you my cigarettes!" The bandits were so astonished, they actually gave them back and said absolutely nothing!

Stuffed Eggs

STALINA GUTMAN

10 eggs, hard-boiled
1 carrot, finely grated
1 small onion, minced
½ tsp prepared mustard
Butter or oil for sauté

Mayonnaise to taste
Salt to taste
Dill, chopped, to taste
10 small cherry tomatoes

Cut hard-boiled eggs in half lengthwise. Remove yolks and set aside.
In small amount of butter, sauté onions and grated carrots over low heat until onions are golden brown. Mash egg yolks with fork and add to the onion–carrot mixture. Add mayonnaise, salt, and dill to taste. Mix thoroughly.

Fill egg halves with the prepared filling. Arrange eggs on a platter with filling up. Place a tiny bit of mayonnaise on top.

Slice cherry tomatoes in half. Remove juice and seeds. Place a tomato half on top of each egg. The mayonnaise should hold the tomato in place.

Dill can be scattered between eggs on platter to decorate.

Refrigerate until ready to serve.

Where Did We Come From?

Russia • The Ukraine • Byelorussia
Moldavia • Estonia • Latvia
Armenia • Azerbaijan • Uzbekhistan

Some of us have also come from:

Iran • Israel • Poland
Romania • The former Yugoslavia

⊞ Ground Herring

LILIYA POPOVA

1 schmaltz herring, skinned and boned	1 cup milk or water
1 onion	½ cup butter, softened
1 apple, cored and peeled	⅓ tsp black pepper
¼ cup white bread crumbs	

Preheat oven to 350°. Place herring in milk or water and soak for 2 hours. Bake the onion in the oven for about 10 minutes or until soft. Put the bread crumbs in the milk or water for a few minutes. Remove the bread from the liquid and drain well.

Dry the herring on paper towels. Using a grinder or food processor, combine the herring, bread, apple, onion, soft butter and pepper. Refrigerate until ready to serve.

⊞ Minced Herring (Farshmak)

STALINA GUTMAN

1 large schmaltz herring, skinned and boned	2 tsp sunflower oil
2 onions	1 tsp vinegar
1 egg, hard-boiled	1 tsp sugar
1 small sourdough roll, day-old	Salt to taste
1 tart apple, peeled and cored	

Dip a dry sourdough roll in water, remove and press the water out.

In food processor, mince together herring, 1 onion, roll, and apple until smooth but not pureed. Add sunflower oil, vinegar, sugar and salt to taste.

Place mixture in a bowl. Sprinkle mashed egg yolk over the top.

Slice 1 onion into very thin rings and arrange over all. Serve.

"When my father was a student at the university, he was poor. His favorite meal was potatoes with herring. It became his habit. And so, for years, we often ate potatoes with butter and herring for breakfast on Saturday mornings."

—RITA GORLIN

Tradition

ISAAC KASHLINSKY
Electrical engineer, Kharkov, Ukraine

Sometimes an ordinary event arouses vague feelings, a sense that something like that has happened before. While watching and listening to the musical *Fiddler on the Roof* recently, I felt a sensation of coming back to my youngest years in the town of Vilneetsa, in the Ukraine. The familiar melodies, the costumes and dances, the views of a small village—all that put me in a reminiscent mood. Fighting tears, I recalled my grandparents....

My grandmother was a short, lean, prematurely gray and stooped woman with a somewhat hoarse voice. She was deeply religious, always keeping kosher and observing the Sabbath. She never missed Shabbos services in the synagogue. If not doing her numerous household chores, she would read and re-read the book of prayers. My grandfather was a tall, bearded man with strict gray eyes. A smile rarely touched his lips. A very quiet man, he seldom spoke to anyone, even to me. As I recall, he served as a part-time cantor in our small synagogue.

I lived near my grandparents. Both of them usually spoke only Yiddish, though to me they used a mixture of Yiddish and Ukrainian. That is where I learned to understand the Yiddish language. They lived in a two-room flat in an old brick house. One room served as a living and dining room. It had one window which faced the brick wall of the building next door. The other room was a bedroom, with no window at all. I would often go to their house for the night. In the evening, a kerosene lantern was lit. The dim light was scattered across the living room. We would drink tea, accompanied by tiny lumps of sugar and pieces of dark rye bread. After tea, Grandmother would usually sew something, repairing worn clothing, while Grandfather sat on an old sofa, murmuring prayers in a quiet voice, interrupted only by the clock's ticking. In this way, we waited for bedtime.

During these long ago years, there was a family tradition which had to be observed without fail. Everyone had to come to our grandparents' house to celebrate the Passover seder on the first night. These celebrations did not last long, because I soon had to leave for another city to find a job. Several years later, my grandparents passed away. And now, while recalling my days with them, I really feel the Jewish spirit of their lives.

❖ Gefilte Fish (Stuffed Fish)

LUCY KASHLINSKY

The Russian version of gefilte (or stuffed) fish bears little resemblance to the white fish balls sold in jars in the kosher food section of the American supermarket. This "made from scratch" version is the same recipe my mother and grandmother used many years ago.

2 medium-sized white fish or carp (2–3 lb)
2 eggs, beaten
1 onion, peeled and finely chopped
2 onions, peeled and sliced
2 slices of dry white bread (without crust),
   or ⅓ cup matzo meal

1 small beet, sliced
1 carrot, peeled and sliced
Salt and pepper to taste
2 Tbs vegetable oil

Clean fish. Cut off heads and remove eyes. Cut off tails and, if possible, remove skin in one piece. If this is not possible, slice fish and scrape meat from strips of skin. Put skin aside for later use. Remove bones and finely grind fish.

Sauté chopped onion. Add ground fish, eggs, salt, pepper and vegetable oil. Soak bread in water until soft, squeeze out liquid and add the softened bread (or matzo meal) to the fish mixture. If you were able to remove the skin in one piece, stuff the fish mixture back into the skin. If the skin is in slices, form the mixture into patties and wrap the skins around the outside of the patties. (If you like, the fish head can be stuffed also, and used to present the appearance of a whole fish when the dish is served.)

In a large pot or roasting pan put sliced onions to cover the bottom. Add the sliced beet and sliced carrot. Put fish on top of these vegetables and add enough cold water to cover the fish. Bring to a boil, then reduce heat and cook over a low heat for about 1½ hours. Remove fish to a plate and refrigerate until ready to serve. Garnish with carrot slices. Serve cold with horseradish.

NOTE: You can cook peeled, sliced potatoes in the liquid from the fish after it has been removed, as a tasty side dish.

There were two major newspapers in the former Soviet Union: *Izvestia*—which means "News," and *Pravda*—which means "Truth."

The Russian people had their own opinions about these papers. The usual joke was, "There's no news in the *Truth*—and no truth in the *News!*"

—GALINA CHYORNY

34

Whenever Russians gather to celebrate any occasion, laughter and conversation usually accompany the opening toast—*Boodtye zdarovi!* (Be healthy!) In true Russian style, the sit-down meal begins with lavish zakooski (appetizers): salads, herring, assorted fish, cheeses, stuffed eggs, pickles, sliced salami, marinated vegetables and, of course, buttered bread with various kinds of caviar. (The number of different kinds of zakooska depends on the number of people—and whether or not it is a special occasion.) This might be followed by hot or cold borscht (depending on the weather), or a chunky meat soup, accompanied by piroshki (filled pastries). Just when you think it's time for dessert, the main course is served! Maybe a beef stroganoff, or a tasty sweet and sour stew…all this washed down with a glass of vodka or wine and enjoyed with animated, friendly chatter. By the time the final mandatory sweets are presented, guests are ready for singing and dancing. Russian hospitality usually culminates with tea (served from a samovar in the old days), often with homemade preserves and followed by cognac. When the glasses are lifted for a final farewell toast, it's time to go home—pleasantly "stuffed" and in a good mood.

Preeáhtnova appeteéta!

The People's Enemy

STALINA GUTMAN
Engineer, Kiev

My childhood began happily. I often recall my birthday celebrations. We sang, danced and played games. It was my father who was the organizer of all those entertainments. He loved his children, and did everything he could to make our lives happier.

I loved to dance, and when a new, wonderful Pioneer Palace was built in Kiev in 1933, my parents enrolled me in the ballet club. In 1934, the defense minister, Voroshilov, came to Kiev. I was honored to present him with a bunch of beautiful flowers. In response, Voroshilov gave me a chocolate bar. I was so happy that I kept the wrapper from it until the beginning of the war. I also remember the New Year holidays, when we danced around the tree with multicolored lights, dressed as snowflakes and ice drops. Our parents were standing around proudly, and our pictures were in magazines. Everyone was given a gift.

And then, suddenly, the horrible year 1937 came. My happy childhood vanished. My father was arrested on July 20, 1937, and accused as a "people's enemy." My mother was left with three little children. To make ends meet, she had to work two shifts in the pharmacy, and at night she sat up with critically sick people.

I was only ten, but I was expelled from the ballet club because I was the daughter of a "people's enemy." Those were very hard days, days of endless tears. It offended all of us. How could such a kind, cheerful, "devoted-to-his-party" person, who loved his Motherland and Stalin so faithfully that he even named me in his honor, be an "enemy"?

Only in 1956, nineteen years later, did we find out that our father was innocent. He was shot on October 20, 1937, and then "rehabilitated" posthumously—*after* his death! He was only thirty-three years old.

Strangers at the Inn

MARIA LITSERMAN
Engineer, Moscow

I was born in 1913 in a small town in the Ukraine called Chechelnik. There were mountains and fields and a nice park nearby. Jews used to have big families, and they spoke only the Yiddish language. Friday nights and Saturdays were holidays, and everyone went to one of the four synagogues in the town. I remember that Passover was always a great holiday. Before it began, people bought new clothes and matzos, cleaned their houses, and got the special Passover dishes out of boxes. Children were dressed in their new clothes, and the matzos were pounded with a mortar and used to prepare tasty Passover foods.

My grandfather ran an inn, where many interesting travelers stayed. Before the holidays, cantors (synagogue singers) came from big cities. In the evenings, they sang songs—all in Hebrew. During the holidays, they sang in the synagogues. Also, Jewish actors often stayed in this small hotel. There were rehearsals in the Yiddish language. I loved to listen to these strangers and their entertainments. On one occasion, my aunt was married under a beautiful chuppa (canopy), and there was singing and dancing to Jewish music. Sweet dishes like strudel and lekhah were served, and it was a very joyous celebration for the whole family.

Unfortunately, it wasn't always so happy. Pogroms upset our lives at unexpected moments. During one brutal attack in 1919, my mother, my little brother and I escaped from the village and hid. Shots were ringing all around us, and we saw many dead people lying in the streets. The killers destroyed our town. After the pogroms, many people left. Slowly, life began to return to "normal." Destroyed plants were restarted. In 1927, the Technical Secondary School was opened. After I graduated from the technical school in 1931, we left for Kiev. From there, my family and I moved to Leningrad. From 1936 until 1993, we lived in Moscow.

After leaving our little town, life changed greatly. Religious observance grew less and less. We began to speak only Russian. We stopped celebrating Jewish holidays and began to celebrate only Russian holidays. Jewish children only wanted to get a good education. Many of them became musicians, journalists, or scientists. But, even when we could not celebrate our holidays, our family always enjoyed cooking and eating our traditional Jewish dishes, as we did at our inn so many years before. All our interesting strangers were treated to family favorites like chopped liver, gefilte fish, strudel, and apple or meat pies. These are recipes from my parents and grandparents. We still enjoy them today.

❀ Pashlet (Poultry Liver Pâté)

TSILYA VENETSKAYA

1 lb chicken or turkey livers
3–4 large eggs, boiled and chopped
1–2 onions, chopped

2–3 Tbs chicken fat
Salt and pepper to taste

Chop the onions and fry them in 2 Tbs chicken fat until brown. Set aside.
Boil the livers, or cut them into pieces and fry quickly in chicken fat.
Chop livers and mix with fried onions and chopped hard-boiled eggs.
Add more fat if needed. Season with salt and pepper and mix again.
Chill before serving.

❀ Marinated Cabbage Appetizer

RITA GORLIN

3 lbs cabbage, chopped
1 medium carrot, chopped
½ bunch parsley, chopped
1 clove garlic, minced

MARINADE
3 cups water
½ cup sugar
½ cup vinegar
½ cup oil
1½ tsp salt

Cabbage mixture: Combine all vegetables. Mix well.

Marinade: In a small pan, combine all ingredients and heat until sugar and
salt have dissolved.

Pour hot marinade over cabbage mixture and refrigerate overnight. Just before
serving, remove cabbage mixture from marinade.

❀ Eggplant Caviar

MILA PASTERNAK

1 eggplant
1 bell pepper, red or green (optional)
3 tomatoes*
2–3 cloves garlic

1 white onion, finely chopped
2 Tbs olive oil
1 Tbs red wine vinegar*
Salt and pepper to taste

*For a creamier version, you can use 1½ Tbs mayonnaise and 1 Tbs fresh
lemon juice instead of tomatoes and vinegar.

Preheat oven to 375°. Pierce skin of eggplant. Bake eggplant and pepper for
50 minutes or until soft. Allow to cool for a few minutes.

Cut eggplant in half, scoop out the pulp and finely chop in food processor,
with all other ingredients, adding salt and pepper last.

Cover and refrigerate until well chilled. Serve with bread, crackers or pita.

A Man with a Vision

Yelena Belyavskaya
Architect, Moscow

Before the Revolution, my mother's family lived in the city of Kursk in Russia. My grandparents had five children. My grandfather was a tailor. Although they were very poor, their children strove for an education. The oldest son, Samuel, was a person of great abilities. He became a tutor because he needed to earn his living while he was studying. He finished the gymnasium (high school) as the best student (number one in his class), and received a gold medal. Even so, he couldn't enter the university because he was Jewish. His Russian friends, who weren't as good students, were accepted, but Samuel was told, "You can't study here. There's no place for Jews!" Samuel was in a bad temper. He understood that the root of all the evil and injustice was in the tsar's government. He had a vision of obtaining justice through revolution. He became a Communist and was the secretary of a committee of the Communist party in Kursk.

In 1917, the civil war began. Samuel was in the Red Army. When the White Army occupied Kursk, he left the city with his regiment. The White soldiers came to the house, arrested his father (my grandfather) and sentenced him to be shot. In shock, he stood with the other prisoners, waiting to die. The officers stood in a line, and the soldiers fired in turn. When the man standing next to my grandfather was fired on, one bullet struck my grandfather's ear, and he fell to the ground. When he regained consciousness, the soldiers had gone. It was the dark of night. The streets were empty. He got up and went home.

Meanwhile, in a somber mood, his wife (my grandmother) and his children sat at the table where they lit candles and offered prayers. When the door opened and my grandfather appeared, they cried out with joy. But when he began to undress, and Grandmother saw the bloodstains, she fell down in a faint. Grandfather's nervous system never recovered from this experience. Before long, he fell ill with cancer and died at the age of fifty-four.

Then, in Russia, there was a victory of Soviet power. My uncle, Samuel Kazatsky, became an important man. He was a supervisor of the budget administration of the Soviet government. For a while, things went well. But he was a Jew, and so in 1937, along with thousands of others, Stalin ordered him shot and arrested his wife. My grandmother died immediately of a heart attack.

My uncle, like many people of his time, had a vision of a better life under the new, revolutionary system of government. Unfortunately, the reality of life for the people, and particularly the Jews, of Russia wasn't exactly what he had in mind.

Armenian Bean Appetizer

VERA OSIPOVA

¼ cup olive oil
2 Tbs lemon juice
¾ tsp salt
⅛ tsp white pepper

1 clove garlic, peeled and crushed
3 Tbs minced parsley
2 cups cooked, drained beans
(navy, kidney, or pea beans)

Beat oil with lemon juice and salt until creamy. Mix in pepper, garlic and 2 Tbs parsley. Pour over beans and mix lightly. Cover and refrigerate 3–4 hours.

Remove from refrigerator, stir well and let stand at room temperature about 20 minutes before serving. Sprinkle with remaining parsley.

Stuffed Eggplant

ANNA OKIN

1 medium eggplant,
    unpeeled, cut in half lengthwise
½ cup olive oil
2 tsp salt
1 large yellow onion, peeled and minced

2 cloves garlic,
    peeled and crushed
3 medium tomatoes,
    peeled and coarsely chopped
⅛ tsp pepper

Cut surfaces of eggplant halves with a crisscross pattern, and sprinkle each with ½ tsp salt. Let stand for 1 hour. Press out as much liquid as possible, rinse in cold water and pat dry with paper towel. Scoop out the meat, leaving the shells about ½" thick. Brush the edges with a little oil.

Cut the scooped out eggplant into ½" pieces.

Preheat oven to 350°. Sauté onion and garlic in ¼ cup oil over medium heat until golden, about 8–10 minutes. Drain on paper towel and put aside.

Sauté tomatoes about 5 minutes and mix with onion, eggplant pieces and seasoning. (Add a little sugar if it tastes too tart.)

Put eggplant shells in a greased casserole dish, fill and bake about 45–50 minutes until tender. Serve hot as a vegetable or cold as an appetizer.

Smoked Salmon Vinaigrette

YEUGENIA KOCHEVRINA

½ lb smoked salmon (lox), sliced
2 potatoes, cooked and diced, cold
2 Tbs capers
2 Tbs minced onion
¼ cup pitted olives, sliced

1 Tbs minced scallions
1 Tbs vinegar
2 Tbs salad oil
1 tsp prepared mustard
Pepper to taste

Cut the smoked salmon into strips or small squares, not too thin. Mix very carefully with potatoes, capers, onion, olives and scallions. Arrange in a dish.

Combine vinegar, oil, mustard and pepper and pour over the top of the salad (do not mix). Serve cold. (Our tester liked this better the next day after the potatoes had absorbed some of the salt from the lox.)

Cucumber and Yogurt Dip

RACHEL LURYE

1½ cups plain low-fat yogurt
⅓ cup sour cream
2 cloves garlic, minced
2 medium cucumbers,
    peeled, grated, and patted dry

1 Tbs chopped cilantro
1½ Tbs olive oil
2 Tbs chopped fresh mint
Whole mint leaves (for garnish)
Toasted pita triangles

Mix cucumbers, yogurt, sour cream, mint, cilantro and oil in a bowl. Refrigerate, covered, for 6–8 hours.

Decorate with mint leaves and serve with toasted pita triangles.

Grandfather Nisl and Grandmother Mirl, c. 1902. Courtesy Mira Bezymenskaia.

Shopping in Soviet Estonia

Riva Sheer

Department store assistant manager, Tallinn, Estonia

First, I'd like to tell briefly what the merchandise in Soviet Estonia was like, and why there were so many shopping problems for the people.

Before 1940, Estonia was an independent, democratic republic. There was also a capitalistic economic system. Most of the factories and stores belonged to private owners, so there was a lot of competition. Each owner wanted to offer the best products for the cheapest price. They did everything to satisfy the customers. In this way, they hoped to have more customers.

After Estonia was occupied by Soviet Russia in 1940, the trade organizations, industry and private properties were taken over by the state. So the capitalistic system changed to a socialistic planned economic system. There was no more competition. That is the reason why all the commodities or goods were similar or alike everywhere. Nobody was interested in turning out a variety of products. Only the quantity of production was important. The "plan" had to be fulfilled.

People didn't have choices. They had to buy even poorer quality goods. The prices of food and other articles were high. Eggs, meat, sausage, poultry, butter and cheese were very expensive. Sometimes, cheaper prices could be found in supermarkets or department stores at the end of the month, when the plan had not been fulfilled. That's what everyone looked for. The stores opened at 9:00 A.M. So we had to go very early, about 6 o'clock in the morning, to begin standing in line, because there were very many people and not too many goods. Actually, we had to stand in two lines. After the purchases were made, it was necessary to wait in another line at the cash register. So it took a long time to finish our shopping. Sometimes we had to go to several stores and repeat this process. All this was very hard, especially for women with families. When they returned home, they were very tired, but they still had so much to do when they got there. We had another problem, too. We couldn't stand in line for hours every day, and we could only get the cheaper food once a month. So we bought everything we could in great amounts.

When we came to America, we were so amazed and delighted at how easy and convenient the shopping is here. We don't need to buy so many things at once. We can even go every day! Also, the service is very good. The salespeople are usually friendly and polite. And that's another story!

The Power of Art

Edit Matov
Shipbuilding engineer, Moscow

I remember the first sound film which appeared on screens in the former Soviet Union. It was in the thirties. (I was nine or ten years old.) That time was very difficult for most Soviet people. It was very hard to buy food, clothes or anything. In particular, it was a difficult time for thousands of homeless children and teenagers whose parents had been killed during the civil war, had been arrested or died of hunger. These homeless children were always hungry. Therefore, they stole, and sometimes they killed people or each other. It was a disaster for the country and a big problem for the government. Then it was decided to organize labor communes where the teenagers could rule themselves, and where they could work and study.

The first sound film, which was called "Passage into Life," told about this experiment. It was a propaganda film, but it was very interesting and well made. Excellent actors played the main roles. In this story, there was conflict between the teenagers who wanted to change and become good citizens and some people who wanted to prevent them and their teachers from achieving their goal. These people killed one mischievous, but cheerful and sympathetic character named Mustahfa. It was a very tragic episode.

However, this was also a very optimistic film. It had some laughable moments. For example, in one scene, a nice young woman stood on a big crowded square putting on her lipstick. While she was doing this, Mustahfa stealthily cut a piece out of the back of her rich fur coat. When she turned around, many people on the square could see her panties through the big hole in her fur coat and dress. All the people in the theater laughed. The audience laughed, and I laughed, too. Really, it was a very funny sight.

But two days later, after school, when I went into the room where we kept our coats and saw instead of my whole coat (made of very cheap fur), only half of a coat, I didn't laugh! It wasn't so funny then. I was upset. When they saw my coat, my parents were even more upset than I was, of course. Then I understood how greatly movies influence young minds. Such is the power of art.

Other Zakooski to Try

Thinly sliced tongue, salami or sausage arranged on a plate will often be found on the zakooski table along with caviar, marinated mushrooms, and various assorted salads. Of course, Russians are also very fond of sardines in any form, and these, too, may be included to complete the array.

Pervoye Blyudo

(First Course—Salads)

The meal continues as the winds of change sweep across the land. The family sits around the bubbling samovar, as through a young girl's eyes the world she knows so abruptly changes....

SALADS

Destiny

Malvina Alexandravskaya
Engineer, St. Petersburg

I was born in 1912. In 1914, World War I began. My mother worked in a large village in a hospital. Next to the hospital, there was a building with four flats for the doctors. Each flat had a garden with fruit trees, vegetables and flowers in it. Behind the garden was the endless Ukrainian steppe. My father, who was twenty-three, and his brother, who was nineteen, decided to emigrate to America. They settled in Fall River, Massachusetts and worked in a green grocery. My father wanted my mother, my two sisters and me to come to America, too. But for a woman with three little children, it was impossible at that time. And so it happened that my father came back to Russia, just as the October Revolution was taking place! Because the war was still going on, the way to the Ukraine was long and difficult. It took my father about a year to make the return trip. When he arrived, we children didn't recognize him. We saw in his photograph that he had a moustache. We thought our mother had deceived us. This man was shaved! But he was so kind and tender that the ice was broken very quickly.

My father's parents lived in a small Ukrainian village with their three daughters. The oldest was married and had three children. There were many gangs roaming around after the October Revolution: the "famous" Machno, the Petlura, and many smaller, but no less cruel groups. In 1919, one gang named "Grigorevtzy" burst into my aunt's home during the night and killed almost the whole family. Father's younger sister jumped out the window and hid in the garden. And one little four-year-old girl lived because she had decided she was lonely. The bandits didn't see her. In the morning, people found the frightened child under her mother's body. After this massacre, my father went to their village and came back with his parents, his sister and the little girl. I remember this day clearly.

We children didn't know the terrible story. The next morning, we woke up, washed ourselves and went into the dining room. We saw a man with a beard, a woman in a head scarf, a sad-looking girl and our parents sitting around the table. On the table bubbled a samovar, and we went to sit down. But Grandfather asked Father in a very stern voice, "How can you eat without a prayer?" Father was an atheist, but he respected his father and told us, "Grandfather will teach you the morning prayer."

From that day, we began to study the prayers and Jewish history from Adam's creation on. I don't know what Grandfather did for a living before then, but the years he lived with us, he was a *melamed* (teacher). The boys came to him every morning. He had a lot of books. I even remember a dictionary in "Hebrew–Russian." He taught us girls, too, but separately—without the boys. He was a very interesting, educated man, and it is sad that he died so young at only fifty-four years of age.

So we and our little orphan cousin grew up in very hard times. We knew starvation, devastation, and grief, but our united family was amicable, and jokes and laughter were often heard in our flat.

My father's brother, meanwhile, got married and stayed in the same town in Massachusetts. They continued to correspond. The letters he wrote were in Yiddish and very interesting. Usually, he read them aloud to my mother, and I liked to listen also. I always remembered the name of the town, and when we came to America, we visited our relatives and had a very good time.

▓ Salad Olivier (Sliced Cold Chicken with Potato)

YEUGENIA ROMM

This is a popular salad, originally created by the French chef of Nicholas II.

1 breast of chicken, boiled or roasted	3 tsp mayonnaise
3 medium boiled potatoes	1 tomato, sliced
2 small dill pickles	6 large olives
1 tsp Worcestershire sauce	2 hard-boiled eggs

Remove all skin and fat from the chicken and slice evenly into very thin strips. Slice the potatoes into ¼" pieces. Peel and slice the pickles very thin.

Combine the mayonnaise and Worcestershire sauce and add to the chicken, potatoes and pickles. Mix together carefully to avoid breakage. Put onto a platter and garnish with wedges of cooked egg, tomato slices and olives.

Music—Food for the Soul

BASYA MASS
Economist, Moscow

I want to tell a story about my son. When he was young, he was a very bad eater. When he was three years old, I went with him to the city of Sochi, on the Black Sea. We had lunch at a restaurant there. An orchestra played while the food was being served. My son liked the music. He had a good ear for it even then. While the music played, I fed him, and he ate. When the music stopped, he was finished. The conductor observed him for several days. Finally, he came to our table and said, "Your son is the best listener! I believe his future will be music."

At an early age, my son began to play the piano. He practiced eagerly for many years. Today, he is an accomplished pianist, preferring only classical music. So, that conductor was right in his prophesy of long ago. The music helped him eat his food as a child, but it became the food for his soul the rest of his life!

The Wedding

Gisya Shvarts
Bookkeeper, St. Petersburg

My mother's family lived in Krementchung in the Ukraine. My grandmother and grandfather had eight daughters and two sons. In 1917, their oldest daughter got married. She was my aunt. She was sixteen years old. Her wedding day was a day the family would always remember.

The young couple stood under the *chuppa* listening to the rabbi chant the traditional prayers, while all the relatives and friends watched them with solemn eyes. Everyone was wearing their best clothes and looked so nice. It was a happy occasion. My aunt held her breath as this person who would be her husband held the wine glass with shaking hands. She was very nervous, and he kept looking secretly at her without moving his head. The tables were all set with the best white lace tablecloths and all kinds of delicious foods that were freshly prepared for the celebration to come. The men and women would have to sit separately, but later there would be music and dancing among themselves just the same.

The groom stomped on the glass and everyone yelled *"Mazel Tov!"* as the ceremony came to an end. Then suddenly, it got very quiet. The guests were looking at the door nervously, where a group of rowdy-looking men were standing staring back at them. Petlura's gang had come to town. They broke into the room, grabbing anyone in their way. Some of them were carrying clubs and looked drunk. They wanted to get the bride and groom and kill them. "Give us your gold or you'll never see this pair again!" one of them shouted. All the guests took off all of their gold and jewelry and gave it to the gang as ransom for the bridal couple. The women were crying and the men looked very worried. They took it, and threw everything in big sacks, but it didn't change their minds. "Wouldn't this make a good fire," somebody said, pulling the cloth from the table as the dishes crashed to the ground.

One of the children had run into the street while the men weren't looking and ran to try to get help. Fortunately, soldiers from the Red Army came into the town just then. It was a miracle. They captured all of the bullies, but not before they had done a lot of damage. The party was over after that. Everyone wished the couple happiness, and went home giving thanks that they were alive one more time.

After that horrible experience, my aunt became sick from nerves and shock. Later, they had four children—three sons and one daughter. Two of their sons were killed in the Second World War. My aunt lived to be eighty-nine years old, but she never forgot her wedding day her whole life.

My Grandmother, the "Legend"

LARISA VILENSKAYA
Engineer, Tbilisi, Georgia

I had a wonderful, beautiful grandmother. Her parents wanted her to marry a widower who was twenty years older. Girls didn't have the luxury of choosing anyone they fancied in those days. A suitable "match" was arranged by the parents. When they told her who they had chosen, her stomach lurched. She knew they loved her and only wanted what was best. But what would life be like with a man so much older?

When she got married, she was sixteen years old. He already had six children. Two of them were almost the same age as their stepmother. My grandmother was a strong and determined woman, even at such a young age. She made up her mind to be a good wife and mother. She later had four children of her own. Altogether there were ten children. All of them loved and respected her because she was intelligent, kind, gentle, and fair.

They lived in a small village. In the early 1920s they experienced a pogrom, and many people were killed. It was a horrible nightmare, and my grandfather never recovered from it. After that he hanged himself. Grandmother was grief-stricken, but she resolved to survive. She worked hard and raised all the children by herself.

In 1925, my father and his family, together with his sister and mother and all the children, moved to Moscow. My grandmother died young, at the early age of fifty-six. All her children and their families came to her funeral. They came from everywhere. She was a "legend." Everybody remembers her struggle to survive and raise her family alone.

▦ Carrot Salad

LARISA VILENSKAYA

3–4 large carrots, peeled and grated 2 Tbs lemon or orange juice
1–2 large apples, peeled and diced* 2 Tbs mayonnaise
1 clove garlic, mashed (optional) 1 tsp sugar

*You can use ⅓–½ cup raisins instead of apples, if desired.

Combine all the ingredients. Serve.

▦ Carrot Salad II

MARIYA KROL

3 carrots 2 Tbs mayonnaise
1–2 garlic cloves, minced 1 Tbs orange juice (optional)
3–4 tsp walnuts, chopped

Grate carrots. Add orange juice, garlic and walnuts. Mix together. Add mayonnaise. (Our tester would have added some raisins or pineapple chunks.)

▦ Beet Salad

MARIYA KROL

2 beets, washed 10–12 prunes, pitted and chopped
1 dill pickle, chopped 2 Tbs mayonnaise

Boil beets, 20 minutes or until tender. Cool, peel and chop into small pieces. Combine with chopped pickle, prunes and mayonnaise. Serve.

▦ Beet Salad II

SONYA SLUTSKER

4 beets, washed Mayonnaise
4 apples, peeled and chopped Dill, minced
16 walnuts, chopped Parsley, minced

Boil the washed beets for 20 minutes or until tender. Cool and chop the cooked beets. Combine beets, apples and walnuts. Add enough mayonnaise to moisten. Add dill and parsley to taste. Serve. (Our tester recommends more mayonnaise and some chopped red onion.)

▨ Chicken–Vegetable Layered Salad

MALVINA ALEXANDRAVSKAYA

1 lb mushrooms, chopped	1 cup mayonnaise
½ lb chicken, boned and chopped	4 eggs, hard-boiled
2 ribs celery, chopped	2 carrots, cooked
Fresh dill to taste	1 cup Swiss cheese, grated
2 large onions, chopped	½ tsp salt-free spices
¼ cup corn oil	(such as Trader Joe's 21
1 Tbs ketchup	Seasoning Salute)

In fry pan, heat mushrooms over medium-low heat. Cover pan and steam mushrooms. Fluid will begin to appear in the pan. Remove cover, keep pan moving, stirring constantly until the fluid has evaporated. Add some corn oil and sauté for 3–4 minutes.

Sauté chicken with celery, dill, salt-free spices. When chicken is cooked, put mixture in food processor and chop. The quantity of the chicken mixture must equal the mushrooms.

Sauté onions until clear—not brown. Combine them with the mushrooms and chicken.

Combine ketchup and mayonnaise in a small bowl.

Separate the hard-boiled egg yolks from the whites. Mash the whites. Place in one bowl. Mash the egg yolks and place in another bowl.

Cook, cool and coarsely chop the carrots.

Layer the various ingredients as follows in a large glass bowl:

Bottom layer: Push egg whites through a sieve and scatter on bottom of dish.

Layer 2: Very thin mayonnaise–ketchup mixture.

Layer 3: Chicken–mushroom mixture.

Layer 4: Very thin mayonnaise–ketchup mixture.

Layer 5: Chopped carrots.

Layer 6: Grated Swiss cheese.

Layer 7: Very thin mayonnaise–ketchup mixture.

Top Layer: Top with mashed egg yolks.

Refrigerate several hours before serving to allow flavors to blend.

⊞ Russian Salad (Vinaigrette)

LIYA MELITSEVA

4–5 potatoes	1–2 dill pickles, diced
3–4 carrots	¼ white onion, finely chopped
2 beets, washed	1 small can peas
1 Tbs lemon juice	2–3 Tbs olive oil
1 tsp salt	Salt and pepper to taste

Boil potatoes and carrots unpeeled. Remove from water, peel and dice.

Add beets, lemon juice and salt to boiling water and boil until tender (20–30 minutes). When finished, chop the beets in the food processor.

Combine the potatoes, carrots, pickles and onion. Add the chopped beets and the peas. Drizzle olive oil over all and season to taste.

⊞ Tenderness Salad

LILYA KHLEBOVICH

2 large potatoes, peeled, boiled and diced	**GARNISH**
2 large carrots, boiled and diced	Whole dill
3 eggs, hard-boiled, chopped	Green onions
1 bunch green onion, chopped	Chopped eggs
1 large apple, diced	Radishes
1 cup hard cheese, grated	Carrots
(cheddar, Dutch, Swiss, etc.)	Olives
2 cups mayonnaise	

Bottom layer: Diced potatoes. Cover with a thin layer of mayonnaise.
Layer 2: Diced carrots. Cover with a thin layer of mayonnaise.
Layer 3: Chopped eggs. Cover with a thin layer of mayonnaise.
Layer 4: Chopped green onion. Cover with a thin layer of mayonnaise.
Layer 5: Diced apples. Cover with a thin layer of mayonnaise.
Layer 6: Grated cheese. Cover with a thin layer of mayonnaise.
Top Layer: Sprinkle any or all of the listed garnishes over the top.

Practicing Medicine in Kazakhstan

MIRA BEZYMENSKAIA
Surgeon, Moscow

I graduated from the Medical Institute in 1953. At that time in Russia, all medical graduates had to work for three years in different provinces of the country. The best students had the right to stay at the Institute for further education, or choose the province they preferred for their future job. I graduated at the top of my class. In spite of this, because I was a Jew, I was sent to Aktubinsk in Kazakhstan, very far from my native city of Moscow and from my parents.

Aktubinsk was a little, dirty town then. All the houses were made of clay, streets were covered with sand, and trees were seldom seen. Plains covered with white salt surrounded the town. Only in spring did the steppe blossom with many colored tulips and become beautiful. The wind blew and blew every day. The climate was continental—cold in winter, and very hot in summer. On the streets, Kazakhs rode small horses. They wore wool coats, fur caps of fox, and one leather glove on their left hand. On the gloved hand sat a falcon for hunting.

Around the town many closed, segregated detention areas (similar to ghettos) were situated. People of many different nationalities (Tatar of the Crimea, Chechen, Cabardins, Germans, etc.) were exiled here for no reason, other than belonging to these nationalities. They weren't permitted to travel more than fifteen miles away, and had to register with the police every day. They worked very hard on the railroad, and many starved. They were unaccustomed to the climate, and there was a lot of sickness among them. Tuberculosis, syphilis and high fevers and disease from drinking bad milk were prevalent. (Milk was not yet pasteurized.)

I worked in a railroad hospital along with another young doctor who had served in the war on the front lines. He was also Jewish. We both wanted to help these poor exiled people. But in spite of our best efforts, there was not much we could do because we couldn't send our patients for the treatment many required. I was a young doctor, with little experience. It was very difficult for me to treat many of the problems, such as appendicitis, or broken arms and legs, etc. One time, I cried during an operation, and my patient, who was an old man, comforted me.

On one occasion, I went by train to a remote station to see a sick child. His parents' house was far from the station in the steppe. I walked alone. It was night, the sky was dark, with bright stars, and wolves were howling. After the treatment, when I returned to the cold railway carriage, I was freezing and lost consciousness.

In January 1953, in Moscow, a few famous doctors were arrested. They were all Jews. They were charged with killing Russian people. All the newspapers and magazines printed articles, and the radio announced: "Jewish doctors are murderers." A special commission arrived at our hospital to check on my colleague and me (the Jewish killers!). They declared that we had received instruction from the murderous doctors in Moscow who had been arrested, and that we wanted to kill people. Everyone was afraid. Patients stopped coming to the hospital, and we waited to be arrested, also.

But, in March 1953, Stalin died. The file on the "doctor/murderers" was closed. Little by little, people began returning to the hospital. My friend and I continued to treat people and to help them as much as possible. It was a difficult time, but I was young. It was my first job and my first experience away from home. I had made friends among the hospital staff, and all in all, I remember it as an interesting and rewarding time.

▨ Satsivi (Chicken Salad with Walnuts)

MIRA BEZYMENSKAIA

This is a very popular cold Georgian dish.

2 lbs chicken	1 cup walnuts, chopped
4 cups water	2–3 cloves garlic, crushed
1 cup mayonnaise	Salt to taste

Place the chicken in a pot. Add water and cook uncovered over medium heat until the water is reduced to 1 cup. Remove the cooked chicken. Bone and dice the meat.

Pour the liquid into a bowl and refrigerate. As the broth cools, it forms a gelatin. Discard the fat that will rise to the top of the bowl.

To the gelatin, add diced chicken, mayonnaise, walnuts, crushed garlic and salt. Refrigerate until ready to serve.

The Ballet Dancer

ELENA TSYNMAN
Music teacher, St. Petersburg

Petrograd. It was the winter of 1920–21. There was hunger and bitter cold. But the theaters were full of people. The Maryinsky Theatre put on the stage operas with the the famous singer Fedor Shalapin and ballets with remarkable dancers like Spessivseva and Viltzak, Lukom and Shavrov. It was necessary to wait all night in front of the box office to buy tickets the next morning. My parents did it, too.

That winter, I was an eleven-year-old girl listening to opera and watching the ballet for the first time in my life. It was the ballet *The Bayoderka.* The main characters were danced by Spessivseva (Nikia) and Viltzak (Solar). After that performance, our apartment was turned into a theater stage, and all the lace and tulle curtains and napkins were transformed into ballet costumes. My cousin Enna and I became ballet stars. Enna was Spessivseva, and I was her partner Viltsak. Or I was Lukom, and she was Shavrov.

In reality, I'm not a ballerina, but I continue to love ballet to this day. The subject of my diploma was the music of the Russian ballets. Sixty-five years had passed since then.

In 1987, I was visiting my son in San Jose. One day he told me that in San Francisco, in the house of his friends, lived a ninety-year-old former dancer from St. Petersburg's Maryinsky Theatre, Anatol Viltzak. "Oh!" I cried. "He is the one I copied in my children's game!" And so, a meeting was arranged between an old woman and an old dancer whose art she had admired sixty-five years before!

Anatol Viltzak told me about his departure from Petrograd to Paris and his European touring. When he finally settled down in San Francisco, he danced and taught the art of ballet. He gave me his photo with an autograph, and my son took a picture of us. I could hardly believe that I had finally met my ballet idol after all those years! He is still living there and is now ninety-seven years old.

Top: Elena Tsynman with her father, Lazar Tsynman, St. Petersburg, 1920. Center: Nemchinova and Viltzak in Les Biches, *1924. Bottom: Anatol Vilzak and Elena Tsyman, 1987*

The Seder

BY JUDITH GELB
Pediatrician, Tallinn, Estonia

When I was ten years old, we had a seder in my grandparents' house. Estonia was an independent country at that time, and religious observance was still allowed. It was always a happy occasion, and we eagerly looked forward to the holiday during the many days of preparation. There was so much to do to make the house ready and prepare the special dishes. When the day finally arrived, we dressed in our best clothes and went early to help Grandmother get everything ready. During the seder we ate eggs in salt water, gefilte fish, horseradish, matzos, charoset, and all the other traditional foods. My grandfather read the Haggadah and the children asked the four *kashas* (questions). On a chair close to Grandfather sat pillows, and under them was hidden the *ahfakomen* (the special matzos the children had to search for). The children crept under the table and the lucky finder excitedly picked up the hidden treasure. It was a big celebration for all the family.

During the war, we spent four years in Siberia. From that time and for the next fifty years, from 1940 until 1992, we quietly celebrated our holidays, but only secretly. Our son and nephews celebrated their bar mitzvahs—but only behind the closed doors of our home, with ten men for a minyan. We couldn't go to the synagogue for these important rituals. It wasn't allowed. We could lose our jobs for such a "crime." We never forgot our traditions, but it would be a long time before we could do it without the fear of someone seeing.

Here in America, we have seders each year again. At these seders, we are now the grandparents, and we celebrate this holiday with our family and all our relatives. Here we don't have to be afraid, and we can celebrate once again as in the days of my childhood.

▦ Vegetable Salad (Vinaigrette)

JUDITH GELB

5 beets, washed and boiled	2–3 sour pickles, diced
3 large potatoes, boiled	Salt to taste
3 carrots, cooked	2 Tbs safflower oil or a mixture of
3 onions, minced	2 Tbs mayonnaise and ½ cup sour cream

Boil potatoes, unpeeled, leaving slightly firm. Blanch quickly with cold water. Peel and dice.

After cooking beets and carrots, cool, peel and dice.

Combine the vegetables with pickles and onions. Mix well.

Add safflower oil (or mayonnaise–sour cream mixture) and salt to taste.

▦ Salad Mimosa

GISYA SHVARTS

1–2 large cans pink salmon, rinsed and drained	1 cup Swiss cheese
3 large potatoes, peeled and boiled	5 eggs, hard-boiled
1 large carrot	Mayonnaise

Bottom layer: Mash salmon and spread on bottom of a large bowl or casserole dish. Apply a light coating of mayonnaise.

Layer 2: Coarsely grate potatoes. Spread evenly over Layer 1. Apply a light coating of mayonnaise.

Layer 3: Coarsely grate carrot. Spread evenly over Layer 2. Apply light coating of mayonnaise.

Layer 4: Grate cheddar cheese. Spread evenly over Layer 3. Apply light coating of mayonnaise.

Layer 5: Separate the hard-boiled eggs: whites in one bowl and yolks in another bowl. Mash whites and spread evenly over Layer 4. Apply light coating of mayonnaise.

Top Layer: Mash egg yolks and spread evenly over Layer 5.

Refrigerate several hours before serving to allow flavors to blend.

The Festival of Freedom—
Pesach (Passover)

Throughout our book there are many references to recollections about the holiday of Passover. It is a holiday of springtime and renewal. This holiday, which commemorates the deliverance of the Jews from the Egyptians and their exodus from Egypt, has special significance to Russian Jews. While most Jewish holidays are observed in the synagogue, Passover (or Pesach in Hebrew) is observed in the home. Jewish families in Russia came together not only to honor a tradition, but to preserve their identity in a openly hostile environment. Even when religious holidays had to be celebrated behind closed doors, they made a special effort to teach their children about their heritage and to maintain this meaningful observance.

Several weeks before the holiday, flour would be ground for the matzos. If not made at home, it was sometimes taken to the synagogue so that it could be baked there under proper supervision. This coarse, unleavened bread is the symbol of Passover—the bread of affliction that was transformed into the bread of freedom when the Israelites carried it out of Egypt in their haste to escape. Meanwhile the home had to be prepared as well, making sure to remove all traces of *humetz,* or food not kosher for Passover. It had to be scrubbed clean so that no crumb of leavened products could be found. Most bread is humetz, but so is any food that contains leaven or fermented grain. (This rite has symbolically been performed with a feather and a candle, so that when traces of humetz are encountered, they can be burned.) Also, special dishes are taken out and everyday dishes put away until the eighth day is over.

The Passover ritual meal is called a seder. It is usually conducted by the head of the family, and all the family members read from the Haggadah, a book which recalls the story of the Passover. Traditionally, the youngest child at the table asks the four questions or "kashas" about this special observance. The first question is always, "Why is this night different from all other nights?" The child's questions are answered and the service continues, until the Passover meal is served. It consists of dishes prepared especially for this time. In the center of the table is a seder plate, a divided dish containing all the symbolic foods: matzos, the unleavened bread which the escaping Israelites hastily prepared during their flight from Egypt; moror, a bitter herb, usually horseradish, for the bitterness of slavery; haroset, a mixture of fruits and nuts, symbolizing the mortar from which the Israelites made bricks as slaves, and also the sweetness of freedom; a roasted shank bone to remind us of the paschal (sacrificial) lamb; and a fresh herb, such as parsley or watercress, which represents spring and rebirth, dipped in salt water, symbolizing tears. Also found on the seder plate is a hard-boiled, roasted egg for the life cycle, the round shape having no beginning and no end.

Keeping kosher and conducting religious services in the Soviet Union was a difficult, if not impossible matter. And yet, the Passover seder, even when conducted in secret, represented a tribute to the human spirit and always meant a joyous family gathering ending with the traditional toast of Jews everywhere—"Next year in Jerusalem!"

The Cantonist

Liya Melitseva
Teacher, Riga, Latvia

My mother's father was a "cantonist" (a member of the tsar's army). Once, when he was ten years old and playing with other children on the street of his little town, soldiers caught him and put him in a sack. So it happened that he began to serve in the Russian army. Under the law introduced by Nicholas I, Jews had to serve for twenty-five years.

Grandfather was forced to become a Christian. Being a young boy, he didn't refuse. But he never forgot his traditions. His Russian name became Grigorii Ivanovich. He finished his duty when he was thirty-five years old and married Grandmother Liza when she was only twelve and still playing with dolls. She had very long braids, and grandfather allowed her to keep them, against the Jewish tradition of married women shaving their heads and wearing a wig. They had eight children—two sons and six daughters. As cantonist's sons, my uncles had the privilege of living in Moscow or St. Petersburg and studying in high school. Daughters didn't have these privileges.

My mother liked to recall that on Saturdays, grandfather would say to his servant, "Masha, you'd like a cup of tea, wouldn't you?" Then Masha would put on the samovar, and all the family was invited to join her in a cup of tea. It was a ritual.

In spite of the great difference in their ages, Grandfather actually lived longer than Grandmother and died suddenly in synagogue right in the middle of the service. Everyone said that he had paid his allegiance to the faith of his fathers after all.

A True Funny Little Story

ESFIR DYNKINA
Technical designer, St. Petersburg

There is no such thing as a "volunteer" army in Russia. Everyone has to go. Young men are called up for military service from eighteen to twenty-seven years old. They have to stay in the army for two to three years. (Not twenty-five years like the days of the tsar!)

A long time ago, in 1938–39, a good friend of mine was doing his time in the service. On the first of May, which was a holiday, I decided to send him a gift by mail. The unit where he was stationed wasn't far off. It happened that about this time, a new food appeared in the stores—bananas. Bananas were a rarity in Leningrad. Most people had never seen them. I thought it would make a good gift, so I packed a bunch in a cardboard box and sent it to him.

After a while, I got a letter from my friend. He was happy to get my package. But when he opened it, he didn't understand what was inside. There was a mass of mush in the box. He thought it was a joke. He called over his soldier friends and stuck his finger into the jelly. He brought it to his lips, and when he tasted it, he was surprised to discover that it actually tasted nice. That was enough. All his friends stuck their fingers in, too, and ate up the rest. When the cardboard box was empty, they were all happy and laughing. We remembered this story for a long time afterwards, and always laughed about it.

Layered Potato Salad

ROSA KINBERG

2 apples, chopped
4 new potatoes, cooked and chopped
5 carrots, scrubbed and chopped
1 onion, sliced into rings
1 beet, cooked, peeled and chopped
5 eggs, hard-boiled and chopped
½ cup mayonnaise

Soak onion rings in cold water for 12 hours. Drain.
Layer the ingredients as follows in a large bowl.
Bottom layer: Chopped apples. Cover with a very thin layer of mayonnaise.
Layer 2: Chopped potatoes. Cover with a very thin layer of mayonnaise.
Layer 3: Chopped carrots. Cover with a very thin layer of mayonnaise.
Layer 4: Layer drained onion rings over all.
Layer 5: Chopped beets. Cover with a very thin layer of mayonnaise.
Top Layer: Sprinkle chopped eggs over all.
Refrigerate several hours before serving. Serve with herring.

✶ Herring Under a Blanket

FAINA BELOGOLOVSKY

1 lb herring filets, cut into small pieces
1 onion, chopped
3–4 potatoes, unpeeled and cooked
1 beet, unpeeled, cooked

1 sour apple, peeled and
   cut into narrow strips
1 cup mayonnaise
4 eggs, hard-boiled and mashed
Olives (optional)

After cooking, peel potatoes and beet. Cut potatoes into small pieces and put one half on a platter. Chop beets and set aside.

Put herring on top of potatoes to make a second layer.

Put half the chopped onion on top of herring.

Cover with a thin layer of mayonnaise.

Add remainder of potatoes, and cover with thin strips of apple.

Spread a thin layer of mayonnaise over apple.

Spread mashed eggs next, and another layer of chopped onion.

Top this with chopped beets and one more thin layer of mayonnaise.

Garnish with sliced apple or olives.

✶ Salad Dressing for Fresh Fruit

SONYA SLUTSKER

Excellent over fresh pineapple, strawberries and nuts.

½ cup sugar
1 tsp salt
1 tsp dry mustard
1 tsp celery seeds

2 tsp minced, grated onion
1 cup salad oil
¼ cup vinegar

Mix all dry ingredients in a small bowl. Add grated onion. Add oil and vinegar alternately, beating with a fork until mixture begins to thicken. Refrigerate. (This will keep in the refrigerator up to 3 weeks if well covered.)

✶ Corn and Mushroom Salad

YEUGENIA ROMM

1 large can sweet corn
½ lb mushrooms, cleaned and cut into pieces
1 onion, peeled and chopped

2 Tbs mayonnaise
Vegetable oil, for frying

Sauté chopped onions and mushrooms in a spoonful of oil. Stir in sweet corn and mayonnaise. Mix well and chill.

Cucumber Salad with Sour Cream

RACHEL LURYE

1 European (hothouse) cucumber,
   thinly sliced
2 Tbs sour cream

1 Tbs dill, chopped
Salt and pepper to taste

Arrange the cucumber in a serving dish. Add salt and pepper. Top with sour cream and sprinkle with dill. Serve chilled.

Meechdah (Dream Salad)

FAINA BELOGOLOVSKY

2–3 cucumbers, peeled and
   sliced into thin strips
2 carrots, peeled
   and sliced into thin strips
¼ head cabbage, sliced into thin strips
1 bunch green onions, chopped
   (including green part)

1 apple, peeled and cut in pieces
2 cloves garlic, finely chopped
Juice of ½ lemon
3 Tbs mayonnaise
2–3 Tbs sour cream
Salt and pepper to taste
2 Tbs sugar

Mix cucumbers, carrots, cabbage, onions and garlic in a large bowl. Sprinkle with lemon juice. Add apples, mayonnaise, sour cream, sugar, and salt and pepper to taste. Mix well. Serve cold.

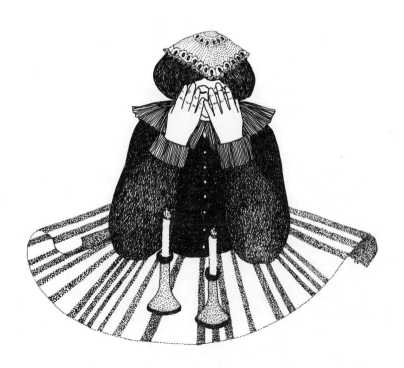

The Lost Package

BORIS ALTSHULLER

Plant manager, Vilnius, Lithuania

My grandfather was a well-educated man. He liked very much to read, and he had a lot of dreams. But he was unlucky. His whole life he worked for a man who owned a big section of forest. My grandpa was a manager of the company. His duties were to organize the felling of the trees, manage the sawing into boards, and oversee the selling of the finished material. He subscribed to newspapers and magazines, and knew a lot of things, but he couldn't found his own business. He tried to do it several times, but each time, he ended up in bankruptcy and had to go back to his old boss.

My grandparents lived in the forest about ten miles from our house. Every weekend, Grandpa came to get me. My grandma loved me very much, and she always cooked my favorite dishes and tried to do whatever she could for me. So, of course, I liked very much to go to their house.

When I was about eight years old, a very frightening thing happened. It was January. My grandpa came to get me as usual in an open sleigh pulled by a team of horses. The frost was very strong (-10°F), and my mother didn't want to let me go in such cold and darkness. But Grandpa insisted because my grandma wanted to see me. I was wrapped up in a warm fur coat and a blanket, and this "package" they put on the sleigh. We drove on the lonely, bumpy road. The sleigh jumped over the bumps, and suddenly with one big bump, I went flying out the back. My grandpa was busy with his own thoughts, and wasn't paying any attention to what was going on behind him.

He stopped in front of the house, went inside and shouted, "Feiga! I brought you your grandson. Come greet him!" But when Grandma came out, she began to cry, "Mendel, are you crazy? Where is the child?" My grandpa was mortified, and he quickly organized a rescue team from his workers to find me. Eventually, they spotted the tightly wrapped little package lying on the road like a piece of wood. This cocoon probably kept me from freezing to death. From that time on, my mother never let me go visit my grandparents in winter—only in summer.

An Important Decision

Riva Sheer

Department store assistant manager, Tallinn, Estonia

I have made many important decisions in my life, but now when I think them over, I find that the most important was one I made a long time (more than fifty years) ago. This decision was important because it saved my life!

It happened in 1941. I was eighteen years old and had just graduated from high school in May. I had gone with my school friend, Sonya, to her grandparents' house in a nearby town for two weeks' vacation. My mother really didn't want me to go because it was a troubled time. The Nazi leader, Hitler, had already started in 1939 to destroy the Jewish nation in Germany, and threatened to kill all the Jewish people in Europe. Suddenly, on June 22 at 4 A.M., World War II broke out. The powerful Nazi army moved very fast. Because of the sudden start, they didn't meet much resistance. So it took only a few days to reach the border of Estonia. All at once I was separated from my family. There was no more telephone connection, and only military transport was allowed on the roads. I couldn't reach my family, and I couldn't get back home.

I can't describe how anxious and desperate I felt. I didn't know what had happened to my family. Where did they go? Many people had decided to stay put, particularly the wealthy. My friend's grandparents did this and urged me to stay with them. So, at eighteen years of age, I was confronted with a very difficult situation. The question was like in Shakespeare's play, *Hamlet*—"to be, or not to be." To stay—or to escape. There was not much time because the last freight train was leaving for Russia early the next morning. I thought very hard about what I should do. I remembered how my uncles and cousins had discussed the Nazis and what they were doing. We had heard terrible stories about how cruelly they treated the Jews. And so I made my decision—to escape to Russia. Besides, I had a feeling (and was hoping) that my family had made the same decision. The next morning I was standing at the station in my light summer dress, a small handbag in my hand, alone, and tears were running from my eyes. I didn't know what would happen or if I was doing the right thing.

After the war ended, I realized that my decision was the right one. It saved my life. When I finally returned home, I discovered, to my horror, that those who stayed in Estonia had not survived. They were all taken to death camps and killed in gas chambers. So it was with my friend, Sonya, and her grandparents. But my mother and sister had found the opportunity to escape, also. Destiny wanted to reunite us, and finally, we found each other once again.

Spinach and Yogurt Salad

MILA PASTERNAK

This popular salad from the Caucasus can also be served as a dip with pita wedges.

2 bunches spinach,
    well rinsed and stemmed
⅓ cup parsley or cilantro,
    finely chopped
¾ cup plain low-fat yogurt

2 small cloves garlic, crushed
¼ cup lemon juice
¼ tsp sugar
Salt and pepper to taste

Bring 3 cups of lightly salted water to a boil in a large saucepan. Add the spinach and cook ovrer low to medium heat until tender, about 2–3 minutes. Drain and cool; squeeze to remove excess water. Chop as finely as possible.

In a large bowl, combine the chopped spinach with parsley, yogurt, lemon juice, garlic and sugar. Mix well and season with salt and pepper. Cover and refrigerate before serving.

Green Cabbage Salad

RITA FAYNSHTEYN

1 head cabbage, finely shredded
1 carrot, finely grated
½ tsp salt

¼ cup lemon juice
    (juice of 1 lemon)
½ Tbs sugar
1 Tbs vegetable oil

Combine cabbage and carrots.

In a small bowl mix together lemon juice, sugar, salt and oil. Pour over cabbage and carrots and toss. Allow to sit for about 30–40 minutes until flavors blend. Serve.

Vtoroye Blyudo

(Second Course—Soups)

Shtetl life was rigorous and generally centered around the family. In spite of hardship, traditions prevailed. Children played, people conducted the business of everyday survival, and there was comfort in ritual like the familiar smell of mouth-watering soups simmering on the stove....

SOUPS

My Little Shtetl

MATVEI KOUCHNIR
Railroad worker, Tashkent, Ukraine

Many years have passed since I left Mahknovka, the little shtetl where I spent all of my childhood. Mahknovka was a village not far from Vinnetsa, in the Ukraine. There was a big river and a forest nearby. My parents were tailors, and I remember well the happy and enjoyable family celebrations we used to have.

Sixty years ago, the central part of the village had dozens of stone buildings, a hospital and a synagogue. The rest of the houses were made of wood or mud, with straw or iron roofs. The windows were small and square, and the ceilings were very low. The floors were made of clay. Most of the houses were old, crooked and rather miserable looking. The streets and lanes were unpaved. After heavy rains, they were covered with thick, impassable mud. We had to get our water from wells, or from the barrels that stood outside waiting for rain. Usually there were cellars, which stayed cool enough to store foods, since refrigerators were not around. We didn't have electricity, indoor plumbing or any other conveniences.

Nevertheless, Mahknovka was appreciated better than many of the neighboring villages inhabited by Ukrainian peasants. Some people even called it a "town." It was actually a very old Jewish settlement. The famous writer, Sholom Aleichem, even mentioned it in one of his stories. The Jews of Makhnovka were mainly artisans, and they often worked for the inhabitants of other villages in the area. I remember many visitors during the market days. They were often clothed in homemade fur coats and high fur hats, with large red sashes. All the men had big, hanging moustaches. They took seats at the table, and drank Ukrainian vodka (*gorilka*), and ate bread with fat. After lunch, they had endless conversations. They were all friendly to my father; or maybe it only seemed so to me then. Some of them could speak Yiddish well enough.

One day, three policemen came to our house, and broke the floor, walls and ceiling looking for gold coins, which they insisted we had hidden. Of course, there wasn't any money to find. So they arrested my father and mother, and took them to jail, where they stayed for seven months. Meanwhile, the seven of us children were left all alone.

When my parents were released, our life again continued. In 1933, there was a period of starvation throughout the Ukraine. All the people in our town were hungry, and half of them died. But we survived. And then, when the war began in 1941, a terrible tragedy befell the Jews of Mahknovka. Most of the remaining population died at the hands of German or Ukrainian fascists. Again, I survived, and went to fight in the war. After the war, I moved to Tashkent.

Before coming to America, I visited Mahknovka once again, and saw the places I had known in my childhood. I visited the Sheshelevski forest, where are left, forever, my mother, my father and my little sister, who was only eleven years old then. Their names are written in the memorial book in the Museum of the Holocaust at Yad Vashem in Israel. There are no more Jewish families in Mahknovka now.

Matvei's Chicken Soup

MATVEI KOUCHNIR AND ROSALIE SOGOLOW

Matvei gave me the following recipe for his chicken soup: "Put the chicken in a pot and cook it...." I thought perhaps a little elaboration might be in order, and decided to embellish slightly with my grandmother's version. Grandma also liked to use chicken feet for a stronger, tastier soup. I recently saw some for the first time in the supermarket. If you can get them, use several. (I also remember everyone fighting over the tiny, little cooked egg yolks that were always in the pot. I haven't seen them in years, and have often wondered why not. I suppose they came with the freshly killed chickens from the shochet [the man who did the ritual slaughtering]. Now that we buy our fowl already cleaned and packaged, those, too, are only a memory from the past.)

1 soup chicken (with bones)	1 whole onion
3½ qts water	2 carrots, peeled
1 Tbs salt	1 bay leaf
2 stalks celery with tops	1 turnip (optional)
Some chopped fresh parsley	

Clean the chicken and trim off the extra fat. Cut the chicken into quarters and put into salted water in a big soup pot. Bring to a boil and cook over medium heat for about an hour.

Add the rest of the ingredients. Cover and cook over a low heat for another 1½ hours or until the chicken is tender.

Take out the chicken and strain the soup. (The chicken can be eaten as is—or, better yet, you can cut it up and use it in salads or other dishes calling for cooked chicken.)

Cool the soup, and then skim off the fat that comes to the top. Reheat, and serve with rice, kreplach (like pelmeni), knaidlach (matzo balls), barley or noodles. Serves 6–8.

Doctors finally admit what Grandma always knew—it's still the best medicine around!

Solyanka

Irina Menshikov
Speech therapist, St. Petersburg

My husband, Rem, and I met in high school in Leningrad in the 1930s. We were in the ninth and tenth grades. Our youth, before the war, was joyful. We went to movies, the theater, museums, exhibitions, and famous parks. We went to dances, and met many well-known people from our country. In winter, we went skiing, skating and for sleigh rides. Our parents lived in Leningrad, also, and our grandparents lived in a small village. I think our lives were much more interesting than theirs.

We and our children liked the New Year holiday best. There was always a nice, big fir tree with many presents and lots of guests in our home. We often cooked our favorite recipes, like cutlets and solyanka. These are nice, nourishing dinner foods. Solyanka is good served with sour cream, green vegetables, pepper, lemon and olives.

Solyanka (Soup with pickles and various meats)

Irina Menshikov

3 qts water	10 green olives, pitted
1 lb beef*	¼ lemon, sliced
3 onions, chopped	3–4 bay leaves
2 Tbs tomato paste	salt to taste
3 Tbs margarine	dill, fresh
4 sour or dill pickles	1 Tbs nonpareil capers,
½ cup sour cream (or substitute)	rinsed and drained

Using a large stock pot, gently boil the raw meat in 3 quarts of water for 25–30 minutes to make a broth. Remove the meat from the pot, cool and cut into small pieces.

In a frying pan, sauté onions in the margarine until transparent and then mix them with tomato paste. Simmer for 10–15 minutes, stirring constantly.

Peel the pickles and cut them into small pieces.

Add to the stock pot: meat, onion mixture, pickles, capers and bay leaves. Simmer for 10–15 minutes. Add salt to taste.

To serve, garnish with a tablespoon of sour cream (or substitute), a slice of lemon, olives and dill. Serves 10.

This soup can also be made with turkey, chicken, sausage, veal or rabbit.

Life in the Shtetl

BERTA TRILESNIK
Engineer, Moscow

My grandparents lived in a small shtetl called Klichev in Byelorussia. The shtetl was about 50 km. distance from a town. A horse and cart were used for traveling. The shtetl's population was made up of about three hundred Jewish families. They worked as tailors, joiners, shoemakers, blacksmiths or small merchants. There were some families whose men had no trade. These families were living as if by air. They were called "luftmenschen." (A job here—a trade there.) Every Friday, the most hearty women went around to the neighbors and gathered a donation for them: some change, bread, eggs, or whatever could be given. My grandmother was such a woman.

There were two synagogues. Nearby were two cheders (schools) for the children. There was one bath house that was open twice a week: on Thursday for the women, and on Friday for the men. The women worked very hard. Besides cooking, cleaning and raising the children, they also had to chop wood for the stove, and carry water for the family's use. Clothes and linens had to be washed by hand in the river, even in the winter. It's a wonder how they survived.

My grandfather was a shoemaker. He worked alone at home. He sewed and sold new shoes and boots mainly for the peasants of the neighboring regions. He also repaired footwear. There were eight children in the family—seven boys and one girl. When they were old enough, they were taught professions which were in the shtetl. Three sons became shoemakers, four sons and the daughter became tailors. In 1905–1909, three of the sons went away to America. They continued to work as tailors there. But it was quite another life from the one they left behind!

Back in Russia, Jews were helpless and deprived of their rights. For example, occasions like the following could occur: the name would be written on a boy's documents in two ways—"Shimen" and "Semen." When the time approached for him to be called up for military service, the young man naturally appeared *alone*. But the chief would demand the "second one," too. The one who "didn't come" had to pay a fine of 300 rubles. But, of course, the Jews couldn't collect such a sum. So the district police would then arrive at the shtetl, confiscate the family's pitiful property and sell it at auction. Life in the shtetl was a difficult existence.

Escape from Baku

Vera Osipova
Professor of physics, Baku, Azerbaijan

I was born in the town of Piatygorsk, in the North Caucasus. My father was a colonel in the Russian army. He was discharged not long before my birth in 1916, because of a bad injury, and became a teacher of mathematics. When I was six months old, he had to run abroad to save himself from execution during the Revolution. He hoped that the revolt would soon come to an end, and he could return. But as it happened, he was not able to come back again until 1956, and died a year later, to my great distress. Meanwhile, my mother had left Piatygorsk for Baku shortly after my father's departure, since that is where her parents lived. Naturally, she took me with her. I lived in Baku my whole life, until January 1990.

Baku was a very international city before World War II. We did not know, and were not interested in knowing, who was who by nationality in our school or university classes. Two languages were used for education in most schools—Russian and Azerbaijanian. Besides these, there were schools in German, Jewish, Armenian, Greek and Georgian languages. We could visit theaters and read newspapers in all of these languages. But after the war, everything started changing, little by little.

The hardest time began in 1988. Persecution of Armenians became more and more severe. In 1989, Armenians were dismissed from their jobs, and forced to leave and vacate their apartments. At first, they were only threatened. Then, on January 12, 1990, the massacre began. People trembled as bands of men burst into houses, beating and murdering innocent men, women and children. On the streets, cars were burned and the people, too. In one week, 200,000 Armenians ran away or were killed in Baku.

My husband, Khachatur, is Armenian and was a colonel in the Soviet army. We were very frightened. We had lived peacefully for many years, and were both respected in our community. We couldn't understand how people could turn against us so suddenly, when our differences had never mattered before. We lived in the downtown of Baku in a four-room apartment. My husband barricaded the doors of our apartment and of our balcony with heavy furniture. Fortunately, when the bandits tried to force our door, we were being visited by an Azerbaijanian acquaintance of ours. This decent man went out to the bandits and persuaded them that it was his apartment, and that we had moved some time before.

He called us after that and informed us that our son's comrades would come to evacuate us between four and five the next morning. One of these comrades was a Jew, and the second an Azerbaijanian. He warned us to take only my little bag and my husband's briefcase. We even forgot our passports. All during this night, I stood next to the door, listening for the bandits to return.

My son's Azerbaijanian friend called about five A.M. to tell us that he and his Jewish friend, Danik, would come soon. I don't mention his name because I am afraid for his safety, even now. (Danik and his family are presently living in Los Angeles.) They came, and we entered the Azerbaijanian's car. He immediately rushed us to his house, driving for some time by different streets, while Danik followed in his car, watching to make sure that we weren't being followed. Our savior hid us in his house for two days. He succeeded in arranging our departure with an airport clerk, and on the night of January 16, he drove us to the airport, risking the lives of himself and his family.

At the airport, we had to wait in a dark and closed service room. We were told that we had to be quiet and must not speak. The room had an exit to a flying field. We and four other people were taken in a car and driven to a plane, which we boarded while it was still empty. We were accompanied by a girl, maybe a stewardess, who told me to change my face's expression because the airplane would be checked by the "People's Front," and they could throw me out of the plane if I attracted their attention.

We held our breaths, but all passed normally, and we flew to Moscow. In Moscow, we had other difficulties, but not such a horror as it was in Baku. I will thank G–d and the people who saved us till my last breath. Many thanks to the American people, who gave us refuge when our native land turned us out. Why must it be so?

Tanov (Armenian Soup)

VERA OSIPOVA

4 cups nonfat yogurt	2 bunches green onion, finely chopped
4 cups water	1 bunch dill, finely chopped
1½ Tbs rice, raw	1 bunch cilantro, finely chopped
1 Tbs flour	Salt to taste
1 large egg, beaten	

Put yogurt in a pot, add water and mix. Add salt and rice.

In a separate bowl, combine the flour with some of the yogurt–water and stir until lumps are gone. Add to the pot. Add beaten egg to the pot. Bring to a boil, stirring constantly. Reduce heat, add green onions and continue to simmer for 15 minutes. Add dill and cilantro and simmer another 5 minutes. Add salt.

The soup is ready to serve when rice is tender. Total cooking time should be about 20 minutes.

❇ Kharcho (Georgian Beef and Rice Soup)

MAINA NEYMAN

Next to borscht, this has become one of the most popular soups in Russia.

1 lb lean beef	½ cup chopped fresh herbs
(bite-sized pieces)	(parsley, dill, tarragon)
3 qts cold water	½ cup rice, raw
2 onions, coarsely chopped	½ cup black olives, pitted (optional)
2–3 cloves garlic, minced	Salt and pepper to taste
1 small can tomato sauce	3 Tbs fresh lemon juice

In a large soup pot, cover beef with cold water and bring to a boil. Remove the heavy foam that rises to the surface. Turn down heat and simmer for 1½ hours, skimming off any foam that continues to appear. Remove pot from heat and cool quickly so that the fat that rises to the surface and solidifies can be easily removed. Reheat stock before adding onions, garlic, rice, black olives, tomato sauce, salt, pepper, lemon juice and herbs. Simmer 30 minutes longer. Serve.

❇ Sauerkraut Soup

REM MENSHIKOV

3 qts water	1 carrot, cut in 1" pieces
1 lb beef, cubed	1 sprig fresh dill
1 lb jar sauerkraut, drained	1 sprig fresh parsley
2 Tbs butter or margarine	8 black peppercorns
2 Tbs tomato paste	3 bay leaves
1 Tbs flour	Salt to taste
1 onion, sliced	1 Tbs sour cream or IMO
1 rib celery, cut in 1" pieces	

To make beef broth, combine beef, peppercorns, bay leaves and 2½ quarts boiling water in a stock pot and simmer for 30 minutes.

In a separate pot, add sauerkraut and 1 Tbs butter to 2 cups water. Cover and simmer for 50 minutes. Then add to the stock pot.

Sauté onion, celery, carrots, dill and parsley in 1 Tbs butter or margarine until onions are transparent. Stir in the tomato paste. Add to the stock pot.

Combine flour and 1 cup broth. Stir until smooth and then add to the stock pot. (This will thicken the broth.) Add salt to taste. Simmer for another 30 minutes.

To serve, garnish with sour cream (or substitute). Serves 10.

Waiting in Line

MARIA KHASIN
Electrical engineer, St. Petersburg

Before moving to the United States, I lived in Leningrad. Everywhere in Russia, there were big problems buying necessary food and modern clothing. Most of the time, store shelves were practically empty. People had to stand in line for hours to buy anything. This was because our country produced a lot of military products, but not enough things for everyday needs of the people. People would see a line and stand in it without even knowing what was being sold. They thought that if there was a line, something would soon be delivered to the store. The whole process was a frustrating ordeal.

I often listened to the radio, and heard one announcer tell this humorous story: A customer went into a store. Seeing nothing but empty shelves, he asked, "Tell me, please, does this store sell groceries or manufactured goods?" The salesman answered, "When there's nothing to buy, what difference does it make what we sell?" It was humor, but it wasn't a joke. Unfortunately, it was true of life for the Soviet people.

Grandfather Grikovsky Sukar, Yalta, Crimea, c. 1900.
Courtesy Mira Bezymenskaia.

My Friend Shostakovich

Raisa Volkhover
Editor, St. Petersburg

I was ten years old when I met Dmitriy Shostakovich. We lived in Leningrad, and he lived on our street. There was a little garden just opposite his house. All the children used to play ball there. Dmitriy was two years older than me, but we all played together, just the same. His older sister, Marusya, looked after him. She only permitted him to play in the garden for one hour each day. Then he had to go home to practice the piano. None of us supposed that a famous future composer played with us.

In 1922, when he was sixteen years old, Dmitriy's father died, and he had to go to work to help support his family. It was difficult to get work, but he got a job in a cinema, playing piano during the silent movies. He worked at night and continued to study at the conservatory during the day. It was not easy for him. Dmitriy wanted very much to hear the music at the Philharmonic Society, but he didn't have money to buy the tickets. Sometimes, he and his friends sneaked in. They stood all night and listened to the music. It drove the controllers crazy, but they didn't say anything because they suspected that one of them might be a future composer or pianist one day.

In 1923, he began to give his own concerts. He often played a little of his work, along with the music of the famous composers. In 1936, sharp criticism of his music began to appear in the newspapers. He became depressed and thought his life useless. So it was for several years.

When the war began, he joined in the defense of Leningrad. He was often up on the rooftops throwing incendiary bombs. That was a terrible time for everyone. However, Dmitriy Shostakovich found time to write his Symphony in F, and Conductor Karl Eliasberg and the Leningrad Symphony Orchestra performed it. Eliasberg was a very talented and popular conductor, and the newspapers wrote good articles about him and the performance. Unfortunately, the government refused to let him conduct after the war because he was a Jew. He had to travel throughout the country in order to work.

My husband and I remained friends of Eliasberg's family for many years. We often talked about our mutual friend, Dmitriy Shostakovich. I certainly never dreamed that my childhood playmate would some day be known all over the world!

From the Days of the Tsar to Revolution

RAISA VOLKHOVER
Editor, St. Petersburg

Before the Revolution in Russia, there was a monarchy. Tsar Nicolas I had his own soldiers. They had to be tall, handsome and not married. They were taken into this elite army as young as thirteen years of age. They were called "cantonists." My grandfather was one of these soldiers. Jewish people didn't have the right to live in large towns at that time, but after serving in this special regiment for twenty-five years, he was given permission to live in St. Petersburg. And so that was where my mother was born. When she married, she moved with her husband to his home town of Dvinsk (now Daugavpils, Latvia). My father was a manager of railway construction in Kalincovichy. My parents, brother, sister and I lived in a very nice house with a garden. There were many fruit trees.

In 1914, the First World War began. It was summer. We had rented a summer cottage and were staying there when the Germans came. One morning, the German soldiers seized our house and garden. They didn't shoot us, but they terrorized us while they proceeded to shake all the fruit from the trees. When they finally left us, my parents decided that it was urgent for us to go immediately to St. Petersburg until the fighting was over. And so we went to my grandparents' home in that city.

My parents rented an apartment opposite a school for officers. When the Revolution came, the Revolutionaries imprisoned and shot all the young officers and policemen. We couldn't go out into the street because the shooting went on all day long. It was so terrible! When the Soviet authority was established, a shortage of food began. We had nothing to eat. My father drove to the country to buy potatoes. From the peel of the potatoes, my mother made pancakes. The starvation lasted a very long time. Meanwhile, in my grandparents' dining room was a very large table. Around this great table could be seated my grandmother, grandfather, their eight children, grandmother's sister and the five of us. Here we spent many evenings together. We never returned to Latvia, but stayed in St. Petersburg until 1991. I am sad when I think that of this wonderful large family, only my sister and I are still alive today.

▩ Borscht (Cold Beet Soup)

RAISA VOLKHOVER

2 qts water, approximately
3 beets, washed
1 bunch green onions
1 cucumber, peeled and chopped
2 eggs, hard-boiled and cut in half

1 tsp sugar
Salt to taste
Juice of 1 lemon
1 cup sour cream
Dill

Cook beets about 30 minutes or until tender. Keep the water (broth). Peel beets and grate on a coarse grater, return to pot of hot water. Add sugar, salt and lemon juice (all to taste). Cool liquid. Before serving, add cucumbers, green onions and ½ egg to each soup bowl. Add 1 cup cold soup broth to each bowl. Garnish with a dollop of sour cream and dill.

▩ Borscht II

SOFIA LEVIN

2½ qts water
2 Tbs oil
2 beets, washed and diced
2 carrots, sliced
1 onion, diced
1 clove garlic, minced
2 small onions
⅓ cup celery, chopped

3 medium potatoes, halved
1 bunch parsley
1 can (8 oz) stewed tomatoes
1 small head cabbage, sliced
Salt to taste
Sugar to taste
Sour cream, optional garnish

Pour 2½ quarts of water into a large stock pot. Bring to a boil.

Sauté the raw diced beets over low heat for about 10 minutes. Remove from pan and put in the stock pot.

Sauté diced onions, garlic and sliced carrots until the onions are transparent. Add them to the soup pot.

Add the 2 raw onions, potatoes and celery to the pot and cook over low heat for 20–30 minutes, or until potatoes are cooked. Remove potatoes and mash. Return the mashed potatoes to the pot. Add parsley, tomatoes, sliced cabbage, salt and sugar and cook for another 20 minutes. Remove small onions.

Garnish soup with sour cream when serving.

Green Borscht

LYUDMILA ORKIS

Can be served cold in the summer or hot in the winter.

4 quarts bouillon or water	1 Tbs parsley
1 onion, chopped	1 Tbs dill
2 carrots, peeled and coarsely grated	Salt and pepper to taste
1 bunch parsley, chopped	Juice of 1 lemon
5 potatoes, peeled and quartered	Sugar to taste
1 lb spinach, chopped	**GARNISH**
½ lb green onions, chopped	Sour cream
1 Tbs rice	Hard-boiled eggs (sliced)

Boil 4 quarts water in a large stock pot. Add rice, onions, carrots and parsley and simmer for 15 minutes.

Add the quartered potatoes and simmer for another 15 minutes.

Add the chopped spinach, green onions and salt to taste and continue simmering 10 minutes more.

Add dill, lemon juice and sugar. Simmer 2–3 minutes.

Serve with egg slices and sour cream.

My husband's grandmother, Olga Vladimirovna Shakhnovich, was a midwife in a little town called Orgheev, near Kishinev in Moldavia. Photo c. 1900. Courtesy Jenny Khorol-Sharal.

▓ Borscht III

GUSTA DOLBERG

2½ qts water
4 beets, peeled and halved
1–2 carrots, grated
1 rib celery
¼ head cabbage, chopped
1–2 onions, sliced
1 Tbs oil
1–2 tomatoes, chopped

2 Tbs tomato paste
1 clove garlic, minced
Salt and black pepper to taste
1 Tbs sugar
1 Tbs lemon juice or vinegar
1 tsp dill
1 Tbs parsley flakes

Using a large stock pot, cook beets in 2½ quarts of water for 15–20 minutes. When tender, remove the beets from water, cool and then slice. Save the water.

In a large pan, sauté onions and carrots in oil until onions are transparent. Add beets. Continue to sauté for another 2–3 minutes. Add tomatoes and tomato paste.

Add the chopped cabbage to the simmering beet water in the large stock pot. Add the contents of the frying pan. Stir and add salt, pepper, dill and parsley to taste. Continue stirring and add lemon juice and sugar to taste.

▓ Borscht IV

LIYA MELITSEVA

SAUCEPAN 1
2 large beets, washed
1 tsp salt
1 Tbs lemon juice (½ lemon)

SAUCEPAN 3
2–3 Tbs olive oil
½ head cabbage, thinly sliced
2–3 potatoes, peeled and cubed
1 large bell pepper, cut into pieces
2–3 carrots, peeled and cut into small pieces

SAUCEPAN 2
4 qts water
2 ribs celery
1 whole onion
Fresh parsley

2 tomatoes, chopped
1 tsp salt
Sour cream, fresh dill, parsley

Saucepan 1: Place beets and water to cover in a pan. Cook beets about 30 minutes or until soft. Remove from water, cool, peel and then grate. Add salt and lemon juice (this will brighten the color).

Saucepan 2: Place onion, celery and parsley in cold water. Bring to boil and cook for 10–15 minutes. Remove onions and celery and discard. Save broth.

Saucepan 3: In olive oil, sauté cabbage, carrots, potatoes and bell pepper for 10 minutes.

Combine the broth from saucepan 2 and the sautéed vegetables from saucepan 3. Add 1 tsp salt (or to taste) and simmer for 7–10 minutes. Add tomatoes and continue cooking 5 minutes. Add beets and simmer 1 minute longer.

Before serving, garnish with sour cream, some fresh dill and parsley.

The Divided City

GUSTA DOLBERG
Engineer/Economist, St. Petersburg

I was born on February 1, 1913, in Ghmerinka, Ukraine. There was a big train station that divided the city into two parts. Under the station was a tunnel. In one part of the city lived the Jewish population. The social buildings and stores were located here. My grandmother had a grocery store. In the second part of the city lived the Russian people. On this side, there were gardens and orchards.

In 1917, when the Revolution began, the city passed from one power to another. A gang of Ukrainian nationals, called Petlura's gang, terrorized us often. I remember the pogroms well. We hid in the cellar, or we ran to the other side and were hidden by some of the Russians there. One time, there wasn't time to run. The bandits found us and dragged us out of the cellar. They demanded gold. They took my mother's earrings and wedding ring. My grandfather was staying with us, and they beat him. Grandfather was very religious. He had a Torah, which was kept in our house. Fortunately, it wasn't harmed, and it stayed with us until my grandmother gave it to the synagogue after grandfather died. It was a very beautiful and solemn ceremony. A short time later, the synagogue was destroyed, and afterwards it was changed into a club.

We were very poor. My father didn't work. My brother and I had only one pair of shoes between us. We took turns wearing them, so we could go to school every other day. In the 1930s collective farming began. It was also the beginning of a famine, and many people starved to death. In 1931, I left my divided city and moved to Leningrad, where I was married, raised my daughter and son and worked. My parents came to live with me until they died. I came to California in 1993.

Russian Humor

When I asked the class who was usually the head of the family in Russian homes, this was their reply:

In Russia we have a saying: "The husband is the head...but the wife is the neck!"

True Love

LIYA MELITSEVA
Teacher, Riga, Latvia

My aunt Nadya was two years older than my mother. She wanted to become a doctor, and at sixteen years of age she left the family in Siberia and went to Switzerland where she became a student in the medical department of Geneva's university. Grandfather thought that only his sons should have a higher education. He felt that his daughters should prepare for family and house duties. That's why he wouldn't give her any money to continue her studies. To help her, my mother left school to work as a cashier at a local cinema. Everything she earned, she sent to her sister.

While Nadya was at the university, she met Zurab, a Georgian nobleman. They fell deeply in love, and later married. After graduation from the university, they went to Zurab's birthplace—Georgia, in Tbilisi. Nadya was not religious, but nevertheless, she didn't accept Christianity, which was Zurab's religion. They had a civil marriage ceremony. When his mother met Nadya, she warned them that people of different nationalities could not be happy. But in this case, she was wrong. Zurab and Nadya loved each other until their very last day.

My mother was the youngest in the family, and after the death of her parents she was left alone. Nadya took her into her family in Tbilisi and took care of her. Nadya and Zurab raised a wonderful and handsome son, named Otar. He dreamt of becoming a doctor some day, like his parents. But he never returned from World War II. He was only twenty-one years old.

An Unusual Village

MINNA VAYSTIKH
Physician, Voronezh

It happened many years ago. I was a doctor in the Russian city of Voronezh. Once, my department had to work on Saturday. The day before that, one of the nurses came to me and said that she couldn't work on Saturday. When I asked her why, she said that it was forbidden by the laws of Judaism, and that she was surprised that I was going to work. I was shocked to hear it from her because I knew that she had a simple Russian name, and that she came from a small Russian village called Ilynca.

Later, I found out that it was an unusual village. A number of years before, the manager of this village had changed his religion to Judaism, and the rest of the people decided to join him. Since then, they had become very observant Jews.

Now the village is empty, because they all emigrated to Israel.

A Determined Man

IOSIF SHUR
Engineer, Riga, Latvia

My father was born in a little Jewish town called Kadino, in the Mogilev district. The family was big. There were ten children—six girls and four boys. Life was hard. The main food was potatoes. Herring was served only on holidays. Then the brine from this was served with the potatoes on weekdays. Clothes were handed down from older brothers and sisters to the younger ones. My father never put on new clothes until he was thirteen years old. Being so poor, one problem was to find a dowry so that his sisters could get married. That's why they were so busy gathering goosedown for pillows beforehand. At least, each girl had good, soft pillows to begin her married life.

All the boys went to *cheder*. The *melamed* teacher was a very strict man. Once, on a particularly cold winter day, my father's older sister tried to put her shawl on his head as he left the house, since he didn't have his own hat. But, because of his pride, he refused and ran to school with a bare head. His sister ran after him and complained to the *melamed*. The unsympathetic teacher punished him so severely that he remembered that incident all his life.

At thirteen, he left his studies behind, and began to earn a living working as a druggist's assistant. He washed dishes and cleaned up the drug rooms. He managed to continue his education only twenty-five years later, when he was married, had children of his own and was working as a tanner. I was already in school, when my father graduated from worker's school and entered the evening classes of the university. He had never given up his desire to get a good education. All the difficulties of his childhood made him a strong and determined man.

✳ Mushroom and Barley Soup

FAINA BELOGOLOVSKY

2 qts water
2–3 soup bones with meat
1 carrot, peeled and
   cut in half lengthwise
1 stalk celery, with leaves
1 onion, peeled and cut in half
1 parsnip, peeled and cut in half

2–3 sprigs parsley
2–3 dried porcini mushroom caps,
   soaked in hot water 20 minutes.
Salt and white pepper to taste
2 Tbs pearl barley, washed
2–3 potatoes, peeled, cut in pieces
   and boiled

Bring meat bones and salted water to a boil. Skim foam, cover, reduce heat and simmer for about 1 hour. Add carrots, celery, onion, parsnip and parsley.

Remove mushrooms from soaking water, dry and chop coarsely. Add to soup. Simmer for 1 hour. Add barley and simmer for 30–60 minutes more.
Add more boiling water, if needed. Cool and remove fat from surface.

Reheat and season to taste with salt and pepper. Serve with cut-up boiled potato.

✳ Bean–Barley–Vegetable Soup

EDITH KRULAN VIA R.S.

My mother loved to make this bean and barley soup, but she often substituted leftover turkey carcass for the soup bones. I like to make a big pot and freeze it in several containers so that we can enjoy it anytime. It's very hearty and almost a meal in itself.

4–6 qts water
2 lbs chuck with bones
   (or turkey carcass)
2 carrots, peeled and diced
2 stalks celery, diced
1 large onion, peeled and diced

1 parsnip, diced (optional)
1 yam, peeled and diced
1 cup dried lima beans
½ cup barley
1 large can stewed tomatoes
1 Tbs salt

Cover beans with cold water and soak overnight.

Place meat and bones in salted water and bring to a boil. Reduce heat and simmer for about 1½ hours. Skim when necessary. (If using carcass, remove and separate turkey from bones. You can return the turkey meat to the pot.)

Wash and drain barley. Drain and rinse beans. Add barley, beans and remaining ingredients and continue cooking over low heat for about 1½ to 2 hours more or until beans are tender. Add more salt, and pepper if desired. Remove meat bones, if used.

Add a chunk of bread and you'll have a great one-dish meal.

The Clever Thief

ELENA TSYNMAN
Music teacher, St. Petersburg

My father and I were traveling by train. It was 1920, and I was ten years old. The journey was long and tiring. I slept most of the way. We had brought along a big baggage basket to carry our things. It was filled with our best clothes and other items we needed for our trip. My father carefully put the basket under the seat. There were a lot of thieves on the trains, and so my father didn't sleep all night, keeping his eyes on our belongings. He sat on the bench with his feet on the edge of our basket the whole time.

When we arrived at our destination, we got ready to get off the train. To our astonishment, our basket was empty. A clever thief had cut out the back wall of the basket from under the bench and taken out all of our things!

Vegetable–Split Pea Soup

MOLLIE GOFFSTEIN VIA R.S.

Mollie was a terrific cook. She gave me some of her recipes during a Hadassah cooking class.

2 qts water	Fresh parsley, chopped
1½ cups green or yellow split peas	1 carrot, peeled and diced
1 large stalk celery, with leaves	Salt and pepper to taste
1 onion, peeled and chopped	

Wash peas. Put into a large soup pot with salted water and bring to boil. Cover, reduce heat and simmer for 1 hour. Add cut-up vegetables and continue to cook for another hour or until peas are soft but not mushy. Stir frequently to prevent scorching. Season to taste.

For variety, add cooked left-over tongue, beef or sliced beef frankfurters.

Izdeliye iz Testa

(Dumplings and Noodles; literally, "made from dough")

With a resourcefulness and strength they didn't know they had, people struggled to make a future for themselves. The older generation clung to the old ways, while the younger one sought an escape through education and assimilation. Through it all, they never lost the wonderful knack of looking at life with their own particular brand of ironic humor. In a way, this was the ingredient in the "stew" of their lives that made it all tolerable.

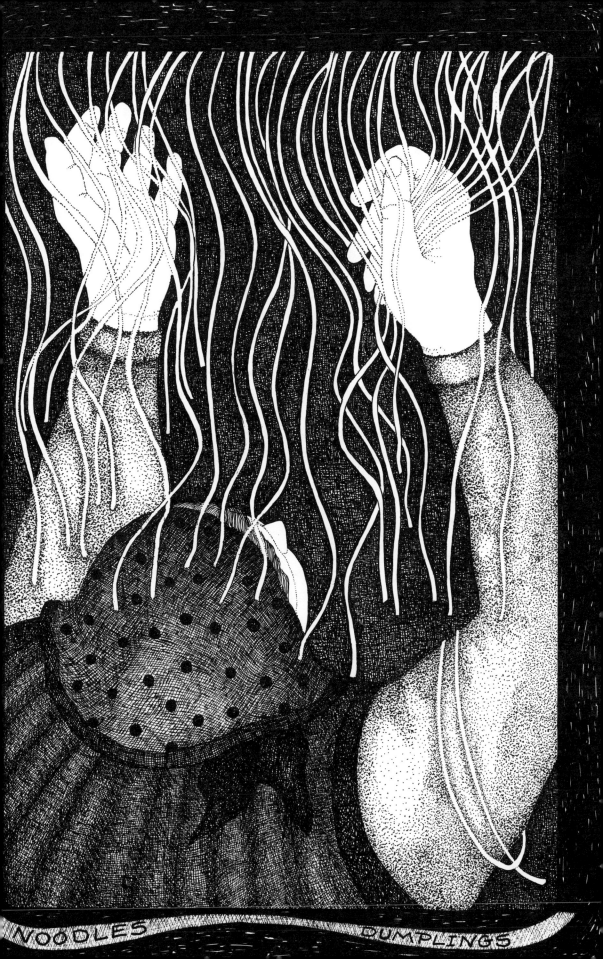

NOODLES DUMPLINGS

Vareniki

VICTOR KOGAN
Builder, Odessa

I was born in a small shtetl called Bershad, which was situated on the border between the Ukraine and Moldavia. It was a wonderful place, with a small river nearby. In any weather, almost all the children of the shtetl were happy to swim and play in its cool water.

The people in this small town were all quite poor, and seldom had celebrations. Our loving parents tried to do their best to make our lives happier. My mother cooked our favorite dishes whenever she could. One of the ones we liked best was vareniki, filled with potatoes or buckwheat.

There were four children in our family. One time, we sat around the table rattling our spoons on the plates (or each other's heads), waiting anxiously for the delectable food. At last, everybody was given a portion of vareniki. We happily began stuffing them into our mouths, chewing greedily. "Woo! Stop! Something is wrong!" I cried. For some reason, I couldn't chew my varenik. I took it out, and found a little piece of cotton in the middle instead of the usual filling. Then an explosion of laughter shook the house. Everyone thought it was so funny. It really was amazing how much pleasure such a simple thing brought to our lives.

Vareniki

VICTOR KOGAN

Similar to ravioli.

DOUGH	FILLING
1 cup sour cream	2 lbs potatoes, peeled and cut into pieces
2 eggs	2 large onions, chopped
2½ cups flour	Butter

Fry chopped onions in butter. Boil the potatoes and mash. Mix together with the fried onion.

Mix the ingredients for the dough and knead until smooth. Roll out the dough and cut into circles. Put a spoonful of filling in the middle of each circle, fold in half and pinch the edges closed.

Boil salted water, and put in the vareniki one by one. After they all come to the top, wait two minutes and then drain. Put on a dish and mix with fried onions, butter or margarine. Serve hot.

⊞ Lokshen Kugel (Noodle Pudding)

ROSALIE SOGOLOW

Kugel was always such a treat at my grandmother's house, that I have been making it and experimenting with it for as long as I can remember. I vividly remember her rolling out the dough with a long broom handle for her homemade noodles. They were then strung out around the kitchen to dry. What a sight! This kugel has been a family favorite for many years. My grandmother made it plain and crispy, without the cream cheese, sour cream or sugar, but my family prefers it just this way. It is a staple accompaniment for our Thanksgiving turkey, or any occasion when a special side dish is desired. It also goes well with Swiss steak or chicken. (Some people like to add apples, raisins, or cinnamon for a sweeter version. You can even add cherries and serve it for dessert.)

1 pkg wide egg noodles
2 eggs (beaten with ½ tsp salt and a pinch of pepper)
½ tsp vanilla
½ large pkg cream cheese
½ pt. sour cream
½ stick margarine
½ cup sugar
Golden raisins, optional
½ cup corn flakes (for topping)

Preheat oven to 350°. Boil noodles and drain. Add eggs with salt, pepper and vanilla. Blend with softened margarine, cream cheese, sour cream and sugar, mixing gently until all ingredients are dissolved and smooth.

Pour into a greased Pyrex baking dish and sprinkle crumbled corn flakes on top.

Bake for 1 hour, or until golden brown on bottom and sides.

This is delicious served hot as a side dish, but my family also enjoys the leftovers cold for lunch the next day.

⊞ Cottage Cheese Pudding (Kugel)

JULIYA GURFINKEL

6 Tbs semolina or farina
1½ cups buttermilk
2 Tbs butter, melted
2 pts. cottage cheese
3 eggs, beaten
¼ tsp salt

Preheat oven to 350°. Mix semolina or farina with the buttermilk and let it stand for one hour.

In a separate bowl, combine the cottage cheese, eggs, butter and salt. Combine both mixtures and mix well.

Coat baking pan with oil or Pam and pour in the mixture. Bake for one hour or until brown. Cool and serve with sour cream or preserves.

Can be served for breakfast or as a main or side dish.

NOTE: This dish has a nice smooth texture but needs accompaniments since it is rather bland alone. If desired, add some sugar and sprinkle with cinnamon.

The Kugel Song

As sung in Yiddish by Judith Gelb and Yelena Belyavskaya

This is a humorous Yiddish folk song about a man whose wife is a terrible cook and gives him nothing but tsouris (trouble). She can't do anything right! Once, she made a kugel from Monday in the morning until Friday at night. When the family cut into it, someone found a stocking inside! Another time, she again made a kugel from Monday morning until Friday night, but when it was time to eat it, she exclaimed, "Oh, my husband, the cat ate it up!"

Ch: Hot a yid a vabbele, hot ehr fum ir tsouris; hot a yid a vabbele, toig zee ahf ka-pouris!

1. Fum Muntig en de frei, biz Fraitig bah nacht, Hot mein vabbele a kugele ge-macht;

Ven iss mer ge-kummen Fraitig tsum essen, "Oy, mein mahn! De katz hot oonga-gessen!

2.

Rochelleh ot a kugel gemacht,
Fum Muntig en de frei biz Fraitig bah nacht.
Ven mer ot dem kugel oongeshnissen,
Eynem hot gefinnen a patyonkee mitten.
(repeat chorus)

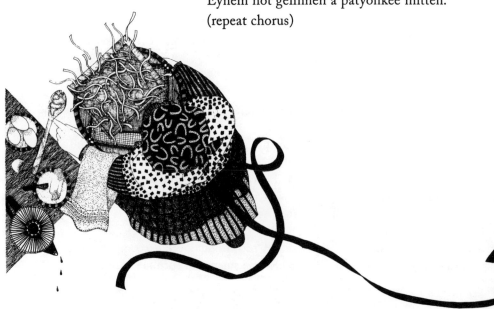

Plum Kugel

VIVIAN HERMAN

6 oz wide noodles
3 eggs
1 cup sugar
1 tsp cinnamon
8–10 Santa Rosa plums, quartered and pitted

TOPPING (optional)
½ cup chopped nuts
2 Tbs melted margarine

Preheat oven to 350°. Cook noodles in boiling, salted water until barely tender. Drain and rinse in cold water.

Beat eggs, add sugar and cinnamon and mix well. Toss noodles in egg mixture. Stir in plums.

Pour into greased 11" x 17" pan, and bake for 50 minutes or until golden brown.

Combine nuts and melted margarine and sprinkle on top if desired.

Makes 6–8 Servings.

Potato Kugel

ETYA NUDELMAN

3–4 medium or large potatoes,
   peeled and grated
3 eggs, beaten
1 large onion, grated
½ tsp baking powder

¼ cup melted chicken fat
1 tsp salt
Pepper to taste
⅓ cup potato starch

Preheat oven to 375°. Grate potatoes and mix quickly with beaten eggs to keep from turning brown. Add grated onions.

Mix potato starch, baking powder, salt and pepper. Add to mixture. Grease a two-quart baking dish with chicken fat.

Bake for 1 hour, or until top is brown and crispy.

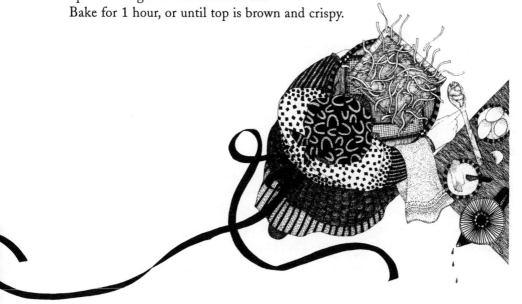

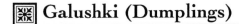

Galushki (Dumplings)

YEUGENIA ROMM

Galushski are pieces of dough boiled in water, milk or stock. This is one of the simplest and most popular of Ukrainian recipes. They can be made from wheat flour, buckwheat flour or a mixture of the two. Semolina or a combination of flour, potato, fresh white cheese, onion and apples can also be used. After shaping them, leave for 20–40 minutes before boiling in salted water, milk or stock. The galushki are ready when they float to the surface. Drain and add a small amount of butter or sour cream, and shake them about in it. Serve hot as a side dish.

3 cups flour	¾ cup water
3 eggs	2 tsp chicken fat (or butter)
1 tsp salt	4 qts boiling water

Beat the eggs, flour, water and salt with a mixer at medium speed, until small bubbles appear.

Boil 4 qts water. Drop dough by spoonfuls into the water. Use a second spoon to push pieces off first spoon. Dumplings should be small as they will puff up when cooked. Continue to cook for about five minutes.

Drain well and mix with fat or butter until all the galushki are coated. Can be served with gravy as a side dish for chicken or meat.

Apple Galushki

YEUGENIA ROMM

10 apples, peeled, cored and cut into tiny pieces	1 Tbs sugar
¾ cup milk	½ tsp salt
4 eggs	1½ cups wheat flour
	4 qts boiling water

Pour milk over the apple pieces. Beat eggs with sugar and salt and add to the apples. Gradually add the flour to the mixture, a little at a time.

With a teaspoon, pick up bits of the dough–apple mixture and drop by spoonfuls into slightly salted boiling water. Test one to see if it is cooked. They are ready if they look dry inside when cut open.

Childhood Pleasures

Malvina Alexandravskaya
Engineer, St. Petersburg

My childhood was spent in a village. The hospital where our mother worked stood on the border of the village on a high hill. In winter, when there was a lot of snow, we flew down the slope on our sleds from our gate to the main street. After that we were forced to climb back up the steep hill, but it was so much fun flying down again!

The hospital occupied a large area. There were three big buildings: the hospital itself, the building with flats for the employees and the barracks, set apart from the others, where the critically ill lay with typhus. In the time after World War I, there were many such terribly sick people. Our mother nursed them. I remember how careful she was in order to safeguard her family. She even cut our hair very short in summer, to help protect us from the disease. There were auxiliary buildings nearby for the cows and the chickens and for the horses, which carried the doctors to the sick people who couldn't come to the hospital themselves. Next to these were gardens. I remember our garden. There were fruit trees: apples, cherries, pears and plums. My parents grew vegetables, too. And how beautiful were the roses!

The whole hospital area was surrounded by a fence, and beyond the fence began the boundless Ukrainian steppe. In summer we children played in the garden every day, or went to the steppe, picking flowers or running hard. Sometimes, running in the steppe without paths, we got lost. But there was one big hill which we named "a guiding star." When we came to this high hill, we would climb up to the top, and then we could find our way home.

We often strolled with our cousin, Sofa, the daughter of my mother's brother, whom we helped in our youth when she became an orphan. At sixteen, Sofa became ill with tuberculosis. Because we lived in the village and my parents could provide her with the best nourishment and care, we took her out of Moscow to live with us. She lived with our family for two years and recovered. Sofa was a dreamer, a bright and kind girl, and we loved her very much.

This is how I lived until I was eleven years old, and my parents decided to send me to school in Moscow. Even though I had studied only at home until then, I was educated enough for a child my age. When I was in the seventh class, our school gave an examination of mental abilities to the pupils in the seventh, eighth and ninth classes. The results exceeded all my expectations—I was third in the whole school!

When I came to stay with Sofa's family in Moscow, she often took me to museums and theaters. How lucky I was to see plays by famous writers such as

Anton Chekhov. I've remembered his plays all my life. In such ways we enjoyed ourselves. And we studied, too, and read very much. My parents had a good library, and so did our neighbors. My best entertainment then—and all my life to this day—has always been reading! These are some of the pleasurable memories of my childhood days.

A Mini Detective Story

ELENA TSYNMAN
Music teacher, St. Petersburg

It was the summer of 1925 in St. Petersburg. It was graduation day, and all the teachers and students gathered for the special event. But the graduation ceremony couldn't begin because one teacher, Vera Nicolaevna, hadn't arrived yet, and she had all of our diplomas. She lived near our school, and so two of the students went to get her. But they didn't come back. After a while, several more students went to see what happened. They disappeared, also. Some other students, following this group, had heard the front door of the apartment open and close. Their friends were allowed in, but nobody came out. They crossed the street and saw a piece of paper falling out of the window. It was a note from one of the girls in the class. She wrote that there was a police ambush in the apartment and nobody was allowed to leave.

This was the time of the white nights in St. Petersburg. A long time had passed, but even though night came, it was still light outside. There were a lot of people in the apartment, and all of them were hungry. We sent several students to bring them food. They didn't come out either. The rest of us were crowded on the street in front of the building, worried and waiting for a glimpse of our teacher and friends. Soon it became clear that the ambush had failed. The door suddenly opened, and everyone came pouring out.

The next day we finally had our graduation party. There was a lot of talk about the events of the previous night. But what really happened? The police wanted to arrest one young man who lived in this apartment. He was a member or a leader of a political group at the university. We never found out what happened to him. Maybe he was the brother or the neighbor of our teacher. We couldn't ask her about this frightening experience. It was such a time and such a country where these questions could be neither asked or answered....

What Did You Say?

Different countries have different proverbs or sayings to express similar ideas. They give us insight into the character of their people. Here are a few ways Russians and Americans attempt to say the same thing:

English: Half a loaf is better than none.
Russian: When there is no fish, a crab is a fish.

English: If at first you don't succeed, try, try again.
Russian: The first pancake is always a flop.

English: You can't have too much of a good thing.
Russian: You can't spoil the kasha with butter.

English: Never put off till tomorrow what you can do today.
Russian: Work isn't a wolf. It won't run into the forest.

English: I wasn't born yesterday.
Russian: Don't hang noodles on my ears!

About Pelmeni

JENNY KHOROL-SHARAL
Radio engineer, St. Petersberg

There wasn't any railroad in Siberia until the twentieth century. People traveled in coaches in summer and by sled in winter. Travelers could change horses at postmail stations, situated along the highway about thirty miles apart. I think that pelmeni were invented in the eighteenth century to feed travelers in winter. Intending to cross Siberia or get to the Far East, people prepared a large quantity, froze them, put them into a bag and knew that they would not suffer from hunger. They could boil them at the way stations. Pelmeni were tasty, nutritious, convenient for traveling and easily stored during the Siberian winters with air temperatures between −20° and −60°.

Now they have lost their former purpose, but they still remain one of the favorite Russian dishes. We eat them the entire year because they are easy to keep in the freezer even in summer.

 # Pelmeni

JENNY KHOROL-SHARAL

Siberian meat dumplings, similar to Chinese wonton or Jewish kreplach.

PASTRY	FILLING
2 cups flour	1 lb ground beef*
½ cup cold water	1 large onion, finely chopped
1 egg	1 tsp salt
½ tsp salt	¼ tsp pepper

Knead the pastry hard. Roll it into very thin sheets and cut into 3" x 3" pieces. Mix the onion with the ground meat and add salt and pepper to taste. Put one teaspoon of the filling on each square and fold over and seal the edges. Put the dumplings into boiling salted water and boil for 4–5 minutes.

When ready, serve with chicken soup or with sour cream. Serves 3–4. (Russians sometimes like to serve this with butter or vinegar.) Can be frozen and stored for many months.

*NOTE: It is possible to use other fillings, including boiled, mashed potatoes with finely chopped fried onions, farmer's cheese mixed with eggs and sugar, or kasha. Dumplings with such fillings are called "vareniki." You can also use chicken or another favorite meat instead of beef.

My Grandfather

Jenny Khorol-Sharal
Radio engineer, St. Petersburg

My mother's father and my own father were the most interesting people in my family. My grandfather lived in the little town of Cherniga in the Ukraine most of his life. He had a big family with many children. Three of them died in infancy, and his youngest son was killed by bandits in 1919, at nineteen years of age. Five daughters and two sons survived. He owned a brick factory and a large house with a big orchard. There weren't any cars in our little towns at the turn of the century, so he used good horses and a carriage. He received a religious Jewish education, but in Russian he could only read and write. He wanted his children to be well-educated and learned people. All his daughters and sons finished gymnasiums (high school). The older son studied at the Medical University in Berlin, but World War I and the Revolution prevented him and the youngest daughter from graduating from the university.

In 1914, on the eve of World War I, my grandfather moved to Odessa. He bought a factory there and a luxurious two-storied country house with an orchard in the suburb of Odessa on the Black Sea, and a large apartment downtown. He lost all of his property in the October Revolution of 1917. All his daughters with their children came to live with him. He had to support the whole family. The old man mastered a new profession. He became a builder. He didn't have any professional license or any schooling in this, but he was a smart and capable man. I remember that he was a chief master when a complex of many houses for homeless children was being built. I passed there four years ago, and saw that his houses are still solid.

He was a very kind, honest and delicate man. I was ten or eleven when he discussed with me the main ideas of his life, religion and his attitude toward G–d, political views and his attitude toward the Revolution. He was very religious, and I didn't believe in G–d. He was against the Revolution, and I defended Lenin and the Bolsheviks. He tried to persuade me, but never was angry or rude. He died in 1931 of a stroke, and I remember him with love and esteem all my life.

People serve pelmeni for ordinary meals and for special occasions. Guests are often invited to a "pelmeni party." According to an old tradition, the cook puts some object like a button into one pelmen, instead of the filling. It is a sign of good luck for the person who gets this special dumpling.

As I Look Back....

Jenny Khorol-Sharal
Radio engineer, St. Petersburg

I remember my life from about the age of three. We lived in a little house with a cherry orchard on the grounds of a sugar factory in Poltava's District. My family lived there until 1918. These were happy years. My parents loved me very much, and I had many little friends and toys to play with. I learned to read at three and a half, and reading has been my favorite occupation all my life.

In 1918, the German army came to our village, and my frightened mother took me and ran away to Odessa where her parents were living. During the next two or three years, we traveled back and forth many times, but returned to Odessa in 1920. These trips were very difficult since a civil war roared in the Ukraine. There were no schedules, no tickets, trains arrived and departed at any time, and all the railroad stations were full of waiting crowds. People sometimes waited at these stations for weeks. They slept on floors and ate only occasionally. There was dirt, lice, typhus and spotted fever. During these journeys, roving bands fired at the trains and uncoupled railway cars. The cars were so full of people that once we had to travel for a whole night and a day on a platform. Sometimes we traveled in cattle cars.

I was eight when we finally came back to Odessa to stay. We lived with my grandparents and all their family—nine adults and four children from two to fourteen years old. The apartment was large, but after the Revolution two of the rooms were occupied by strangers. Most of the family didn't have jobs, so we were poor. I couldn't go to school because I didn't have any coat or shoes. I studied at home with some private teachers. Most of my teachers taught me for nothing or for only a modest sum. I studied mathematics, grammar, Russian literature, piano and French. I was able to attend school only in the sixth and seventh classes. There weren't any high schools then in the Ukraine, only seven classes of working "labor" schools.

But my main education I received in the Children's Library. I spent every free minute there every day. I wanted to know everything! Several young women who worked as librarians were clever, well-educated and experienced teachers. They organized many exciting "circles" or groups. We put on many interesting performances for the children, such as "The Discovery of the North Pole," "The Search for the Amundsen Expedition," and so on. My life was happy and full of interests. I am thankful to these wonderful women for my childhood and adolescence. The last of them died a year ago in Moscow. She was ninety-three. My little comrades from the library became my friends for life.

From 1920 until World War II (1941), I lived in the beautiful town of

Odessa. Odessa is a young town. This year it celebrated its 200th birthday. The streets are straight and planted with big trees, the houses have three or four floors, and all around there is the Black Sea. Really, it isn't black, but blue or green or turquoise, depending on the weather. Most of my life I've lived in many other different cities, but everywhere I've gone I've always remembered and loved my Odessa.

Before the War

JENNY KHOROL-SHARAL
Radio engineer, St. Petersburg

In 1929, our country (the USSR) began to industrialize. I had been unable to obtain work until then, but with many new jobs opening up, I became an employee of a library, where I met my future husband. He was hired the same day as I and was a student of the Institute of Electrical Communications. I also wanted to study in some institute, but didn't have the necessary training. My first attempt to enter Odessa University was unsuccessful. In 1931, I tried to enter the Institute of Electrical Communications. My exam marks were excellent, but it was not enough. The Communist party and the Soviet state wanted to train their own intellectuals and allowed an education only to "workers" and their children. I was just an office worker and was not accepted. But state industry badly needed engineers because many old engineers had been shot, and many new factories had been built. So in April of 1932, I was finally received as a student at the institute. (There was famine in the Ukraine at this time, and of the forty freshmen in my class, only eight made it to the next year!)

At this time, I was already married. Our marriage in 1931 was not celebrated or marked in any way. Then there were no wedding ceremonies, no festivities in our country. We came to a little, untidy, dark room in the building of our district Soviet. Posters hung on the walls of this room instead of pictures. They showed patients with features of different venereal diseases and some inscriptions, such as "Kissing spreads infections." We were very young. I was eighteen, and my bridegroom twenty-one. We loved one another, so we only laughed about such scenery. Nobody congratulated us. The clerk only asked if we had any diseases. After our marriage, we lived separately for two years, each with his parents, because we had no money and no apartment. Nobody knew that we were married. Only in 1933, when my husband graduated from the institute did we begin our common life. We lived together for fifty-seven years, until my husband died in 1989.

My husband was a very clever, well-educated and smart person. He loved our children and me dearly, and our life was happy. After he graduated, he stayed at the institute for the postgraduate course and received his master's degree. At the same time, he worked as an assistant lecturer, as a teacher at the college of Electrical Communications and as an engineer at the Institute's workshop, which produced special radio instruments for merchant ships. He earned enough money so that the last year at the institute, I was able to manage well without working. I, also, stayed at the institute for the postgraduate course. But this course was eliminated because our only professor, a Doctor of Technical Science, was arrested and exiled to Siberia.

After our daughter was born, the three of us continued to live in one little room of our communal flat. My mother, her second husband and his daughter occupied another two rooms, and two strange families resided in the remaining two rooms. There was no bathroom at all, and only one lavatory for all the residents. The only sink and faucet were in the kitchen. (We could not have another apartment until 1940, when our institute gave us a big room, also in a communal flat.)

In 1938, my father was arrested and shot in prison. I had to inform the Komsomol committee about that event. We were both active members of Komsomol, and my husband was already the professor of the radio chair and director of the workshop. The summer of 1938 I'll remember till my death. We lived in a rented country cottage with my little daughter (eight or ten months) and my poor father's daughter (fifteen months). Every night we waited for the KGB to come and arrest my husband. Sometimes people asked me, "Where is your husband? Is he arrested?" The questions to him were even more forward. "Oh, aren't you arrested yet?" The cause of arrest wouldn't be some crime or fault, but the official position of some person in charge. We lived in fear that whole summer, but we were lucky. He somehow remained free and alive.

In 1939, World War II began. Some of my friends took part in the annexation of Poland and in the war with Finland. We were indignant about the union of our country with fascist Germany, but were powerless to do anything about it. In 1940, life became easier. Mass arrests ceased. We hoped that all would be good and that life would be peaceful and happy in the future....

My father, Jacob Khorol-Sharal, in Kiev, circa 1912. He was a student at the University of Kiev at this time. In 1938, at age fifty-three, he was arrested and shot. In 1958, twenty years after his death, his name was cleared because he hadn't committed any crime.

The Years of Darkness

JENNY KHOROL-SHARAL
Radio engineer, St. Petersburg

The war began at night, but we were informed of its beginning only at noon on June 22, 1941. It was a joyful, sunny day. I was at home with my little three-year-old daughter. The news was like thunder in a clear sky. The next night, my husband had to leave for his military unit on the Romanian border. My mother and daughter were hiding in an air raid shelter near our house, and I accompanied my husband to the railroad station. German planes bombed it as we waited for the train's departure in a nearby cellar. After two hours of waiting, my husband left and didn't return. So I went home and didn't know if he was alive or dead.

In the middle of July, a political commissar from my husband's military unit came to Odessa and brought to the officers' wives credentials necessary for evacuation. I could take only my daughter and my husband's parents. My mother and stepfather weren't listed on my documents and had no right to evacuate. We set off by ship and then by train for Stalingrad, where in my father's house lived his wife and my little four-month-old sister. At this time, Stalingrad seemed very far from the front lines. But the German army moved forward very fast, and in October my husband was already in Sevastopol (Crimea), and the Germans were near Stalingrad.

Sevastopol's defense was one of the most heroic pages of the war's history. The naval fortress was surrounded by land and sea by the enemy army. It was bombed from the air and shelled from land. They resisted for two hundred and fifty days. Most of the defenders died during the siege, and Jews were killed after the town's defeat. My husband had been transported to the Caucasus before the end, because he had discovered the secret of a new German underwater mine, which had been raised from the bottom of the sea by our minesweepers. He had to report this secret to the Black Sea naval staff. He stayed in Novorossiysk, became a naval officer instead of an army one and was sent to the Mine Unit.

In October 1941, it was already clear that we must leave Stalingrad and go somewhere in middle Asia. My uncle had been evacuated to Leninabad (formerly Khodjent), a Tajhiks town. We decided to go there, too. My mother, my stepfather, my aunt (my mother's twin) and my young seventeen-year-old cousin were then in Stalingrad, too. At the beginning of November, all my family (all eight persons) went by ship down the great river Volga to Astrakhan—a big seaport on the Kaspiy Sea. There we were forced to live for twelve days and nights under open skies, without food or hot water. It snowed, it was cold, and ten or fifteen thousand people had to wait in such inhuman conditions for some means of transportation. At last, a small trader ship took us. All adults were on the deck. Only my child had a little place under the stairs inside the ship. We traveled across the sea maybe ten or twelve days, because all the seaports were frozen, and our ship got stuck in the ice, too. Finally, a small ice breaker came and pulled us out.

A measles epidemic, complicated by pneumonia, broke out. When we came to the seaport of Krasnovodsk, we brought ashore fifteen dead children and two or three dead adults. My daughter was ill also. I wanted to put her in the local hospital, but my mother-in-law and my stepfather, who were both doctors, persuaded me to continue our travels. They didn't think it was dangerous for the child. Five days later, our trip was finished. I put my stepfather into the hospital with frozen toes, and took my little girl to the Children's Hospital. But it was too late. She died of meningitis as a complication of the measles and pneumonia.

I didn't want to live any more. But I had to support my relatives—five feeble and ill seniors and one very young girl. I received my husband's salary, and I began to work as a technician at the radio station. My mother-in-law became a doctor in a military hospital. My cousin also worked at my station, so we could rent an apartment and buy some food. My stepfather endured amputation of his toes, after which he also began working as a doctor at the hospital. Some months later, I became the chief engineer of the district management of communications. I didn't have sufficient training for such a position, but all the men were at the front, and women—even the inexperienced—were drafted to replace them.

But I wanted to take part in the war, and in the spring of 1943, I obtained permission to join my husband. Then for two years I worked at the sweep workshop of the Black Sea navy. At first, my husband and I lived in the town of Poty. Then Sevastopol was liberated in 1944, and we were transported there. It was a Black Sea naval base. All our workers were its residents. I was a commissar of the train, which transported all the workers, their families and equipment home.

We traveled across ruined towns and villages of the Ukraine. But the most terrible was the sight of an uninhabited Crimea. All the houses in the villages were empty—no people, no animals. By Stalin's order, all Tartars had been deported to Siberia or to Kazakhstan. Sevastopol was ruined, and ninety percent of the houses were demolished. I walked from the railroad station, across the town to the bay, because I had to inform the command of our arrival. I didn't meet any people, any cats or any dogs. I worked in Sevastopol for fifteen months, and my husband was transferred to Leningrad.

In Leningrad, he acquired a new profession: specialist of a new naval weapon—torpedoes. I accompanied him to Leningrad, and it was the beginning of a new life. We thought that after such a war and such a victory all would change. No anti-semitism, no injustice, all people would be satisfied. Alas! It was not to be so.

I worked as an assistant to a professor at the Institute of Electrical Communications, but in 1950, I was dismissed with many other Jews. My husband was demoted to a lower position because of his nationality. In 1953, many trains were ready to deport all the Jews from Leningrad, Moscow and other cities to Siberia. Stalin died on March 5, and it was our great chance. We were left in peace....

After the War

JENNY KHOROL-SHARAL
Radio engineer, St. Petersburg

My husband and I joined the Communist party in 1944, during the war. We knew about the multiple arrests in the late thirties, but we believed that they were necessary, though sometimes there were judicial mistakes. After the German assault, all the Soviet people were ready to sacrifice their lives for the defense of our homeland, and we were sure that after the war everything would be changed in our country. Rank and file communists were the first in battle and the first at work. We wanted to be in the first ranks, also. So we joined the Party.

My son, Yevgeniy, was born in 1948, and my daughter, Svetlana in 1957. From 1950 until 1976, I worked at the College of Electrical Communications. At first I was a teacher of radio subjects, then a head of the radio department. I was in charge of 500 to 600 students of three to four specializations. I liked my work very much and loved my children dearly. Life was full, but it wasn't easy.

In 1947, the monetary reform was fulfilled and product distribution cards (a legacy from the war) were canceled. There was enough food in Moscow and Leningrad, but it was difficult to buy shoes, dresses, coats and so on. And the most difficult was for the whole family to live in one single room of a communal flat. It became possible to buy an apartment in a housing cooperative only in 1964. We bought a small one with two bedrooms, one living room and a little kitchen. It had nearly 400 square feet of living space. It was impossible to move, but as my husband was a doctor of technical sciences, a colonel in the navy and a Lenin prize winner (one of the highest Soviet awards), after being on the waiting list for five years, we were allowed to purchase a bigger, four-room apartment in a suburb of Leningrad.

After Stalin's death, secret documents about the years of terror were published. It was awful. We learned about the millions of innocent people who were shot or exiled without trial, by decision of a "troika" (three persons) appointed by the KGB. The leadership of the party told us about all of these acts. After the death of Stalin, there was a "thaw" period. Most of the political prisoners were rehabilitated, and Jews could find jobs or enter the university. We believed in the "thaw" and in the change of the party's policy. But the "thaw" lasted for only a short time, and our leader, Khrushchev, was not a clever man. He made many mistakes, and nobody was allowed to correct him or point out the defects of his policy because he was a dictator with immense, unlimited power. He was sent away in 1964, and the leaders after him were foolish, uneducated and rough people.

In 1964, the situation in the Communist party changed. Brezhnev became general secretary instead of Krushchev, and life in our country began to deteriorate. Neither of my children were able to find jobs after finishing the institute, even though they were excellent students. In 1974, my son applied for permission to leave the USSR for Israel, which was his historical homeland. Many young people wanted to do the same. The government dealt harshly with them. They were dismissed from their jobs, excluded from the university, and often imprisoned for some absurd cause. Their parents, also, were expelled from the party, and dismissed from their jobs. They were accused of treason and labeled "traitors." Yevgeniy applied for immigration on February 1, 1974. My husband was dismissed on February 3. He was the director of a big military torpedo laboratory, which worked under his management very effectively. He had already retired, but continued to work at the laboratory since this work was very important for the Soviet navy. But that didn't matter, because he was a "traitor's father." He was also dismissed from the shipbuilding institute where he was a professor. I continued to work because nobody in my college knew anything about my son. Yevgeniy ended up working odd jobs in garden park management, and finally as a night cashier at a bank. (He had graduated in 1970 as a mathematician.) Meanwhile, he was arrested on a false charge of acting against the militia. He was freed thanks to the efforts of his father and his wife.

We were used to bad leaders, but supposed that leadership would be on a collective basis. The newspapers, radio and television informed us about the successes of our industry and agriculture. At the same time, living conditions continued to get worse. Shops were empty, and in order to buy something, you had to waste a lot of time in lines. We understood that everything was bad, but were used to suffering and felt it was our duty to work and support the country.

In 1975, Yevgeniy found a job as a programmer in an office and worked there until 1988, when he was finally allowed to leave the USSR and go to Israel. While he was in transit in Vienna, he decided to go to California instead, because his good friends and sponsors lived there.

My daughter also had many troubles with her work. After three years, she was discharged from her first job and began to search for another position. She found many openings, but everywhere she was told that "It's not for Jews." She worked temporarily as an engineer of safety and a part-time guide at the Pavlovsk Palace. Only in 1979 did she find a job in a research institute of the printing industry as an electrical and then a patent engineer.

It wasn't until the 1980s that we understood the falsehood of the whole system and of the Communist ideology. My husband died in 1989 of an awful illness. Many of his pupils, former colleagues, naval officers and friends came to his funeral, which was a military ceremony. It was after his death that my daughter and I decided to emigrate to the United States. We joined my son in San Jose on March 22, 1991. Our life here is not free of troubles or mishaps, but the social atmosphere here is optimistic and living conditions are good. There are many good people. I like America very much and I'm thankful to it. But my heart still worries about my native land and its misfortunes.

Matzo Balls with Beef Filling

ROSA KINBERG

½–1 lb ground sirloin	2 tsp salt, and pepper to taste
1 onion, chopped	7 eggs, beaten
4 Tbs oil	1 cup water
2 cups matzo meal	Butter or margarine, melted

In a frying pan, brown beef and onions in a little oil. Drain off fat and set aside.

Combine matzo meal, salt and pepper. Combine eggs, oil and 1 cup water. Mix together dry and wet ingredients and refrigerate for 1 hour.

To make matzo balls, wet hands and roll a small amount of mixture into a ball. With your thumb, make a pocket in each one and fill with some beef–onion mixture. Add more matzo mix if necessary to enclose meat. Drop the stuffed matzo balls into a large pot of rapidly boiling water. Boil for 20 minutes. When finished, carefully remove from pot, drain and serve with melted butter or margarine, if desired.

NOTE: For lighter matzo balls, separate 3–4 of the eggs and reserve the whites. Before forming balls, beat egg whites until stiff and stir into mixture.

Potato Dumplings with Chicken or Meat

EDITH KRULAN VIA R.S.

6 potatoes, peeled and boiled
3 Tbs chicken fat
⅔ cup matzo meal
3 eggs

¼ tsp pepper
2 cups cooked chicken or meat
 (ground or cut fine)

Preheat oven to 375°. Mash potatoes with chicken fat. Mix with 2 beaten eggs, meal, salt and pepper. Bind meat with other egg and season to taste.

Take a spoonful of potato, place some meat on it, cover with more potato and roll into a ball. Place on a greased pan and bake until brown (about 20 minutes).

Soup Mandlen (Soup Nuts)

ROSA GOLDSHTEYN

2 eggs
2 Tbs water
1 Tbs vegetable oil

¼ tsp salt
1 cup flour

Preheat oven to 350°. Combine all ingredients and beat until the dough reaches a creamy consistency. Grease a cookie sheet with oil and drop 1 tsp of batter to make each piece. Bake about 20 minutes. Makes about 3 dozen.

Serve in soup or bouillon.

The Jewish Village

ASYA CHERNOMORDIK
Engineer, St. Petersburg

I was born in 1914 in a village in Byelorussia. It was called Litsevo. This village was interesting because there were only thirteen families there, and all of them were Jewish. I remember that they all plowed the soil. There was enough land for everyone. One man was a shoemaker, and there were dressmakers, also. My uncle had nine children, five sons and four daughters. He had two houses, a cow and a horse. The most interesting thing was that the big house was our synagogue. On the wall, there was a closet covered with a very nice curtain. A *Mogen David* (Star of David) was embroidered on it. And the Torah was inside. People came to my uncle to pray on Fridays, Saturdays and all holidays.

My parents also had a house, a storage shed, a cow and some poultry. I remember that on Chanukah and Passover, geese and turkey were served. During the war, the fascists destroyed our village, and all the remaining inhabitants. My parents had moved to the city of Nevel in 1924, to my father's parents' house. They had ten children, but by the time we got there, they had all moved away to different cities. One of my uncles had even gone to America.

What can I say about the happiness of a seven-year-old child? Our parents loved us so much. We had a good time. I was the eldest, and I was often taken to my grandfather's cheder. He wanted me to study, but I didn't want to. I became a pioneer. Now, I do not even know the Hebrew alphabet, though I remember all the rules and traditions. I always think about the holiday dinners with gefilte fish, and horseradish made with beet juice, tzimmis with chicken or turkey, and broth with knaidlach (dumplings), rice or homemade noodles. And, of course, on Passover, dishes made with matzos. My mother used to make a wine with raisins to go with it all.

Once the war came, all those good times changed. But, now I'm in America. It's a long way from my little village. But our family still continues the old customs and traditions. And we can still enjoy all our favorite foods.

Living in a Prison

ETYA NUDELMAN
Pediatrician, Kiev

In 1945, I lived in the city of Kuybeeshev, where I finished high school. I wanted to enter the medical institute. First, I had to pass four examinations. I did very well, and passed them all. I became a student at a first-year pediatric faculty and went to live in a hostel. This hostel building had a history. Some years before, it had been a prison. It was a very big building. A famous revolutionary, for whom the city was named, was imprisoned in this place. These cells have been turned into a museum. Some students lived in these small rooms, but new students lived in the basement.

Twenty other girls and I lived in one of these basement rooms. It was awful. At night, the rats visited us and ran across the tables. I was the only Jewish person in our room, but I didn't experience anti-Semitism at this time. Life was difficult. My parents had returned to Kiev. I had to live on my stipend and whatever they could send me, such as Ukrainian fruits, beans and millet. But I wanted very much to learn, and I studied hard. I was always joyful because I was young.

In 1949, I came back to Kiev, and was a student at the Kiev Medical Institute. Here I felt what it meant to be Jewish. I thought I wanted to become an ophthalmologist, but I was forced to specialize in pulmonary therapy. It wasn't my choice. After I finished my studies, I began working in Dunbas. Fortunately, my chief was an understanding man. Since I was interested in pediatrics, he helped me to continue my studies and become a pediatric pulmonologist.

Goodbye, My Dear Place

Yelena Belyavskaya
Architect, Moscow

In the center of the heart of the capital town of Russia, Moscow, there is the house of the Moscow government. It is one of the most beautiful buildings in the city. It was built in the eighteenth century by the great Russian architect, Kazakov. A statue of a horseman, the Tsar General Skobelev was there. After the Revolution in 1918, this statue was destroyed. Another monument was erected in its place. It was called the Monument of Freedom. It was a big obelisk with a woman holding a torch on the top of it. On the obelisk were written the words of the first Russian constitution.

In 1946, Stalin destroyed the Monument of Liberty, and the space received a new name: Soviet Space. It took eight hundred years to build Moscow. The founder of the city was Uriy Dolgorukiy. In 1947, on Moscow's eight-hundredth birthday, a new statue of Uriy Dolgorukiy on a horse was installed and has stood till this day.

I was born and lived many years near this spot. In my childhood, I often walked and played with my friends there. When I was a student of architecture, I had dates with boys there. I have always liked it. Before I left my city for the last time, I went there to have one last look, and to say, "Goodbye, my dear place!"

Pirogi and Piroshki

(Filled pies, large and small)

The Communists copied a page from Ivan the Terrible's gruesome history. During Joseph Stalin's era of the gulag in the 1930's, the soil of Mother Russia was littered with victims of his cruelty. Stalin's unspoken but well-known policy of discrimination against the Jewish population affected every aspect of their lives.

But neither the confinement of the shtetl nor the repressive policies of Stalin's regime discouraged people from searching for a better way of living. After World War II, there was a loosening of some restrictions, but on the whole life still presented a challenge, which a determined people strove to overcome. Like the pastries which they love, they, too, were filled with surprising flavor and diversity.

PIROGI   PIROSHKI

The Biggest Robbery of All

Maria Khasin
Electrical engineer, St. Petersburg

After World War II, with government encouragement anti-Semitism increased. I finished my studies at the institute in 1951, but because of this discriminatory policy, I was unable to get a job. In 1953, after Stalin died, things got a little better, and I began working at a military factory. Shortly afterwards, the factory received a plot of land outside of the city that the employees could use for gardening. The boss of the trade union promised that whoever wanted to garden would own their own piece of this land. Many people refused to take the garden plots because they were afraid that after putting in all the work, the government would take over, like after the Revolution.

At that time our family lived together with our parents and children in a small room of a big communal apartment. It was very difficult to live there with such a big family. We wanted to improve our lives by having our own house near Leningrad. So my husband and I became gardeners. We worked very hard there all of our free time after our jobs, on weekends and during our vacations until 1957. We built a big wooden house with several rooms, including a kitchen, closets and other sections for our parents, children and ourselves. Later, when our daughter and our son got married, their children (my grandsons) grew up in this house. We had a big garden with vegetables, fruit and berries. In summer, it was very comfortable living in our own house, in spite of working hard. We enjoyed it very much.

There were problems with occasional robberies when people left in the fall. Robbers broke doors, windows, and sometimes took what they could find. There weren't any valuable things like jewelry, gold or expensive objects. However, it was terrible because after those incidents, we had to repair everything and clean up the mess. In 1991 robbers broke our door and windows, drank all the wine and vodka that was left in the bottles and ate all the cans of food in the kitchen. They even took an old record player and an old record that was in it. They stole a bicycle from our neighbor. But I really don't think they were professional thieves, but probably just young people walking in the woods on their way to the train station, looking for a place to eat and rest on their way.

Unfortunately, we soon had another much bigger robbery. It happened when we were ready to leave the Soviet Union for America to join my son's family. It was time to sell our beloved garden house that we had enjoyed for thirty-four years. The boss of the trade union told me that we would have to take the house down and sell it somewhere else, because the land belonged to the factory! What could we do? How can you sell a house without land under it? How could we sell it after it was taken apart? It was awful. In spite of past promises, we understood that this was the greatest robbery of all.

Finally, we did receive a little money for our "property"—just enough to buy some toilet paper for our bathroom in America!

✶ Samsa (Piroshki with Pumpkin)

YEVGENIA YAROSHEVSKAYA

Uzbek cuisine.

DOUGH *

1 pkg active dry yeast	1 egg, beaten
2 tsp sugar	½ tsp salt
⅔ cup warm milk	3–4 cups flour
2 sticks sweet butter	

FILLING

3 lbs pumpkin	1 tsp sugar
(or 3 large cans of pumpkin filling)	1 tsp salt
1–2 onions, chopped	Pepper to taste
½ lb lamb fat, cubed	

Combine the yeast, sugar and milk in a large bowl and let stand about five minutes until foamy.

Add egg, butter and salt and mix well. Mix in the flour, a little at a time, stirring well. Knead gently for about three minutes on a floured surface until dough stays together without being sticky. Divide dough into three balls, cover and let stand for about ten minutes.

Scoop out pumpkin and cut into small cubes. (Or use canned pumpkin.) Chop the fat and onion and mix with pumpkin. Add sugar, salt and pepper as desired.

Preheat oven to 350°. Roll out one section of dough at a time on a floured surface until about ⅛" thick. Cut rolled-out dough into 3" circles with a glass or cookie cutter. Flatten slightly with hands, putting a spoonful of filling in the center of each cut piece. Fold in half and pinch the edges to seal. Pat into an oval shape. Place on baking sheet, seam side down about an inch apart.

Bake for about 30 minutes or until lightly browned. Makes about 50.

For those wishing to follow Jewish dietary laws, see recipe for plain yeast dough, without butter or milk, on page 122.

⊞ Pirog (Large Pie)

MARIA KHASIN

This is a one-dish meal. Serve with tea.

1 pkg dry yeast	⅓ tsp salt
⅓ cup water, warm	1 egg
1 tsp sugar	2 sticks butter, melted
3–4 cups flour	2 cups milk

Combine and let stand for 5 minutes: yeast, warm water and sugar.

Put flour and salt in a mixing bowl. Add egg and mix well. To this add melted butter and 1 cup milk. Let stand 3–5 minutes. Mixing by hand, add remaining cup of milk and the yeast mixture. Put the mixing bowl in a warm place and allow to rise for about 5 hours. During that time, punch the dough down 3 times. When the dough is finished, roll it out and fill with prepared filling. Roll up lengthwise. Pinch together to seal. For individual piroshki, cut into circles, fill, fold over and pinch to seal.

Preheat oven to 350°. Place on a greased pan and bake until light brown (approximately 30 minutes).

NOTE: For those wishing to follow Jewish dietary laws, see recipe for plain yeast dough, without butter or milk, on page 122.

MEAT FILLING

2 lbs beef, cooked	½ cup rice, cooked
1 onion, chopped	1 tsp salt, or to taste
2 Tbs oil	

Cut beef into pieces and put through food processor. Sauté chopped onion in oil. Mix together beef, onions, rice and salt.

CABBAGE FILLING I

1 small head cabbage, cut into thin strips	2–3 Tbs oil
1 onion, chopped	Salt to taste

Sauté onions in oil. Add cabbage and continue cooking for several minutes. Add seasoning.

CABBAGE FILLING II

1 small head cabbage, cut into strips	3 hard-boiled eggs, chopped
½ stick butter, melted	Salt to taste

Plunge cabbage into boiling water. Cook for 1 minute. Do *not* allow it to get soft. Drain. Add butter, salt and chopped eggs.

The Miracle Cure

SAMUEL ZALTSMAN
Radiologist, Tallinn, Estonia

After the end of World War II (1945-1953), the situation of the Jews in the Soviet Union was very intense. The single Jewish theater in the country, in Moscow, was closed. Also, publication of one of the more popular of two Yiddish newspapers was stopped. More importantly, many Jewish artists, writers and performers were executed in April of 1948. (Memorials are still held in their honor every year.) The Bible was forbidden, and Hebrew language and literature were neglected. Works by authors like Sholem Aleichem were stricken from the shelves. Fictitious stories were circulated about medical professors, which blamed them for attempts to kill high-ranking Soviet workers.

At this time I was involved in a dangerous affair. In the Russian medical journal, *Klinichnaya Medicina,* a biological researcher named Olga Lepesinskaya published an article about the miraculous effects of a baking soda solution (bicarbonate) on the development of plant, vegetable and animal embryos. She also recommended a baking soda dilution bath for the treatment of tuberculosis. Stalin supported Lepesinskaya's scientific work, and critical comments were excluded. I was a professor at the Medical Institute at this time. Shortly after publication of this article, I attended a small party of my colleagues and happened to mention my opinion that this work was wide open to criticism. I also thought it was a wonder that a serious medical journal would include this article for publication.

The reaction to my comments came immediately. A few days later, I was called to a special institution where I was questioned for two and a half hours. The party member in authority accused me of consciously discrediting a Soviet scientist and Soviet science. This criticism was even worse because it came from a Jewish doctor. He told me that my comments might have serious consequences. I went home and waited for the worst. Fortunately for me, Stalin died in March 1953, and my interrogator's dire prediction had not yet taken place. One or two months later, another article was published in the same journal stating that Lepesinskaya's theory may not have been correct. Her "miracle cure" was open to criticism after all.

War's End

MIRA BEZYMENSKAIA
Surgeon, Moscow

It was the beginning of summer 1944. Our troops successfully took the offensive on all fronts, liberating one city after another. In spite of the difficulties of all the Russian people, hope appeared that the war was finally ending with victory. In June, it became known that the German prisoners of war would pass through Moscow.

It was a wonderful, sunny day. Along all the flower-lined streets stood rows of women, children, old men and disabled soldiers. I had finished with my ninth-grade classes and, together with my friends, stood on the hill where I lived. The faces of the women were emaciated, tired and worn. All the people were pitifully thin and poorly clothed.

The German army appeared. In front of the ranks were a lot of generals, led by General Paulus. They went without order. Behind them came thousands of soldiers. They wore dirty, torn uniforms. On their feet were puttees (leggings), and mess tins hung loosely from their belts. They were unshaven, and a terrible stench emanated from them. The line went on for about four hours.

Behind the column, came cars watering the streets. A lot of soldiers passed by hanging their heads, with guilty expressions on their faces. But there were also faces full of hate. There was no sound from the watchers on the streets. It was as quiet as a coffin. Even the children were absolutely silent. This silence was more terrible than any crying or shouting could possibly be. The Russian women's hatred turned to pity for all the unhappy people, their misfortunes and the dear ones that they lost.

It has been over fifty years since that day. But this picture stays in front of my eyes, and can never be forgotten.

Shifra and Velvel

ROSALIE SOGOLOW
Teacher, Chicago, Illinois

My grandmother, Shifra, was born in 1892 in a small Jewish town in the Ukraine called Laudizhinka in Kiev gebairnya (the region of Kiev). It was a little village next to a meandering river where the children liked to fish. There were many cherry trees, and most of the houses had grass roofs. She was the youngest of eight children. Each child was assigned his own task. Hers was to sew. Her older sisters did the cooking. One of her sisters married a man who owned a leather factory in Odessa and, as a young girl, she went to live with this sister and work in the factory.

My grandfather, Velvel, was from the town of Dubover. (I think it is now called Dubrovitsa). He was the youngest of five sons in a second marriage. There were also five other sons from his father's previous marriage. His father had died, and his mother had no money to support him. And so, when he was six years old, he was sent to live and work with his uncle as an apprentice tailor. He began by sweeping floors and worked his way up. At seventeen, he was a full-fledged tailor. His uncle could teach him no more. It was time to go out on his own, so he decided to try his luck in America.

He managed to steal across the border and attempted to make his way to Hamburg. There were many crooks and sinister-looking men along the way. A burly man on the train, seeing a young boy alone, decided to befriend him and became his protector for part of the trip. When he reached the seaport, he tried to buy passage on a ship for the new land. When he told the ticket salesman he wanted to go to America, the man asked him, "Which one?" "What do you mean, which one?" he asked. "How can there be more than one America?" "There's a North and a South," he was told. What a dilemma! He didn't even know there were two, and now he had to make a choice. "I'll tell you what," the man said. "Go to South America, and if you don't like it there, we'll bring you back in thirty days."

He quickly got a job, and for the next three years, he tried to make a life for himself as a tailor in South America. But the life and morals there bothered him. He had also been receiving disturbing letters from his brothers telling him that the army was looking for him. The time was approaching when he was due to report for duty. His brothers had been threatened with dire consequences if he didn't show up. The Russian army wasn't a healthy place for a Jewish boy at that time. Discrimination was rampant, and many young men never made it home again.

His brothers were obviously very worried, so he decided to return home

*"Shifra and Velvel,"
Sophie and William
Tarantur, Laudizhinka,
Ukraine, c. 1912. Courtesy
Edith Tarantur Krulan.*

*Velvel and his uncle's
family, Ukraine, c. 1909.
Courtesy Edith
Tarantur Krulan.*

and try to buy himself out of the service. When he got back, he approached the officer in charge with his savings. For the price of 300 rubles, a "substitute" was found, and he was permitted to escape this ominous obligation. For the time being, his family was spared. Having solved this immediate problem, he decided it was time to find a wife.

In 1912, at the age of twenty-one, his marriage to my grandmother was arranged. They both sewed. It was a perfect match! Her family was in the horse business. One was a blacksmith, one did hauling and one ran a livery stable. But my grandmother's father, whom everyone called "Big Red" because of his fiery hair, also had a "sideline." He helped desperate people escape over the border. Pogroms were frequent, and one of my grandmother's brothers had been tied to the back of a train by one of the roving gangs and dragged to death. The future looked bleak, and so the young couple decided to flee and make a new life for themselves in the *real* America. One night, they accompanied my great-grandfather under cover of darkness. When they reached the border, my grandfather asked, "Where is the dowry you promised?" "You have her!" was the reply.

So, with only their meager possessions and high hopes, they made the long, arduous journey to their new home. Since two of my great aunts had already settled in Chicago with their husbands, that was their obvious destination. The new bride didn't know how to cook. But Tanta Pasee and Tanta Brana took her under their wings and taught her all the old recipes. She became a terrific cook.

In my mind's eye, I can still picture this dear little lady, always so busy in her kitchen, preparing her dishes for the family's enjoyment. A special family favorite were her knishes. They were usually filled with cheese or rice, but could sometimes contain potatoes, meat or beans as well. These delicious morsels were always eaten with delight.

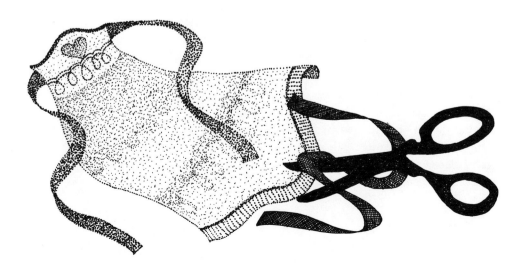

Grandma's Knishes

ROSALIE SOGOLOW

DOUGH	RICE FILLING	CHEESE FILLING
7 cups flour	1½ cups rice	2 lbs farmers cheese
2 tsp baking powder	3 cups milk	(or dry cottage cheese)
3 eggs	½ cup sugar	1 tsp salt
½+ cup oil	½ tsp salt	3 eggs
1 tsp salt	1 tsp vanilla	Pepper to taste
½ cup sugar		
1½ cups water		

Dough

Combine all ingredients. Knead until well mixed. Form into sections and allow to stand covered for at least 1 hour. Roll one section of dough at a time until paper thin. Oil and cut into strips about 2" wide. Stretch as you fill. Keeping dough very thin, roll and shape cheese knishes round and rice knishes long.

Rice Filling

Bring rice and milk to a boil and then reduce heat. Cover and simmer for about half an hour, or until liquid is fully absorbed. Add other ingredients. Cool before filling.

Cheese Filling

Mix all ingredients and fill.

Bake on a well-greased pan at 350° for about 45 minutes or until golden brown. Brush tops with butter, if desired, for a glossy look.

Plain Yeast Dough

ROSALIE SOGOLOW

For pies with meat fillings, if you wish to use a yeast dough without butter or milk, this recipe provides a traditional crust.

1 package active dry yeast	2¼–2½ cups flour
¼ tsp sugar	½ tsp salt
¾ cup warm water	2 Tbs vegetable oil

In a large bowl, combine yeast, sugar and ¼ cup water. Let stand until foamy, about 5 minutes. Add the rest of the water, oil, flour and salt. Mix well.

Put dough on a floured surface and knead until smooth and elastic, about 5–10 minutes. Shape into a ball and place in a greased bowl. Cover and let rise in a warm place until dough doubles in size, about an hour. Punch dough down, divide into sections, and proceed as recipe describes.

Where There's a Will,
There's a Way

JULIYA POLOVETS
Physician, St. Petersburg

My parents were born in Mogilev. I was also born and raised there. It is a city in Byelorussia. There are a lot of trees, flowers, parks and interesting sights there. It is an industrial city. My family was large. There were eight children. We all lived in a two-bedroom apartment. My father was a math teacher, and my mother was a bookkeeper. They were very smart, beautiful people. My father died when I was eleven, at only forty years of age. My mother was the only one working. We lived very poorly, and my childhood was very unhappy. We had to work very hard to exist. But, we loved each other, and that helped keep us alive. Our neighbors helped us very much, and sometimes they gave us old clothes and food.

My older brother moved to Leningrad when he was sixteen. After a couple of years, the rest of the family went there to join him. All of my brothers and sisters began working very early. Six of us studied at the university in Leningrad, and worked at the same time. Four of us received engineering degrees, and two are doctors.

Now, my life is much better than my parents' lives were. I live in a democratic country and have a good life. I am very grateful to America for everything. Here, my family can live in freedom and enjoy all kinds of things. Some of our favorite foods are still the old Russian pies, with many different kinds of fillings. I would like to share a few.

Pastry dishes play an important part in Russian cooking. Pies and tarts are the pride and joy of any Russian housewife.

"A home is made by pies, not by walls."
"A birthday is not a birthday without pies."
"Arrows complete a quiver, and pies a dinner"

These Russian sayings bear witness to the long standing popularity of pies. You don't see them on the table every day, but when you do, it means there's something to celebrate and that guests are expected.

▨ Meat Pie / Mushroom Pie

JULIYA POLOVETS

DOUGH *

½ cup chilled butter
2 cups flour

½ tsp salt
6–8 Tbs cold water

Work butter into flour–salt mixture with the fingers until the mixture becomes crumbly. Make a well in the center and gradually pour in the cold water. Continue to work with the fingers until the dough can be formed into a ball but, at the same time, does not stick to the fingers or bowl. Allow the dough to rest, covered and refrigerated, for a minimum of two or more hours. When ready to roll, bring the dough to room temperature. Lightly flour a flat surface, roll the dough to a ⅛" thickness. Cut the dough into 5" squares and fill with about ½ Tbs filling. Fold diagonally (2 opposite corners together). Seal by moistening the edges and pressing together. Bake on a greased baking sheet at 350°, approximately 30 minutes or until golden brown.

Our tester used this food processor method of preparing the dough:
Add the 2 cups of flour and salt to the food processor bowl.
Cut the butter into ¼" pats and add to bowl, spreading evenly.
Mix until the butter–flour mixture breaks up into pea–sized pieces.
Add chilled water while mixing until dough forms a ball. Proceed as above.

MEAT FILLING

1–1½ lbs ground meat
1–2 onions, chopped
1 clove garlic, minced (optional)

½ cup rice, cooked
Salt and pepper to taste
Oil for sauté

Sauté ground meat and set aside after pouring off excess fat.
Sauté onions and garlic in a small amount of oil. When golden brown, add ground meat and the rice and mix well. Season to taste. Fill the prepared dough.

MUSHROOM FILLING

1 lb mushrooms, sliced
2–3 onions, finely chopped
1 clove garlic, minced (optional)

½ cup rice, cooked
salt and pepper
Oil for sauté

Sauté mushrooms with a small amount of oil. Set aside.
Sauté onions and garlic until golden brown. Add mushrooms and rice. Season to taste. Mix well. Fill prepared dough.

*See page 122 for plain yeast dough without butter, for use with meat filling if desired.

▨ Beliashi (Tatar Meat Pies)

LEAH SVERDLOV

These are usually made from a yeast dough, but I have found that Pillsbury buttermilk biscuits work just fine and make a delicious substitute.

2 pkg Pillsbury buttermilk biscuits (10 each)	1 tsp salt
1 b ground beef	Pepper to taste
1 large onion, chopped fine	Vegetable oil for frying
	¼ cup finely chopped parsley or dill

Separate biscuits and allow to stand until room temperature. Mix the meat well with the chopped onion, parsley, salt and pepper. Flatten the biscuits. Place 1 tsp of the meat filling in the center of each biscuit. Moisten the edges with cold water and fold them toward the center leaving a small, round opening in the middle. Press the edges to make sure they stick, so they won't open during frying.

Fry a few beliashi at a time, open side down first, until golden brown. Turn and cook for 2–3 minutes more, or until brown on both sides. Drain on paper towels and keep warm until ready to serve.

Pirog—a large pie; piroshki—many small pies

Piroshki are traditional Russian favorites. They are good as finger foods or accompaniments for soup. They can be made with many different fillings. Besides the ones given, you could also try:

Chopped egg with scallions, seasoning and butter
Ground veal with mushrooms
Flaked, sautéed fish with hard-cooked eggs
Chopped calf's liver with lots of onions.

No matter how you fill them, they're sure to disappear within minutes.

Kulebiaka (A large flat pie)

LEAH SVERDLOV

Kulebiaka has been popular for centuries. This dish can be made with ground meat, chicken or turkey, or with cabbage. Fish is also a common filling. Sometimes there are two or three layers of different fillings: for example, boiled rice, meat filling, and then a layer of hard-boiled eggs, cut into rings. The flaky, buttery crust is wrapped around a tasty filling.

PASTRY DOUGH *

3 cups flour	2 sticks sweet butter, chilled
¾ tsp salt	2 large egg yolks, lightly beaten
½ tsp baking powder	⅔ cup sour cream

Combine flour, salt and baking powder. Cut in butter with knives or pastry blender until it forms coarse crumbs. Mix most of the egg yolks with the sour cream and add to flour mixture (reserve a small amount of yolk for glaze). Knead for about 30 seconds on a floured surface. Divide into two equal parts. Wrap pastry balls in plastic wrap and refrigerate for 1 hour.

FILLING I

1–2 lbs ground chuck, chicken or turkey	⅓ cup beef broth
1 large finely chopped onion	3 Tbs sour cream
2 hard boiled eggs, chopped	Vegetable oil for browning
¼ cup matzo meal or flour	1 tsp salt, pepper to taste
2 Tbs chopped parsley	

Fry the onions until well browned. In a large bowl, mix the meat, fried onion, eggs and rest of the ingredients.

FILLING II

1 lb fresh salmon	1 Tbs butter
2 hard-boiled eggs, chopped	Salt and pepper to taste
1 onion	

Poach salmon in seasoned water. Skin and flake the fish.
Sauté the chopped onion in butter. Mix fish, eggs and onion with a little of the fish stock.

Assembly

Preheat oven to 350°. Divide yeast dough in half. Roll out on a floured surface and trim to an oval shape about 12" long. If commercial dough is used, do the same to one piece. Carefully place on a floured baking sheet.

Place filling mixture in center of dough. Roll out second piece and trim to a slightly bigger size than the bottom piece. Put this piece over the filling. Fold up the edges of the bottom piece of dough and pinch to seal. Leftover scraps of dough can be cut into decorative pieces and placed on the top. Prick surface with a sharp knife in several places. Brush with remaining egg yolk mixed with 1 Tbs water.

Bake for about 1 hour or until golden brown. Cut into slices to serve.

See page 122 for plain yeast dough without butter, for use with meat filling, if desired.

The Dress

LEAH SVERDLOV
Pediatrician, St. Petersburg

Shopping for stylish clothes in the Soviet Union always presented quite a challenge. Several years ago, my friend was walking down the busy street Nevsky Prospect in what was then Leningrad. It was a lovely day, and she was enjoying her stroll and looking in the shop windows. As she passed one shop, a beautiful red dress caught her eye. She thought it would be perfect for her daughter. She entered the establishment, and after several minutes caught the attention of a solemn-looking saleswoman. "Excuse me, please," my friend began. "I would like to see that dress in the window. I think I would like to buy it for my daughter." The sales clerk looked at her as if she was crazy. "Oh, that dress isn't for sale," she said. "That's only a decoration for the window!"

Grandfather's Orchard

SOLOMON KUMKES
Editor of a geographical publishing house, Moscow

My mother's father, Tevye Mechanik, lived in the state of Slutsk in Belarus, where my parents and I were all born. His basic profession was a joiner/furniture maker. But besides that, he was an amateur gardener and selectionist. He had a big orchard near his home, about sixty trees. The orchard's pride were pear trees. They were single, but he carried out experiments on them, and was able to produce five different kinds of pear from each tree by grafting. This was a new idea.

By developing a brand new sort of pear, he received fame and was even mentioned on the pages of the *Encyclopedia Brockhaus*. I was excited to receive a letter from the editor-in-chief of the *Jewish Encyclopedia* (in the Russian language), which was published in Jerusalem, informing me that Tevye and his work as a selectionist was mentioned in the seventh volume. Because of his work in his beloved orchard, my grandfather became famous.

One Step from Death

ZALMAN KHASIN
Electrical engineer, St. Petersburg

A miner or an electrician can be mistaken only once. In 1972, in the territory of a chemical center called Fosforit in the Leningrad region, the construction of a powerful enclosed electrical exchange complex began. Completion of the electric mounting work was to be carried out by the district. I was a leader of this district.

After the first stage of work was finished, we adjusted the high tension from the Leningrad atomic power station and turned on a few transformers for private needs. Then it was necessary to dry the reactors. We decided to dry them all around the clock—twenty-four hours a day. We did it with hot air. We set up electric fans inside the premises of each reactor. As a strict rule, the doors to all areas of high tension had to be locked with a padlock.

During this drying period, I decided to check the work of the fans at night. On arriving, I saw that the door to one of the reactor sections was open. I went into the dark area and found that the fan wasn't working. I couldn't turn on the light because I would have to go to another area of low tension to do this. I looked around the premises and saw blue flashes on the wires. I smelled the scent of ozone and heard a crackling noise. I realized that I was in a room of high voltage. The padlock had been taken off the door by thieves. Now I knew that I was next to death. If I had taken one more step, I would have been electrocuted! I have never forgotten this very close call.

A Little Uneducated Woman

YEVGENIA YAROSHEVSKAYA
Teacher, Tashkent

My grandmother's name was Rebecca Olshanskaya. At the end of the last century, her family consisted of eight people: her husband, his parents, and their four daughters. During a twenty-four hour period, the town was taken over, and they were deported from their farm. They were put on a carriage, and sent into the darkness.

They arrived in Lugansk and decided to stay there. My grandfather was under great stress, and developed mental illness. Grandma was still a young woman. She was left with a sick husband and four children, who ranged from one to sixteen years of age. She looked after her husband for nineteen years, until his death. Her oldest daughter got married to a rich man when she was sixteen, and my grandmother started working with him in his store. She raised the rest of her children and helped them get a good education.

My grandmother became a successful business woman, and a lot of men in Lugansk came to her for advice. That was a pretty big achievement for a little woman with no education.

Cabbage Pie

MIRA BEZYMENSKAIA

FILLING

4 lbs cabbage	½ tsp black pepper
5 hard-boiled eggs	½ tsp salt
1 bunch green onions, chopped	1 Tbs sugar
2 sticks butter or margarine, softened	

Cut cabbage into quarters. Boil for 5–6 minutes, drain and finely chop. Add chopped eggs, green onions, salt, pepper, sugar and softened butter. Set aside.

PASTRY—METHOD 1

2 cups milk	1 pkg yeast
2 sticks butter or margarine, melted	¼ cup warm water
2 eggs	3 cups flour
½ tsp salt	

Add melted butter to milk, sugar, salt and slightly beaten eggs. Stir well. Combine yeast and warm water, stir to dissolve. Add to butter and milk mixture. Add flour. Knead well and allow to stand in warm area for 1 hour. Preheat oven to 350°. Divide pastry into 2 parts. Roll out each part separately. Spread filling on one part and cover with second pastry. Seal edges and brush with egg. Pierce with fork. Bake 40–45 minutes until golden brown.

PASTRY—METHOD 2

½ stick butter or margarine	1 Tbs sugar
3 cups flour	½ tsp salt
½ cup buttermilk	

Combine flour, salt and sugar. Cut butter into flour mixture until it has the consistency of cornmeal. Add buttermilk. Work the dough well until a ball is formed. Place in freezer for 2 hours. Preheat oven to 350°. Roll out dough into a thin layer. Spread with filling. Roll up lengthwise (as for strudel). Brush with egg and bake for about 40–45 minutes. Slice and serve.

Blini

(And Other Russian Pancakes)

Conflicting images throughout the land present a contrast almost too jarring to be real—the past and present somehow existing simultaneously. In the countryside, quaint *iz bas* (log huts) with floral motifs dot the landscape. In small, rural villages peasants farm the land in much the same manner as their ancestors did for hundreds of years. Meanwhile, throughout the rest of the country, the "Party"—a Big Brother with its finger in every pot—is busy doling out apartments, jobs, admittance to universities, and just about every other commodity. It is, also, a source of constant fear.

BLINI AND OTHER RUSSIAN PANCAKES

The Black Raven (Chyorny Voron)

INNA EYDUS

Oncologist, St. Petersburg

The idea of injustice and cruelty by the government and some of the people of the country where I was born and grew up occurred to me long ago. I first ran into those phenomena while still at school. The big building across from mine in the center of the city was beautiful and different from all the others around it. Famous people like artists, writers, generals and leaders of the NKVD (later the KGB) lived there. The school in our area was called an exemplary school, and children from this house across the way studied with me in the same class. Of course, I always walked to school, but these children were driven in luxurious cars.

I was about ten years old in 1937, when a big terror began in the Soviet Union. Every day some children were absent from school. Each evening a black car, which people nicknamed "The Black Raven," stopped near that beautiful house, and every day, people from that building disappeared. A janitor who worked there was heard to say, "Yesterday the floor above you, today the floor under you, and tomorrow—your turn!"

Once, a boy who was my friend (I was often in his home) didn't come to school. He was the oldest boy in his family. He had two brothers—six and three years old. His father was one of the chiefs of the NKVD. Of course, he was a communist and called his boys Marx, Engels and Felix. The father had been arrested, and after that, his wife did nothing but sit by the window. It seemed that she had lost her mind. The "Black Raven" had come and taken the children to an unknown place. They were gone forever. So, every day I lost my school friends, girls and boys. I was afraid to return home, I was afraid to go past that "damned house," and I was afraid that I might not see my parents again.

My childhood years passed by under this fearful cloud. When I was fifteen years old, I fell in love with a Russian boy. He liked me, too. Soon the Second World War broke out, and my mother and I were evacuated to the Urals. The boy was with the Military Medical Academy in Samarkand (Uzbekhistan). During the war we wrote letters to each other, and when we came back, we decided to marry. But his family was against it because I was a Jewish girl, and the marriage didn't take place. That was a big shock for me. I couldn't understand why this made such a difference. I found out that being "in love" was not enough.

This was not the only lesson I was to learn. After finishing the Medical Institute, young doctors were sent to work. The country needed doctors, especially in pediatrics, which was my first specialty. Russian doctors got work easily, but not Jewish ones. I felt like I had been struck a blow again. After my mother's death of cancer, I decided that I wanted to devote my life to trying to defeat this disease. I approached a professor of oncology whom I knew, and appealed to him to help me achieve my goal. He took me under his wing, and in this way I was able to specialize in oncology, though I had to work for a whole year without salary in order to "prove myself." Later, they put me on at half pay. I didn't really have a choice if I wanted to continue to work and study. It was a very big, four-hundred-bed hospital. While working at the hospital, I tried not only to treat my patients, but to do research at the same time. My professor gave me a very current theme for my dissertation. When I had almost finished my preparation, it was 1953—the famous year of the "doctors." It was a terrible time. Doctors were called "murderers in white coats." Most of these doctors were Jews. They were dismissed from work, arrested, put in prison or killed. My professor said that it wasn't a good time for me, as a Jewish doctor, to defend my dissertation.

At the height of that affair, I chanced to find myself in the hospital with an attack of appendicitis. I was pregnant and expecting a baby in two months. During that difficult time, one of my former patients—a Russian woman—sent me a big basket of fruit. It was winter, and fruit was very expensive. In that way, she wanted to show her attitude about this phony "doctor's business." I'll remember her family all my life—Vishnyevskaya. When I write about it now, I still feel a lump in my throat. Shortly afterwards, I "accidentally" became a department head at the hospital. The personnel department of Health Services made a mistake and took me for an Estonian. I didn't really like administrative work. I wanted to be a researcher at the Oncology Institute. From time to time there was a vacancy, but only Russian doctors could be accepted.

Then my son began to experience anti-Semitism. After finishing school and the institute with high marks, he still couldn't get work for a long time. It was necessary to make an important decision about leaving or staying in the country of my birth. I understood that my children couldn't live in the Soviet Union. I wanted to see them happy in a country where they could show their abilities and advance according to their efforts. Now I am happy. My dreams have come true. Thanks to the creator for letting us out of such a bloody country—a country where "the Black Raven" could come without warning in the middle of the night.

With Easy Steam!
(S'Lyohkeem Parom!)

MARIA KHASIN
Electrical engineer, St. Petersburg

There are a lot of proverbs and sayings in America, as there are in Russia. They are examples of folk wisdom, culture, traditions and customs of the country. But there is one saying in Russia, "with easy steam," which is never heard here. If you ask me, "Why not?" I'll tell you about it....

A long time ago, most Russians lived very poorly in big communal apartments, some without bathrooms or hot water. The only good living they could see was in the movies. Every week they usually went to the bath house (the Russian word for it is *bahnya*), where everybody could wash themselves. There were different sections of the *bahnya*, separated for women and girls or men and boys. Sometimes people had to stay in line for an hour for their turn. Each common area had a reception room, a washing room and a steam room where people could relax in the hot steam while washing with birch branches. It was very enjoyable, and when they left everyone could feel better about themselves.

Now most Russians in big cities have their own apartments with a bathroom. But some of them, and those who still live in communal apartments, continue the old habit of visiting the *bahnya*. In my opinion, there isn't such an expression in America because Americans are used to having their own bathrooms and can take baths any time they wish. They aren't accustomed to the camaraderie of the *bahnya*. And so, while Americans often like to part with a customary "Have a nice day!" Russians say instead, "With easy steam!" It's an old Russian tradition.

*My husband's family, c. 1908,
in Orgheev, Moldavia.
Courtesy Jenny Khorol-Sharal*

My Meeting with Krupskaya

Elena Tsynman
Music teacher, St. Petersburg

In 1935 I met Nadezhda Krupskaya. She was Lenin's widow and worked at the Ministry of Education. I was a conservatory student. During winter vacation, our group was rewarded with a trip to Moscow. We visited theaters, museums and had a meeting with Krupskaya.

Nadezhda was very punctual and came fifteen minutes earlier than the appointed time. She sat down behind the desk, an old, tired woman with very modest clothing and coiffure. She wore a dark jacket, and placed an old fashioned fur cap on the desk in front of her. Krupskaya reminisced about their life in Paris. She told how Lenin liked to listen to French songs in pubs.

We told her about our problems. I complained that we didn't have a professor of music history. It was my major. She talked about the importance of self-education, and reminded us that Lenin had graduated from the University as an "external" student. We were all impressed by this quiet, unimposing woman and her stories about her famous husband.

I don't know.... Maybe it was coincidence, but when we returned from our vacation, we found that we had a professor of music history. And I have never forgotten my meeting with such an important and interesting woman.

Krupskaya died one year later, in 1936.

✖ Carrot Pancakes

GENIA KANTOROVICH

My recipe is from a Latvian kitchen. I ate it when I was on a diet.

1 lb carrots, peeled and coarsely grated	1 tsp salt
2 Tbs butter	1 tsp sugar
¼ cup water, boiling	1 Tbs flour
1 egg, beaten	3 Tbs toasted white bread crumbs
2 Tbs farina	Sour cream

Sauté coarsely grated carrots in butter. Add ¼ cup boiling water to carrots and braise. When the carrots become soft and the liquid has partially evaporated, add farina and mix thoroughly. Let the farina expand and absorb the liquid. Allow the mixture to cool.

Add a beaten egg, salt, sugar and mix well.

Shape pancakes, coat with mixture of bread crumbs and flour.

Fry in oil-coated pan.

Serve with sour cream.

The Man from KGB

EDIT MATOV
Shipbuilding engineer, Moscow

This happened about twenty-five years ago. My cousin had relatives in Israel, but nobody knew about it. It was her big secret. She raised two children all alone, because her husband had been killed by bandits. She suffered hardship and many difficulties. But she was very careful and she never complained. She had a good job, and she was afraid of losing it more than anything.

One day, a man came to my cousin's door and told her that he was from Israel. He said that her relatives in Israel were worried about her and her children and wanted to help her. "Please, tell me what you need," he said. My cousin thought, "It can't be true. This man isn't from Israel. He is certainly from the KGB. He came to test my loyalty." She told him that she and her children needed nothing, that they lived very well, and they had everything because they lived in the best country in the world. She said that the best government in the world took care of them, and she didn't have relatives in Israel. My cousin was proud of herself and her decision.

Two days later, when she got to work, the special chief (from KGB) called her in and asked, "Who came to visit you two days ago? Who was that man? What did you have a conversation about?" My cousins answered, "That man was from KGB." "Who?" wondered the chief. "He was from KGB," she insisted. Well, that chief had a sense of humor. He laughed for maybe ten minutes. Then he told my cousin, "Okay! Don't worry! You can relax!" She breathed a sigh of relief.

Several years later, she received a letter from her Israeli relatives. They said how happy they were to know that her family was doing so well. For a minute she was puzzled. Then she finally realized her mistake. The strange man at the door that day was from Israel, after all!

A Surprising Treat

BERTA TRILESNIK
Engineer, Moscow

In 1935, my husband was a young chemical engineer. He was sent on a mission from Moscow to America. At that time, Franklin Roosevelt was president of the United States. It was the beginning of diplomatic relations between our two countries. The ambassador in Moscow, Mr. Bullit, was not able to give out visas yet. My husband had to go to Germany. He had to stay in Berlin for ten days before receiving permission to leave for America. He departed from Bremen on the fast-going steamship *Europa* to New York. (There were no airplane trips to America that year.)

The ship was very large and comfortable. The journey lasted for six days. The passengers were of different nationalities. Only four of them were Russian. They sat together at one table in the dining room. None of them spoke English or French. It was not easy for them to order food. They indicated to the waiter a line from the menu. But very often they were mistaken. Instead of meat, they received some fish, and so on. So they had to order again and again.

Every day, in the middle of every table, they saw some "decorative thing." It had a bunch of green leaves on the top. The last day, after dinner, the Russians saw passengers at the neighboring table cutting and eating this "thing." My husband and his comrades decided to try it, too. They were surprised to discover a very delicious, juicy fruit. What a pity! They had never seen a pineapple before. They could have enjoyed this excellent dessert all six days of the trip!

❊ Blini (Russian Pancakes)

MAINA NEYMAN

1½ cups flour	3 eggs, separated
1 tsp sugar	2½ cups milk
¼ tsp salt	2 Tbs butter for frying
2 Tbs butter, melted	Fruit, preserves or caviar (optional)

Beat the egg whites until stiff. Set aside. Mix ½ cup milk with 3 egg yolks. Add dry ingredients and mix until lumps disappear. Stir in melted butter. Gradually add the rest of the milk. Gently fold the egg whites into the batter.

Melt a small amount of butter in a frying pan. Drop some batter onto a hot fry pan, just enough to cover bottom. Keep thin. When the first side begins to brown, flip and cook the second side. Repeat until batter is gone.

Fold pancakes into quarters and dust with powdered sugar. Serve with fruit, preserves or caviar. (These can be wrapped inside or served outside the delicate pancakes.)

❊ Blinchiky (Blini or Blintzes)

BERTA TRILESNIK

2 eggs	½ cup flour
1 Tbs corn oil	1 cup milk
½ tsp salt	butter (for final browning)
1 tsp sugar	

Batter

In an electric mixer, mix eggs with oil, salt and sugar. Add ½ cup milk. Gradually add flour and the rest of the milk. Continue mixing until the mixture is smooth.

Shell

Melt a small amount of butter in a medium-sized fry pan. Using a soup ladle, pour a very small amount of batter to cover the bottom of the pan with a thin coating. Keep pan moving. It should cook less than a minute, only long enough to set and slightly brown. Turn onto a large board which is covered with a cloth. (Cloth prevents sticking.) Continue making shells until the batter is gone.

CHEESE FILLING

1 lb cottage cheese	½ cup sugar
Vanilla (optional)	1 Tbs Cream of Wheat (optional)
1 egg	Raisins (optional)

Combine ingredients. If too thin, add Cream of Wheat to thicken.

CABBAGE FILLING

2 lbs cabbage, chopped	1 tsp sugar
2 eggs	½ tsp salt
2 Tbs corn oil	

Heat oil over medium-low heat in a large pot. Add cabbage and sauté for about 10–15 minutes. Remove from heat. Add eggs, salt and sugar. Mix well.

BLUEBERRY FILLING

2 cups blueberries	2 Tbs flour
2 Tbs sugar	

APPLE FILLING

2 cups peeled chopped apples	2 Tbs sugar
2 egg whites	Cinnamon, to taste
⅓ cup chopped nuts (optional)	

Assembly

Spread 1–1½ Tbs of filling along one side of a shell. Fold sides and roll, moistening the edges with water to hold them together. When ready to serve, fry in butter until the outside of shell is golden brown.

As light as air....

One of the most popular treats in Russia are the delicate pancakes known as blini. Their filled cousins are called blinchiki. Favorite Russian fillings include caviar, smoked fish or cabbage. In America, the Jewish version of the Russian blinchiki are known as "blintzes." These usually contain cheese or fruit and are traditionally served with *smetana*—sour cream. Making these takes a little bit of practice, but it's definitely worth the effort!

Some things never change— dachas *and* izbas *dot the landscape.*

An izba *near Zagorsk, Russia*

Enroute to Sergei Pasad, Russia.

Strings of small kiosks abound, selling anything from water and alcohol to books and toys. The sign reads "Trading Row."

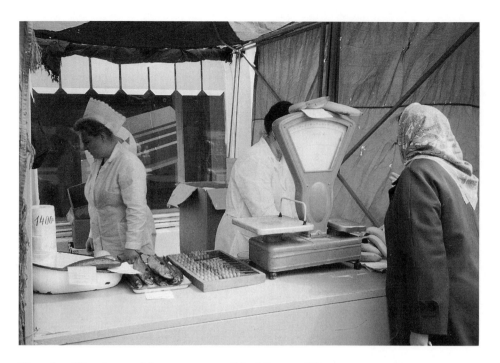

Shopping "Russian style" at a street stall in Moscow. The ever-present abacus takes the place of a cash register or calculator.

A babushka sweeps the steps in the Kremlin's Cathedral Square.

The Master of My Fate

BERTA TRILESNIK
Engineer, Moscow

I was trying to think about the most serious decisions I have made in my life, and I suddenly realized that all the important decisions were actually made for me! It began when I was fourteen. It was a time when the administration was looking for a new form of education. They wanted to have more specialists. So, after graduating from the seven-year school, everybody had to choose two-year courses with some specialization.

I liked reading very much, so I entered the librarian's courses. But when I arrived for the first class in September I was told that this specialty had been changed and that the country was in need of chemists. So I became a chemist. After working as a chemist for a time, I entered the Chemical Institute to become a physicist-chemist. But after finishing the second course, a special faculty was organized. All the best students were taken to this faculty. We were told that the country now needed ammunition engineers. So my specialty became explosives.

After graduating from the institute, during the years of World War II and for the rest of my life until pension time, I never did have a chance to decide my own fate...until now. The last serious decision—to go to America—my husband and I made together. He wasn't so young or in very good health. We have lived here for almost two years, and he now has a second breath. Finally I could choose what I wanted to do, and I think the decision was quite right!

As Easy as Ah, Beh, Veh, Geh....

The Russian language looks and sounds as "foreign" to us as English does to Russians. First of all, the Cyrillic alphabet is completely different from our own. But it is a rich language, filled with nuances and fascinating history. It is difficult for others to truly understand the Russian people without understanding their language. It is a language of great literature, with works of poetry and prose to rival any in the world. Great writers such as Gogol, Tolstoy and Dostoevsky, plus many others whose writings are still unknown to us, have long cast magic spells over their readers with works covering a wide range of humanity and emotion. If only there were a magic recipe that would allow the peoples of the world to automatically understand each other.

Save the Children!—
The Horror of Chernobyl

Meri Fiterman

Pediatrician, Kiev, Ukraine

Before 1986, Chernobyl was a beautiful place. People used to go there to have fun. They swam in the river, caught delicious fish, pitched tents and enjoyed wonderful fruits and vegetables which were grown in the fertile ground surrounding the town.

Then, on April 26, 1986, at 1:23 A.M., a terrible explosion tore through the sky. Everything was brilliantly illuminated, as a stream of fire shot out of the fourth block of the Chernobyl Atomic Power Station. Frightened inhabitants rushed out of their apartments, sleepy children were crying, and fire trucks roared toward the blazing inferno. The fire brigades were the first rescuers—and the first victims—of Chernobyl. The operators of the power station tried to stop the nuclear process, but they only made matters worse.

My family and I were in Kiev when the nuclear accident happened. I first heard about it on the radio and TV several days later. Only then was an announcement made. Everyone was alarmed and frightened, but people weren't told the full truth and remained ignorant of the consequences. At first, we couldn't imagine how big the disaster was. Offices were open as usual, and people lived like every day before, except that nobody could leave the city. All the exits were blocked.

May first had always been a big holiday in the Soviet Union. This year, as in the past, there was a big demonstration and public merry-making in the streets of Kiev, which was about forty miles from Chernobyl. There was music, a parade and presentations of flowers to government officials. People with children, unaware of the danger, watched their families enjoying the outdoor festivities, as they unknowingly absorbed large doses of radiation, drank contaminated milk and ate poisoned foods.

Not until ten days later did the authorities begin an evacuation from Chernobyl and adjoining districts. They created a twenty-five mile danger zone. But the evacuation was badly organized, and poorly prepared with a shortage of materials and equipment. People were given iodine tablets, but this was less than useless against the radiation they had received. Nobody knew much about radiation or its effects. A new city was built not far away, called Sosnovy Bor (Pinewood.) There was no other way out, so people settled there. Volunteers from Russia and other countries tried to help, and donated a lot of materials, food, etc.

Each hospital provided a team to help the victims. At that time I was working at the Third Children's Hospital in Kiev. Doctors' brigades were sent into the devastated area to take out the children and bring them to different hospitals, where they could be helped by experienced physicians and given specialized treatment. I was among the doctors who went in to get them. The children were weak, apathetic and sleepy. Some of them vomited. We were short of medical supplies, but we worked enthusiastically and did the best we could under extraordinary conditions. We did what was possible, and sometimes what was impossible, to save the boys and girls. People wanted to send their children to some other places outside of Kiev, but it was impossible to obtain tickets for trains or airplanes. There was a big panic, as everyone wanted to leave.

Meanwhile, the level of radiation exceeded hundreds of times that of Hiroshima. Fires and radiation destroyed the beautiful pine forests, as well as most of the animals. At first, people didn't understand the danger, because they were inexperienced. The Communist party and the government concealed the true information. So, as a result, a lot of people became sick, many died, and babies with deformities continue to be born.

Shortly afterwards, on October 9, 1986, I became ill. I found myself at the Kiev Republican Radiology Institute of Oncology for treatment. It was directed by Professor Kudzelsky, who had given help to the first victims and rescue teams. Professor Kudzelsky worked with an American, Dr. Robert Gale, and together they succeeded in performing complicated operations for the transplantation of bone marrow. I underwent treatment there, but I am still sick and fighting the effects of my exposure during that terrible time.

No one lives in Chernobyl now. This once beautiful place will never be the same again. The danger of radiation from that awful disaster can't disappear either now or in the foreseeable future. Not in our lifetimes, or those of our great-grandchildren. Maybe not for a thousand years! And yet, political events and hard times turn people's attention away from this unpleasant happening. Memories are short, and people forget. There is even talk about the question of returning to Chernobyl. They still don't understand how dangerous it is! How will people survive? I don't know.... It's such a tragedy!

Potato Pancakes

BENTSION PETRUSHANSKIY
Design engineer, Kazan, Tatarstan

My parents and I lived in Kiev, in the Ukraine. Father worked as a general accountant, and Mother was a housewife. I was a student. In August of 1941, we were evacuated to Kazan, Tatarstan. My adolescence was over.

I do not remember my grandparents, but I know that one grandfather had a kerosene store. The other grandfather was a merchant. My father's brother was killed in a pogrom. His sister had epilepsy, after being beaten in the pogrom. My mother's sister developed schizophrenia after her terrifying experience in the pogrom. My uncle, aunt and cousin were murdered in 1941 at Babiy Yar. So my family history is a tragic one.

But, every Sunday and every Jewish holiday, our relatives and friends came to visit us. They drank tea, and Father sang Jewish songs.

I learned to cook potato pancakes from my mother. I made them on Saturday or Sunday or any special occasion. They are good to eat with sour cream.

Potato Pancakes (Latkes)

BENTSION PETRUSHANSKIY

4–5 potatoes, peeled and grated	1 pinch baking powder
1 onion, finely grated	2 Tbs flour
2 eggs, beaten	Oil
1 tsp salt	

If grated by hand, squeeze excess liquid from potatoes. Combine the grated potatoes and onions and add eggs, salt, flour and baking powder. Mix well. (You will need more flour if potatoes are grated in the blender or food processor. Onion can be grated this way, as well. Add eggs to blender, too, if done this way.)

To prepare pancakes, heat oil in a large frying pan. For each pancake, drop 1 Tbs of the potato mixture into the hot oil and brown. When nicely browned, turn over and cook the other side. When the potato pancakes are finished, drain on paper towels and keep warm. Don't crowd the pan. Add additional oil as needed. Serve with applesauce or sour cream.

Cabbage Pancakes

VICTOR KHODOSH
Mechanic, Minsk

I was born in 1918, in Bobruysk, which was a small town in Byelorussia. After finishing middle school, I began to work in a big factory where railroad cars were repaired. In 1939, I enlisted in the Red Army and fought in the Great Patriotic War. After the war, I was demobilized and, for more than forty years, I worked in the Ministry of Railroad in Minsk. I have one son and one daughter, and also two grandchildren. My wife died about ten years ago.

In my childhood I loved horses. Next to my house there was a stable, and I often spent my time there. When I was eleven, I was considered one of the best horsemen. My father liked to invite guests, and enjoyed entertaining them. He prepared for holidays like Passover by himself, and many friends and relatives came to our house for the first seder. The children always had a separate table. Always, there were matzos and many tasty Jewish dishes. I like to prepare some dishes, too. I often make pancakes of cabbage. My neighbors like this dish very much. They are good cooks themselves, and they always praise it. My late wife taught me this recipe, and I make it in any season. It is good served warm, with sour cream. It is okay for any meal—breakfast, lunch or dinner. Come to me please, any time. I would be happy to make them for you.

 ## Cabbage Pancakes

VICTOR KHODOSH

1 small head cabbage
2 eggs, beaten
Dry bread crumbs (enough to coat)

Salt and pepper to taste
½ tsp sugar

Method I

Cut cabbage in half and boil with 1 Tbs salt and ½ tsp sugar for about 4–5 minutes. Cabbage should be soft, but only half cooked. Remove from water and squeeze out as much liquid as possible. Slice across cut end, making slices about 1" wide. (There will be many layers to each section.)

Beat eggs in a bowl. Add salt and pepper to taste. Dip cabbage sections into egg mixture and then coat with bread crumbs. Heat oil in a fry pan and fry "pancakes" first on one side and then the other until golden brown on both sides.

Method II

All instructions are as above, except: After removing cabbage halves from the boiling water, cut into short, narrow strips. Mix all cabbage pieces with egg mixture, coating thoroughly. Place by spoonfuls into bread crumbs and then into heated oil. Fry as above. Serve with sour cream or preserves.

A Sad Story

Esfir Dynkina
Technical designer, St. Petersburg

This story isn't happy. It was in time of war, during the German blockade of Leningrad. The Germans had been bombing us, and we were under fire. There wasn't any light in Leningrad. There wasn't any water. We melted snow. There was hunger. There was frost. Many people died. The siege lasted for 900 days!

Dear Rosalie, you asked what we had to eat. A jelly from leather bands (which we obtained by trading for other goods), once a day, (not every day). And to us it was delicious! Besides that, a soup from yeast and a piece of bread, 125 grams for each. This wasn't a normal bread as we know it, but a soggy concoction…made from what—we never knew. Only during the coldest months, when Ladoga Lake was frozen over, could we sometimes obtain a little more. Then it was possible to travel by lorry over the ice to other nearby places. During these months, we called the river "the way for life." But we were moving targets there, and this was still risky.

I was working in the war industry in Leningrad at this time. One day, we got a little gruel of buckwheat at work. I got a glass jar and was very happy to take it home. My sister was there, and I knew she was very hungry. My home was far from my job. I had to cross bridges, which the Germans liked to bomb. People were often killed on these bridges. It was slippery, and I fell. My glass jar broke, and the gruel mixed with glass and snow. To collect it was to risk my life. I went home empty handed and wept all the way. That was approximately fifty years ago, but I can never forget it.

An Interesting Neighborhood

Leonid Segal
Mechanical engineer, St. Petersburg

In Leningrad, I lived on Hertzen Street. Before the Revolution in 1917, it was the street where the famous jeweler Faberge lived. His old shop was located across the street from my house. There was a rumor going around that before he went abroad to escape from the Bolsheviks, he had hidden his treasures somewhere in this house. My friends and I often talked about finding this great treasure. One day, when we were feeling very brave, we decided to try to find it. We were about twelve years old at the time. We made our plan, and when the coast was clear, we snuck into the building. We searched the basement, the walls and floorboards. While we were busy looking, the janitor came. Of course, he discovered us and chased us away. We never did find what we were looking for, but we kept talking about it for a long time.

My school was opposite the famous Isakiy Cathedral. Pushkin, the great Russian poet, mentioned this place in his work "Eugeny Onegin." In 1939, I finished school and was called up for military service a year later. After the war, my former classmates and I met at our old school every year for a reunion. More than half of our students had perished in the war and during the blockade of Leningrad. Many of us who had survived had become scientists, engineers and Olympic champions. But the most well known among us was Yelena Bonner, the wife and assistant of the famous scientist and public figure, Andrei Sakharov. Her mother was a Jew, and her father was an Armenian. She lived a hard life. Her father had been killed in 1937 by the Stalin regime. Now her children and grandchildren live in the United States. I think you could say that we had a pretty interesting neighborhood.

Buttermilk Fritters (Oladushki)

MILA SHULMAN

2 eggs, separated	1 cup flour
1½ cups buttermilk	1½ Tbs sugar
1 Tbs vegetable oil,	¼ tsp salt
plus enough for frying	½ tsp baking soda

In a large bowl, mix egg yolks, buttermilk, and 1 Tbs oil.

Mix dry ingredients together and add slowly to buttermilk mixture until blended. Let the batter stand for one hour.

Just before frying the fritters, beat egg whites until stiff and fold them into batter.

Heat 1 Tbs of oil in a fry pan over medium heat. Drop about 1½ tsp of batter into pan for each fritter. Fry on both sides until golden, about 3 minutes on each side. Keep warm until ready to serve. Serve with jam, honey or sour cream. Makes about 20 fritters.

Filled Pancakes

YEUGENIA ROMM

This Ukrainian pancake mixture is made from egg yolks, cream, sugar, spices and, sometimes, butter. The mixture should have a runny consistency. To make it even lighter, a few beaten egg whites are added at the very last minute before frying. When cooked the pancakes are filled with jam or apples and more beaten egg white is poured over them before they are baked in the oven. Sometimes the mixture is baked all together with the egg whites on top rather than making separate pancakes.

APPLE PANCAKES

¾ cup flour
1 cup cream
10 eggs, separated
1 lb apples, peeled

¼ lb butter
½ cup sugar
2 tsp dried lemon peel or
  grated peel of 2 lemons

Preheat oven to 400°. Make a batter with the flour, egg yolks and cream.

Cut the apples into thin strips and fry in butter together with the sugar and lemon peel. Then stew gently until soft.

Fry four individual pancakes. Fill the pancakes with the apple mixture, roll up and place in a baking dish. Cover with beaten egg whites and bake for about 5 minutes, or until golden brown.

SOUR CREAM PANCAKES

1¼ pt. sour cream
½ cup flour
⅔ cup sugar

2 Tbs butter
1 tsp vanilla

Preheat oven to 350°. Whip the sour cream and mix it with the other ingredients, adding the vanilla last. Spoon the mixture into a pan and bake at about 30 minutes or until golden.

Chremsel

SOPHIE TARANTUR, VIA R.S.

3 matzos
½ tsp salt
1 lemon, grated rind only
4 eggs, separated

1 cup sugar
¼ cup raisins
1 tsp cinnamon
¼ cup almonds, chopped

Soak matzos until soft, then press thoroughly, draining off excess water. Stir matzos to a cream, add lemon, salt, sugar and beaten egg yolks. Add raisins, almonds and cinnamon. Beat egg whites until stiff and fold into mixture.

Drop by tablespoons on hot, slightly greased griddle or fry pan, and fry until lightly brown on both sides. Serve hot with stewed prunes.

A Remarkable Woman

MIRA BEZYMENSKAIA

Surgeon, Moscow

I had a wonderful grandmother. She was the founder of our large family. She had five sons and two daughters, fourteen grandchildren and seven great-grandchildren. She lived to be one hundred and six years old. Her mind and memory were still strong to the very end.

She was born in 1870, in a small town in the Ukraine, near Berdichev. She grew up without a mother. My great-grandfather was a poor tailor. Grandmother was very beautiful. She had blond hair, big blue eyes, and perfect features. She wasn't tall, but she had a resolute disposition. Her elder brother worked as a bookkeeper in Warsaw, and sometimes she went to visit him. She loved the big city and dreamed that her children would study and live there someday. She always dressed her children very nicely, just like in the city. She sewed, embroidered and knitted very well. She was very skillful. I don't ever remember her not being busy.

She arrived in Moscow in 1929. During the war, she knitted for the soldiers and taught us, her granddaughters, how to do it, too. All of her children, except my father, and her sons-in-law were in the army, and came back with injuries. Grandmother believed in G-d, but she didn't teach religion to her children. When she was alive, all of her family gathered around her. We all came together for holidays, such as Passover. It was our tradition. She cooked everything herself. Good, tasty things from matzos, and latkes (potato pancakes) from potatoes with matzo flour. I have never eaten such delicious food.

In 1944, when her grandson began going to school, she was seventy-four years old. She decided to study, too. She began to learn Russian grammar. She started to read Russian newspapers and magazines, and watch TV.

When her last grandchild got married at the restaurant Metropol in Moscow, she was one hundred years old. Her grandsons sat her down in an armchair, and to the music of Mendelssohn's "Wedding March," brought her to the banquet room on the second floor. She was so happy. She first congratulated the younger generation, and drank a goblet of wine, toasting them and wishing for their happiness. It gave her pleasure to give us souvenir gifts and toys. We all loved our remarkable grandmother very much. She was a wise old woman, and we always think about her and observe the anniversary of her death.

Garneer

(Side Dishes)

Over and over, our emigrés shake their heads with wonder. "We knew our lives were hard," they say, "but we never imagined that everyday living could be so different in other places. For such a long time we accepted our fate because we didn't know any better."

So effective was their isolation behind the notorious Iron Curtain, so controlled their information from the outside world, people just assumed their hardships were a fact of life. And yet, with determination and sheer will, they persevered and even managed to find pleasure in ordinary things....

GARNEER

The New Suit

BORIS ALTSHULLER
Plant director, Vilnius, Lithuania

When I was fifteen, I graduated from the seven-year school and entered a special school to study working skills and professions. After finishing there, I started working in a plant as a craftsman. I also assembled motors. I remember very well my first salary. To me it was remarkable.

It was a time when people were starving to death on the streets. The whole country was starving. My mother tried to help as many of these people as she could, but our resources soon came to an end, and we, too, awaited the same fate. The only thing that kept us going was a ration of bread and potatoes which I received each month, along with my pay, because I was a worker at a government plant.

Well, my first salary was twenty-eight rubles. I brought it to my father, but my father told me to keep it for myself. "Take it," he said, "and buy whatever you want. The next pay you should give to the family, but the first one is yours alone."

I had a dream. The dream was to have a good suit. I never wore a coat, so I wanted to have a real suit and look like a solid man. So, I went out and bought my suit. I bought it in spite of my starvation. (I was hungry constantly.) I could have bought food or other things, but my dream was stronger. I also bought a cap. The suit was a little long in the sleeves and the pants. I have a picture of myself wearing this suit. Whenever I look at it, I smile. I think that I made the right choice.

Just in case...

It's rare to see anyone venture forth without his or her handy string shopping bag tucked neatly into a pocket or purse. These magical bags seem to expand indefinitely and to hold a multitude of things. They are called *aloska*—which loosely translated means, "maybe I can find something."

✳ Pilaf with Almonds and Raisins

MARINA TSESINA

A tasty rice dish from Azerbaijan.

1½ cups long-grain rice
3 cups boiling chicken stock,
   canned broth or water
1 cup carrots, grated
Zest of 2 oranges, grated
⅓ cup slivered almonds

4 Tbs (½ stick) unsalted butter
   or margarine
Salt to taste
¼ tsp ground turmeric
⅓ cup raisins

Melt the butter or margarine in a heavy saucepan. Add carrots and stir over medium heat for about 5 minutes. Mix in the almonds, orange zest, raisins and turmeric and continue to cook for another 3–4 minutes. Add the rice and keep stirring until the rice is well coated—about 2 minutes.

Pour in the boiling stock and continue to boil for about 2 minutes more. Add salt, reduce heat to low and simmer until all the liquid is absorbed, about 15–20 minutes. Let stand, covered for 10 minutes. Fluff with a fork before serving. Serves 4–6

Childhood Years

RITA GORLIN
Nuclear engineer, Moscow

My childhood was happy, but it was like a little magic island in a stormy ocean. The surrounding life was fearful. Anybody could be arrested, exiled or imprisoned without trial or judicial inquiry. The official authorities sometimes prosecuted people simply for the purpose of confiscating their possessions. People from the GPU (later called the KGB) burst into homes at night and conducted ruthless searches. They particularly looked for gold coins.

In the apartment upstairs from us lived a plumber named Ivan Sychev. He was a drunkard. Since 1904, he had been a member of the Communist party and had the honorary title of "Old Bolshevik." He often came to my father, Phillip Feldman, and demanded, "Give me vodka! If you don't give it to me, I'll write to GPU and tell them you have a lot of money." My father always gave him a drink. We never knew if he executed his threat or not, but one winter night we were awakened by a loud banging at the door. I saw that my parents were very frightened. Father opened the door, and three men in identical dark gray suits burst into the room. They ordered us to sit down, showed a claim to search and began to look everywhere.

The search continued for about three hours. They found nothing. Then they ordered my parents to put on their clothes and took them away. My mother cried and asked for permission to inform her sister that her two little girls were alone. (I was six years old and my sister, three.) She didn't receive an answer. The door closed with a bang. I took my sister to the sofa, and we sat there for a long time. Then my sister fell asleep. I cried all night. The next morning, my mother returned home. She was very tired, pale and unhappy. Afterwards, she told us that all night the preliminary investigator demanded that she show him the place where the gold was hidden. We didn't know where my father was. A month later, the two men from GPU returned to our house. They showed my mother two papers. The first was the order stating that my father was being exiled to the North because "he refused to *give back* his hidden gold." The second paper was an order to remove all valuable things from our apartment. They took away all our furniture, Mother's fur coats, silver things, pictures and books. The main thing they took away were two bookcases with Brokhaus and Efron Encyclopedias. My father eventually returned from exile, which happened very seldom during those years. But fear accompanied all my childhood from then on.

Once my father returned, our family life was happy. We loved each other, and our parents had enough to provide for our needs. My sister, Tanya, and I studied at school and music lessons, went to parties, walked together, attended theaters, museums and the conservatory. But, again, our happy existence was interrupted, this time by the war. We were evacuated to Siberia. It was a difficult time. In 1942 our father died. When the war was over, we returned to Moscow. The three of us began to live again, but it was another life altogether.

Family Portrait

RITA GORLIN
Nuclear engineer, Moscow

My father, Phillip Feldman, came to Moscow when he was sixteen years old from a little shtetl called Izaslvl in the Ukraine. He finished his studies at Moscow University and became a chemist. My mother was from a large family named Sutin. A famous artist, Chaim Sutin, was from this family. Her parents were wealthy. They had a wood manufacturing factory near Minsk in Smolevichi. They died when my mother was a child, and she moved to her elder sister's in Moscow.

I was born in Moscow. It was a terrible time in Russia. All life was accompanied by fear. Many people, especially the educated and cultured, were arrested and often killed. All our relatives and friends waited each day for this to happen.

In 1930, my father was arrested and sent into exile. It was very common then for innocent people to be arrested for no reason. My mother went to a very famous photographer named Napelbaum, and asked him to take a picture of her daughters and herself to send to her husband while he was away. "I'll make a portrait, and hang it on my studio wall until your husband returns," he said.

Afterwards, my father told us that this photo was with him wherever he went. After two years in exile, he was able to come home. He went to Napelbaum and thanked him. "I believed that you would come back," the photographer said. "Now, I'll do a new portrait of your family and hang that on my wall."

Anna Feldman, Rita and Tatyana, Moscow, 1923.
Courtesy Rita Gorlin.

Recollections of Postwar School Life

YEUGENIA ROMM
Teacher, Odessa, Ukraine

Just after World War II, my family came back to our native city of Odessa in the Ukraine. The country suffered greatly from the lack of daily necessities, such as food, fuel, electricity, paper, etc. I returned to my school to teach the children. Living conditions were awful, and our poor youngsters were sitting in classrooms with almost no heat in the severe winter cold. They were poorly fed, and had no paper to write on. Pieces of old newspaper were used instead. In my school, there were stoves (no central heating), and these were heated only once a week. Naturally, everyone tried to preserve the precious heat and not allow it out of the room. So, when I entered the crowded classroom, with about forty students present, I could hardly breathe because of the stuffy air. (I already had my heart condition at that time.) I was ashamed to ask them to open the window. I understood how important the heat was for them in school, since most of them had no heat at all in their homes.

Before long, my students noticed my uncomfortable condition and began asking me if I would like the window opened. I had to agree. After that, there wasn't a single class when the children forgot to refresh the air throughout the entire winter. I felt their attitude towards me as a person who could give them some knowledge, and it encouraged me to work more and more devotedly. Very soon we became very good friends. My students felt my love for all of them, and they realized that I not only wanted to teach them the necessary subjects, but also to educate them to be real people.

Almost always, when I entered the room, I saw very pleasant greetings for me written on the blackboard. They even tried to look up special expressions for the occasion. I remember those years well, and those students with special fondness. They longed for a good education, in spite of terrible life conditions.

Eggplant Slices

YEUGENIA ROMM

A Caucasian recipe.

3 medium eggplants
Coarse (kosher) salt
Olive oil
Chopped fresh basil or cilantro

Sauce
1 cup plain low-fat yogurt
2 medium garlic cloves, crushed
Salt to taste
Mix and refrigerate overnight

Preheat oven to 425°. Wash and remove stem from eggplants. Cut into ½" slices. Put into a colander and toss with a generous amount of coarse salt. Let stand for 30 minutes. Rinse and pat dry with paper towels.

Brush with oil and bake for about 20 minutes. Sprinkle with chopped basil or cilantro and serve warm with sauce spooned over the top.

Sonya's Vegetable Surprise

YEUGENIA ROMM

This recipe was a secret for a long time. My mother, Sonya, won a big prize when she cooked this vegetable dish. Nobody could guess the ingredients of this delicious food.

SAUCE
3 medium tomatoes,
  peeled and chopped
  (or 1 can stewed tomatoes)
1 tsp lemon juice
1 Tbs oil
Salt and pepper to taste
1 tsp sugar
1 cup water

CAKES
2 onions, peeled and quickly grated
(or they'll get watery)
2 eggs, beaten
2 Tbs flour
1 tsp baking powder
Salt and pepper to taste
Oil for frying
Sour cream, as a garnish

Sauce

In a pot, boil the tomatoes with water, lemon juice, sugar, salt, pepper and a small amount of grated onion. Mash tomatoes to make a sauce. Keep sauce hot. If the sauce is too thin, you can thicken with flour.

Cakes

In a mixing bowl, mix the rest of the onions, eggs, flour, baking powder, salt and pepper. Heat some oil in a fry pan and drop the onion mixture by teaspoons into the oil. Brown on one side and then gently turn and brown the other side. They will puff up as they cook.

Carefully transfer the cakes to the hot sauce. Reduce heat to low and cook for 10–15 minutes. Serve with sour cream. Serves 4–6.

160

Victory Day

SONYA SLUTSKER
Engineer, Odessa

When we lived in the Soviet Union, the greatest holiday after the war was May 9—Victory Day. It was the day that marked the end of World War II for our country. It was a holiday for all the people of all nationalities. On this day everyone had tears in their eyes because so many of us suffered so much during that war.

On the eve of this holiday I worked hard and cooked some very delicious foods with meat, fish, and salads from different vegetables. I also baked piroshki with meat and cakes with cream. It was spring, so the weather was always nice and warm at this time. The trees were blooming. All the windows would usually be open, and the sound of music was everywhere.

In the evening, our guests would come to celebrate with us. Everyone greeted each other and wished us the best and for peace in the world. We drank vodka and wine, and then dinner began. After dinner, we sang songs and danced. We often saw a concert on TV of the best performers. Now, very often, I am reminded of my young years, my city and our celebrations with our guests.

Eggplant and sauce

IDES KRUKER

1 eggplant	1 carrot, grated
Flour	1 onion, chopped
Salt	1 (15 oz) can tomato sauce
⅓ cup oil	½ tsp sugar

Cut eggplant in 1"-square pieces and lightly salt. Coat the eggplant with flour and fry in the oil. In a saucepan, combine the eggplant, carrot, onion, sugar and tomato sauce. Cover and simmer for 10 minutes.

Serve as a side dish.

▨ Potato–Onion Casserole

SONYA SLUTSKER

2 lbs potatoes, peeled and boiled	3 Tbs butter or margarine, melted
4 eggs, beaten	1 Tbs oil
3 onions, thinly sliced	Salt and pepper to taste
1 cup milk, warm	

Preheat oven to 350°. Mash the potatoes with milk and butter. Add eggs, salt and pepper. Mix well.

Sauté onions in oil.

Spread one half of the potato mixture on the bottom of a buttered baking dish. Layer the sautéed onions over and top with remaining potatoes. Brush with some melted butter or beaten egg.

Bake for 20–25 minutes until golden brown. Serve warm.

May be served with fish fritters; see recipe on page 181.

▨ Passover Carrot Pudding

MOLLIE GOFFSTEIN VIA R.S.

3 cups carrots, peeled and grated	1 tsp baking soda
1 cup matzo meal	½ cup brown sugar
3 eggs, separated	1 tsp cream of tartar
1 tsp salt	½ cup vegetable shortening

Preheat oven to 350°. Mix dry ingredients. Cream sugar and shortening. Beat egg yolks until light.

Add egg yolks and dry ingredients to the creamed mixture. Mix well.

Add grated carrots.

Beat egg whites until stiff. Fold into mixture. Bake in a well-greased mold or pan for about 40 minutes. Serve hot or cold.

▨ Steamed Zucchini

ARKADY KUTIKOV

1 lb zucchini, cut in 1" pieces	1 tsp salt
4 large carrots, diced	3 tomatoes, sliced
3 bell peppers (red, yellow, and green)	Dill and parsley, chopped,
4 Tbs oil	to taste

Slice bell peppers in diagonal strips. Steam all the vegetables until tender.

Add oil and mix well. Place in a serving dish and sprinkle generously with dill and parsley.

My Family

RITA FAYNSHTEYN
Metallurgical engineer, Odessa

My father was born and lived in a little town called Ochakov, on the Black Sea. He was the eldest son in the family and began to work early, at fifteen years old, in a fish factory. He worked all his life in the fishing industry, first as a foreman of the salting, and than as an inspector of quality. He fought in World War I and in World War II, during which he perished.

My mother was born and raised in her childhood village. Her father worked for a German landowner. This landowner was a good man. He liked my grandfather very much and was nice to him. My mother played with the landowner's daughter, and they were good friends. When the pogroms began in their village, the landowner hid all of the family. Mother moved to Ochakov when she was eighteen. First, she worked at different jobs, but then she studied and became a bookkeeper, which she did all the rest of her life.

My childhood in Ochakov was cordial and carefree. I remember how my grandfather put me on his knee and taught me Jewish words. He showed me objects and called out their names in Yiddish. I had to repeat them. When I was five, my parents moved to Odessa. I lived there until World War II began. At that time, I evacuated with my mother to the Orenburg District, in the country. There I finished school and worked as a secretary in the area prosecutor's office. In the fall of 1943 I went to Moscow to the institute. The war continued.

As a student, I experienced cold and hunger, but life was still relatively carefree. During the first year, I lived in a hostel in a room for fifteen girls. On April 10, 1944, my friend and I organized a "feast" in our room in honor of the liberation of Odessa from the fascists. We cooked a bucketful of millet with potatoes, thickened with fried onions. We all stuffed ourselves. Then we sang, danced and had a good time.

I was always satisfied with my life, in spite of all the difficulties. We considered our life good, because we didn't know any better life. I had a good family, a good husband and good children. But my husband died young. We complemented each other. He was a graphic artist and something of a musician. I was a technologist. We passed these abilities on to our children. They finished music school, as well as receiving a general education. Our children liked music and mathematics, but they chose mathematics and became programmers.

My life was better than the life of my parents because they faced persecution and couldn't obtain a higher education. Now, I live here in America with my children and grandchildren. My children work in their specialties as programmers. Their lives are better than mine was. I hope that my grandchildren grow up to be good people with good educations, and that they will be happy in this free country.

▦ Mamaliga

FAINA BELOGOLOVSKY

A Moldavian recipe. Mamaliga is made from stoneground cornmeal. It can be eaten fried for breakfast, or sprinkled with feta cheese and baked for lunch. For dinner it serves as a base for a hearty stew, and for dessert, slices can be topped with powdered sugar or jam. It is similar to polenta. Constant stirring is the secret to a good, smooth mamaliga.

3½ cups water	5 Tbs butter,
Salt to taste	unsalted, cut into pieces
1 cup yellow cornmeal	8 Tbs (1 stick) unsalted butter, melted

Combine water and salt in a heavy saucepan and bring to a boil. Slowly add 2 Tbs cornmeal and whisk until the water returns to boiling. Gradually add the rest of the cornmeal, stirring constantly. Reduce heat and simmer, covered, until thickened and cooked through, about 10 minutes.

Add butter, a piece at a time, stirring constantly. Continue stirring until the mixture doesn't stick to the sides of the pan, about 5 minutes more.

Spoon the mamaliga into a medium-size oval bowl and flatten with a wet spoon. Let stand for 5 minutes. Turn onto a plate and sprinkle with melted butter.

Some Traditional Ways to Serve Mamaliga

• Sprinkle with 1 cup feta cheese and bake at 400° until golden and bubbly, about 10 minutes. Serve with melted butter.

• Cut into ¼" slices, coat with cornmeal and fry in butter. Serve for breakfast with jam or powdered sugar.

❖ Vegetable Ragout

RITA FAYNSHTEYN

3 potatoes, peeled and cubed
1 carrot, sliced
1 onion, chopped
½ head cabbage, coarsely chopped
2 tomatoes, chopped

1 small can cut green beans, drained
1 small can green peas, drained
3 Tbs vegetable oil
Dill

Fry onions until transparent. Add potatoes and carrots, cover and cook. Place the potato–carrot–onion mixture in a large pot. Add cabbage, pepper, salt and water to cover. Simmer until tender. Then add the green beans, peas and the tomatoes. Simmer 5–10 minutes. Sprinkle with dill and serve.

The Town of Ribnitsa

YEFIM LITVAK
Circus manager, Odessa

Until 1935, I lived in a small town called Ribnitsa in Moldavia on the banks of the River Dnestr. The left side of the river belonged to the Soviet Union, and the right one to Romania. It was the border between the countries. All the streets started from the church, which was surrounded by a marketplace. On the main street, there were three little shops, many street vendors, a fire company, a cinema, a hospital and a grocery store. A nice little park was next to the river. There was also a train station in town, and trains came through once every three days. There were two schools (one Ukrainian and one Jewish), and three synagogues, which were divided by occupation. Everyone knew each other, and on weekends and holidays, people got together to exchange information and to visit.

The main product of Ribnitsa was sugar. There were many plum and pear trees in the sugar collective farm garden, and when I was a little boy, I once jumped over the fence to gather fruit to eat. When my father came home, he was very angry and punished me. My grandfather and my father were both roofers. There were four children in our family, and my mother stayed home and took care of them.

I had a little dog named Sharik. One day, a man grabbed her and took her away. Many pets were being stolen and killed to make soap. I discovered where they were kept, and when the bandit left to catch other animals, I ran and opened the door so they could all run out. I was a secret hero. Nobody knew that I was the one who did it.

In 1930, when I was ten years old, there was a big flood. The first synagogue closed right after this. It became a hostel. In 1933, the second synagogue closed. It was turned into a club. In 1935, the third synagogue closed, too. The director of the Jewish school was arrested, and so was the rabbi. The last Jewish school was shut down at the same time. After six months, the principal and teacher were shot. All the children began to study at the Ukrainian school. People prayed at home. Many left to go to Odessa. It was the end of the Jewish community in Ribnitsa.

Getting an Education— Soviet Style

ILYA MATOV
Shipbuilding engineer, Moscow

In the Soviet Union in the 1920s and the beginning of the 1930s, only the workers or workers' children could matriculate to an institute. My older brother wanted to study in such an institute very much, but even though he had all excellent marks on his entrance examinations, he wasn't accepted because our father wasn't a "worker." Each year, for three years, he tried to enter the institute, but each time he was rejected. Because of this, he became very depressed for many years. Therefore, when I was twelve years old, I began to work in a factory after finishing school. For five years I worked at the factory during the day, and in the evening I studied in a special mid-school which prepared workers to enter the institute.

One year after I entered the institute, the Soviet government decided that the country was in need of good specialists for industry and scientists for developing sciences. Since many capable, young people were not permitted to enter these institutes or universities up until then, a change was required. Therefore, the rules were altered so that all young people, under thirty-six years of age, from that time on, were to be allowed to enter these places of learning. This was the case until the end of the Second World War, at which time secret limitations were introduced for young Jews wishing to enter many universities and institutes. For this reason, my son had many difficulties trying to get his education.

An Unexpected Sight

Mira Bezymenskaia
Surgeon, Moscow

My husband and I traveled to the Caucasus in October 1960. On the way back, we took a Black Sea voyage from Suhume to Sochi on a little cutter ship. The weather was very good. It was warm. The sun was shining. The sea was quiet and caressing. There wasn't any wind. We were sitting on the deck and admiring the view. Suddenly, a strong wind came up, black clouds appeared, lightning sparkled and thunder roared. It was dark all around. The storm hit hard. Our cutter was thrown from side to side and lifted high into the air, as high as a house! After that the ship was thrown down like a little nut. It was terrible. We sang songs to help us take our minds off the danger. During the storm, my husband and many other people became very seasick, but the singing seemed to help me avoid this problem.

Suddenly, dolphins appeared—now here, now there. They jumped around the ship and over it. They were very large animals with shiny, brown skins. It was a very beautiful picture, but also very frightening. We had seen these creatures from far away before, but we had never seen anything like this. They swam alongside the ship and accompanied us to Sochi. They helped calm us. When I got off the ship, my legs felt very weak, and only then did I become seasick. We were afraid of death, but now only the good memory of this strange sight remains.

Baked Cabbage Casserole

Manya Reyzis

1 lb cabbage, sliced	5 Tbs flour
1 small onion, minced	3 eggs, beaten
¼ tsp salt	½ cup sour cream
2 tsp baking soda	½ cup mayonnaise
1 tsp sugar	

Preheat oven to 350°. Combine all ingredients and bake in a preheated oven for 15–20 minutes.

Like Joseph's coat, a myriad of colors...

Many people, when they think of "Russia," see only visions of frozen Siberian wilderness. Covering one sixth of the globe and spanning eleven time zones, there is so much variety it is difficult to describe. From the deserts of Uzbekhistan to the mild Mediterranean waters of the Black Sea, each region has its own distinctive topography, foods, customs and personality. There are over 100,000 large rivers and more than three million lakes. It's no wonder that fish is one of the most popular foods!

When we think of Russian food, we immediately conjure up images of potatoes, cabbage and, of course, borscht. Russians are very fond of potatoes, using them in salads, soups and stews or simply all by themselves. And borscht is a long-time favorite of both peasant and tsar, appearing in countless varieties, which can be served steaming hot on cold, winter days, or clear and refreshingly chilled in summer. In fact, I've been told that if you ask fifty different people for their recipe for borscht, you will receive fifty different versions, each with its own distinct flavor.

Just as there is great diversity of climate, customs and history, each region is known for its own cuisine—depending on what is available in the area. Ukrainians love foods in pastry crusts. (You'll find quite a few here.) Armenians are fond of soups, cheeses and vegetables and also like to stuff grape leaves with meat, rice and spices. Azerbaijanis often cook their meat with apricots and raisins, and Georgians fancy lavosh and shashlik. The Estonian diet includes lots of fresh fish, while Lithuanians favor yogurt, sausage, buttermilk and sour cheeses. Lamb and game birds are popular all over, just as blini, caviar, sour cream and kasha are staples in every Russian home. And since many of our Russian homes were also Jewish homes, we can't forget those great traditional Jewish dishes as well. These are our favorites...all part of our memories...all "Russian." Not to mention delicious!

Glavnoye Blyudo

(Entrees; literally, "main course")

With an enduring love of the rich culture of their land, Russian hearts seek the "soul" that their famous composers and writers portrayed. They speak about it as if it were a tangible thing. No matter how unsettling daily life became, solace could be found by listening to the stirring music of Tchaikovsky or Rachmaninoff. Or they could turn to their beloved poet, Alexander Sergeyevich Pushkin, who wrote about passion and regret and of "noble hearts in a cruel age." Pushkin instilled in the people of Russia a romantic image of themselves. Their affection for his work has never diminished.

> *It's time, friend, time! For peace the spirit aches—*
> *Day chases day, each passing moment rakes*
> *Away a grain of life, and while we, you and I,*
> *Would rather have lived on, lo, all at once we die.*
> *Here happiness is not, but peace and freedom are.*

—UNTITLED, 1834

ENTRÉES

Three Generations

Riva Sheer

Department store assistant manager, Tallinn, Estonia

I'd like to tell about the lives of my family during three generations, and how our lives were different from each other. The differences depend upon the historical epochs in which they lived.

Our first generation

I don't remember my grandparents, but my mother told me about them. It was a hard and joyless life. They lived in a shtetl called Rujew, in Latvia, on the border of Estonia.

Since the eighteenth century, the Baltic states were provinces *(gubernia)* of tsarist Russia. Therefore, the persecution of the Jewish people was terrible. Often, there were pogroms. There was no "justice for all," only injustice. For example: Jewish children might only study at elementary schools with three to four grades. Jews didn't have the right to live in the capital or big cities, only in small towns or shtetlach. They couldn't move to other places to look for work. So, they didn't have an opportunity to get more education or a better job.

They had to work hard for their existence. They produced most of their own household necessities. Everyone had a small piece of land, where they grew vegetables. They had some animals—one cow, or a goat, and maybe chickens or geese. Their houses were poor and small. Mostly, they lived in one room together with many children. Most of the people were craftsmen. My grandfather was a tailor. They did whatever they could to survive. But through everything, they kept their religion, traditions and their native language, which was passed on from one generation to the next.

But people were looking for a better life, particularly for their children. So, around 1890, the large emigration to America and other European countries began. One of my uncles went to Scotland, and my aunt went to America.

Our second generation—my parents, aunts and uncles

After my parents got married in 1920, they moved to Estonia, where my mother's sister and her family lived. Just at this time Estonia became an independent republic, after the end of World War I (1914–1918). Because Estonia was a democratic republic, there was no discrimination. There was equal justice, but life was not easy. My father had to work hard for a living. He owned a small workshop, where he made pipes for smoking and repaired umbrellas.

My mother took care of us children and our home. They didn't have time for a joyful life, but sometimes they got together with friends or relatives.

I remember that my parents loved Jewish traditions. On holidays and Saturdays, they went to synagogue. Nobody worked on these occasions. They celebrated all of the holidays My mother prepared wonderful holiday meals. I remember the table was set, covered with a white tablecloth, the candles were lit, and we all enjoyed eating delicious foods.

Our third generation—we, the children, who were born after 1920

Our lives changed, step by step. The dark, difficult time that our grandparents and parents had when they were young, was over. We felt free. In summer, we enjoyed swimming and hiking around the lake. In winter, we loved skiing, ice skating and sledding. Our whole family loved animals, and we always had dogs and cats to play with. We all liked to read. We attended movies, theater and parties, and had fun walking together with our friends. Almost all of us finished high school, and many of us studied in universities. We loved our language—Yiddish, and we all speak it very well. We had a wonderful childhood, but we didn't forget that we soon had to find a job and to help our parents.

Suddenly, our good time was over. I was eighteen years old when World War II broke out. Because the occupation of Estonia by the Nazis came so quickly, to save our lives we became refugees. We left all our possessions and escaped to the east—to Russia. This was a very hard period for us. My parents died there in 1943. We were in Russia for four years. After the war ended in 1945, my sister and I came back to Estonia. But we found nothing. Our home was destroyed, and another very difficult time began for us.

But we were young and hopeful. I continued my education, got married, and worked more than thirty years in a big department store in Tallinn. My husband of thirty-two years worked as a lawyer before he died. Now I live with my nephew and his family in the USA. We have found a new homeland. We are very thankful that the next generation will have an easier life than the ones that came before.

Beef Stew in Sweet and Sour Sauce

RIVA SHEER

My mother was a very good cook. She cooked and baked excellent dishes. She prepared many wonderful meals. One of them I have not forgotten because it is delicious. So I will try to remember the recipe. The name of this meal is Beef Stew in Sweet and Sour Sauce with Potatoes and Prunes. It is an old Jewish recipe. In Yiddish the name is Floimenzimes.

2½ lbs beef; must have some fat	3 Tbs sugar
8–9 potatoes, peeled	3 Tbs vinegar
1 lb pitted prunes	5 cups water
1–2 onions, sliced	Salt to taste
Oil for browning	

Preheat oven to 350°. Cut potatoes in half. Soak the prunes in hot water. Combine the sugar and vinegar in 1 cup water.

Cut the beef into 3" pieces. Place meat and onion slices in a large pot and bake uncovered until the meat is brown. Add 1 cup water to the pot. Cook approximately 1 hour.

Transfer the meat and onions to a large roasting pan. Add potatoes, prunes, salt and the sugar–vinegar mixture. Add 3 cups water to the pot. Stir well. Place in oven and continue cooking for another 2 to 2½ hours, until the meat is tender.

 # Myeena (Liver and Potato Pudding)

PATRICIA MARKMAN

My parents, Morris Sheinfeld, of Ackerman, Bessarabia (which was part of Romania at the time) and Gloria Handler of Uman, Ukraine (near Kiev), were married in New York City in 1927. They enjoyed preparing this dish for family and friends. It is still prepared by their children, both in New York and California.

1 lb beef liver	2 Tbs vegetable oil
1–2 large onions, chopped	Salt and pepper to taste
2 eggs	3 lbs peeled, boiled potatoes

Preheat oven to 350°. Fry beef liver in oil. Add chopped onions. Chop coarsely in food processor, adding eggs, salt and pepper to taste. Mash potatoes, add to liver mixture and finish blending by hand until firm.

Turn into a baking pan greased with chicken fat or oil. Bake until a thin brown crust forms on sides and top (about 30–40 minutes).

A Lucky Day

BORIS MOYZHES
Physicist, professor, St. Petersburg

It was in 1952, the last year of Stalin's era. I was working as a teacher at a technical school in a small town. All my vacations and Sundays, I performed calculations for my Ph.D. thesis. But before I could receive it, I had to pass examinations in my specialty.

Because I am a Jew, it was impossible for me to find a technical university which would agree to accept exams from me at that time. Then I asked the director of our school to find out if the technical university of our ministerium would agree to accept them. After she returned from a busy trip to Moscow, she told me that it was possible that the Moscow Technical University of Communication would agree to accept me for examination.

It was just before the summer vacation. I quickly collected exams from my students and left for Moscow. I went to the waiting room of Professor Nadenenko, the vice president of the university. My turn came, and I entered his office. I was very frightened. I didn't know what to expect. An elderly man in uniform greeted me, gave me his arm and said, "I have read your papers in journals. Now I am glad to meet you."

I was astonished. Nobody had ever told me before that they had read my papers. And at such a crucial moment! After our first meeting, Professor Nadenenko helped me often. He was the first person to congratulate me on my Ph.D. degree. But our first meeting I remember in a special way.

Many times in my life, I have been in very difficult situations. But every time, somebody helped me. There have been so many good people in my life!

Boris Moyzhes is an internationally known physicist. His papers have been published all over the world.

⊞ Beef Stroganoff

MAINA NEYMAN

1 lb beef, filet mignon or other tender cut	1 Tbs flour
¾ cup sour cream	1 small can tomato sauce
(or IMO or non-dairy creamer)	½ cup sliced mushrooms
2 onions, chopped	Salt and pepper to taste
3 Tbs oil	

Slice the beef into thin strips and pound until thin. Season with salt and pepper.

Sauté onions in oil. Add beef strips and continue to sauté another 5–6 minutes until browned. Sprinkle flour over beef to thicken. Stir in sour cream, tomato sauce, sliced mushrooms, salt and pepper. Continue to cook over low heat about 15–30 minutes more or until meat is tender.

Serve over noodles or with fried potatoes.

Service at a Russian Restaurant

RITA GORLIN
Nuclear engineer, Moscow

My husband, Jonathan, and I decided to have breakfast at a restaurant one morning. The waitress set the table and went away. Jonathan noticed that she had forgotten to leave a teaspoon. He called, "Waitress!" In a few minutes, the server came to our table. She carried a tray with dirty dishes and cups. "You forgot to give me a teaspoon," my husband said. "Oh, sorry," exclaimed the girl. Then she took out a teaspoon from one of the dirty cups, shook it and put it on the table. "I don't think this is very clean," Jonathan said politely. "Don't worry," answered the waitress. "There was only tea in the cup—not coffee!"

Pomsteak (Fried Meat)

RITA GORLIN

2 cups bread crumbs
1 lb meat
2 eggs, beaten

Salt and pepper to taste
Vegetable oil for frying

Cut meat into bite-size pieces and put into a bowl. Mix eggs, salt and pepper and pour over meat. Allow the meat to marinate for 30 minutes. Roll meat in bread crumbs. In a hot fry pan, sauté meat on both sides in oil for about 15 minutes or until meat is cooked. Serve with salad, potatoes, pickles.

Shashlik

RITA GORLIN

I think this dish originated with the Mongols. They skewered their meat on swords and roasted it over open flames. Ivan the Terrible drove them out of Russia during the sixteenth century, but not before he claimed their shashlik. It made its way to Moscow kitchens in the 1700s, where the meat was marinated and then cooked in its own juices. Shashlik has been a favorite dish all over the country ever since.

2 lbs lamb, cut into 1½" pieces
3 medium onions, cut into large chunks
2 Tbs vinegar or lemon juice
    (Or use your favorite marinade.)

1 Tbs vegetable oil
Salt and pepper to taste

In a large dish, combine the lamb and the onions. Add salt, pepper and vinegar (or lemon juice). Stir well. Place in the refrigerator or 2–3 hours (or more).

Thread the lamb on skewers. Alternate with onion chunks. Broil or barbecue. If you wish, the lamb and onion can be sautéed in a frying pan.

NOTE: For variety, pieces of green pepper, pineapple and tomato can be alternated with the meat and onion to add color and additional flavor.

No Place to Hide— The Communal Apartment

RITA GORLIN
Nuclear engineer, Moscow

Many people in big cities in Russia have lived in communal apartments for many years. What kind of dwelling is it? It's one apartment with several rooms, where two to seven or more families live together. Each family has one or two rooms. Each door looks onto a common corridor. The apartments have one kitchen, one toilet and one bathroom. Many common apartments don't have any bathroom, only a sink in the kitchen where neighbors wash themselves as best they can.

In the kitchen, there is a stove and many small tables and shelves for each family. (Five families, five tables; seven families, seven tables.) The best place is near the window. In the morning, people stand in line to use the toilet and bathroom. The corridor, the kitchen, the bathroom and toilet are called "the places of common use." Each family cleans them once a week, according to a schedule. Each apartment has a representative, who is in charge of paying the bills for telephone, gas and electricity. How much each family pays depends on the number of people and how many bulbs or other electrical equipment they have in their rooms.

People live in very crowded conditions, often with four generations sharing one room. Divorced couples are often forced to continue living together. I know a case where the divorced husband, after the wedding, invited his second wife to live in the same room as his ex-wife and their son. As you can imagine, this kind of situation can make for miserable living. But moving isn't easy. When someone wants to receive a new apartment, he has to stand in "the line for improving dwelling conditions." But, no one can stand in this line unless they presently have less than five square meters (about six square yards) per person living space. People have sometimes stood in this line for ten years or more, and often died before receiving a new apartment!

There is no such thing as privacy in such places. Communal apartments have destroyed what might have been happy relationships. Married couples have many strikes against them, and divorce is common. There is just no place to hide...no place to be alone...no place to call your own. In the 1960s, many of Russia's cities began constructing bigger, more modern buildings. But a lot of people still live in a common apartment.

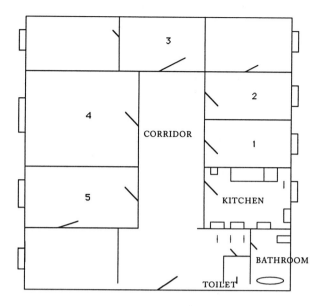

Apartment for five families.

Beetochkee (Chicken Patties with Mushrooms)

FAINA BELOGOLOVSKY

1 lb ground chicken
2 slices white bread
½ cup milk or non-dairy substitute
½ lb mushrooms,
   cleaned and chopped

1 onion, chopped
2 Tbs butter or margarine
1 cup dry bread crumbs, seasoned
Salt and pepper to taste
2 Tbs sour cream or IMO

Soak white bread in milk, non-dairy creamer or water, and squeeze out excess liquid. Mix with ground chicken. Add salt and pepper to taste.

Sauté chopped mushrooms and onions in butter or margarine until onions are golden. Add sour cream or substitute.

Make small patties of the chicken mixture. Put one spoonful of filling mixture into center of each patty and mold to close.

Lightly coat patties with bread crumbs and fry until brown on the outside and done inside—about 10–15 minutes. (Turn once.)

Serve with green peas and potatoes or pasta and salad. If desired, finished patties can be garnished with additional sautéed mushroom and onion slices.

Dolma Golubsi (Grape leaves stuffed with meat)

VERA OSIPOVA

An Armenian recipe.

1½ lbs ground beef or lamb	1 cup water, boiling
1 small onion, finely chopped	½ tsp salt
1 egg, beaten	¼ tsp pepper
1 bunch mint, finely chopped	1 large jar of grape leaves (50+ count)
1 bunch cilantro, finely chopped	2 cups Mountain High nonfat yogurt
1½ Tbs rice, uncooked	1 clove garlic, finely minced

Combine ground meat with egg, onion, mint and cilantro. Add rice, water, salt and pepper. Blend mixture well. Rinse grape leaves, remove the stems but set them aside (do not discard!).

On each leaf put some of the meat mixture and wrap up. These are called dolmas.

Line the bottom of a shallow pan with the remaining grape leaves. Place prepared dolmas on top and, lastly, distribute the stems over all. Pour boiling water over the dolmas until barely covered. Cover the pan, bring to a boil. Then decrease the temperature and simmer for 1½ hours.

Dressing

In a separate bowl, combine yogurt and minced garlic. Mix well and set aside, allowing the flavors to blend. Serve with dolmas.

Combined Dolma

VERA OSIPOVA

4 small eggplants	1 bunch mint
4 medium green pepper	1 bunch cilantro
4 large tomatoes	1 cup water
4 large apples	½ tsp salt
1½ lbs ground lamb	¼ tsp pepper
1 small onion, finely chopped	

Sauté ground lamb with finely chopped onion, mint, cilantro, water, salt and pepper. Peel eggplant, remove the core, pour on the boiling water and press out moisture. Cut off tops of peppers, tomatoes and apples and scoop out the seeds.

Stuff the prepared vegetables with the lamb mixture and place layer by layer with open ends up in a deep pot or Dutch oven. The eggplant on the bottom, then the pepper, the tomato and, lastly, the apple. The stuffed part of the vegetables must be on top. Four columns of stuffed vegetables will be cooked together in the same pot.

Pour hot salted water to ⅓ height of the vegetables but *not* over the top of the eggplant. Using low heat, cook in a covered pot or Dutch oven for 1–2 hours.

Each vegetable column will serve one person.

Golubtsi (Stuffed Cabbage)

MINNA PETRUSHANSKAYA

1 head cabbage	½ cup sour cream or IMO
¾ lb ground meat	1 Tbs tomato paste
½ cup rice, cooked	1 tsp sugar
1 onion, chopped and sautéed	1 cup water
1 Tbs flour	1–2 tsp salt
2 Tbs butter or margarine	¼ tsp pepper

Preheat oven to 350°.

Put the head of cabbage into boiling water and cook for 5–7 minutes, then into a colander to drain. Carefully remove the cabbage leaves from the head.

Combine the ground meat, sautéed onions, cooked rice, salt and pepper. Mix well. Place some filling in center of each leaf and wrap.

Melt butter or margarine in a large frying pan, and lightly brown cabbage rolls. Place in a large baking dish.

Combine water, sour cream or IMO, tomato paste, flour, salt and sugar. Mix until well blended. Bring to a boil and simmer about 5 minutes, stirring constantly. Pour sauce over the cabbage rolls. Bake in oven 30–40 minutes.

Siberia

SONYA SLUTSKER
Engineer, Odessa

I was a student when the Second World War began. When the Fascists approached Odessa, our family evacuated to Siberia. There I worked in a military factory. We worked twelve hours a day, without stopping for weekends. If it was necessary, we worked sixteen hours and more in the bitter cold. Sometimes, we had to load our production on railway wagons outdoors in winter, when the temperature was −40° to −45°C (−32° to −35°F). It was very hard. When I walked to work, early in the morning, I saw dead bodies being carried out of the factory. They were covered. They had died from hunger and cold.

The conditions we lived in were very difficult. Six people lived in two small rooms. Hunger was common. We sold our clothes to buy potatoes and other food. The water was a long way from our house, and we carried it in two pails with a yoke. It was hard work to bring enough for washing. To rinse the linen, we went to the river Belaya. In winter, the river froze over, and we could walk on it. But in spring, when the ice broke up, all the houses nearby became flooded. During the summer, we were sent to the forest to cut down trees, and in the fall we had to harvest the crops.

It was especially hard on my mother. Our family was big, and she was always busy. She was a gentle woman, tall and thin, with brown hair and gray eyes. I loved her more than anyone in the world. She never complained in spite of her hardship. She often had to go to the market in freezing weather to sell things. Sometimes she earned some money and was able to buy us some food, and sometimes she came home without anything, shivering from the cold, and very sad. I can never forget one particular episode. We didn't have water in our house, so we had to bring it in buckets from the well. I usually did it, but this time I was in a hurry to go to work, so she decided to do it by herself. As she was coming back, she fell on the ice and the water spilled all over her. There was a hard frost, and it froze very quickly. Her wet coat was heavy and hard and she couldn't move. I'll always regret that I wasn't there to help her. If I had been late for work the administration would have brought action against me in court. I'll carry this tragic picture for the rest of my life.

My Life in the USSR

Semyon Nudelman
Mechanic, Kiev

Before I came to the United States, I lived in Kiev. It is the capital of the Ukraine, one of the republics of the former USSR. Now it is a separate, independent state. I worked for thirty years at a factory where cars were repaired. The work was very tedious, and I was often nervous. I went to work at seven o'clock in the morning, and worked for twelve hours a day, often on Saturday and Sunday, too. This happened often at the end of the month, as the planned work had to be completed at any price. At the end of the day, the director of the factory gathered all the leaders together and discussed any problems that might have occurred.

After work, I had to think about how to buy food for my family. This was always troublesome. I had to stand in line for long periods of time to buy what was needed. Even then, I often came home without anything. Meanwhile, my son waited for me to help him with his studies. This was repeated day after day.

Fish Fritters

Sonya Slutsker

1 lb white fish fillet, boned and skinned	3 Tbs flour
¼ lb onions	2 Tbs vegetable oil
1 egg, beaten	Parsley, salt, pepper to taste

Cut fish and onions into small pieces. Using a food processor, combine parsley, salt, pepper, onions and fish. Process for a few minutes until the mixture has a fairly smooth consistency. Form the mixture into thin patties. Dip into beaten egg and then coat with flour. Fry patties in preheated oil until golden brown, turning once. Drain on paper towel before plattering.

Serve warm with Potato–Onion Casserole (see recipe on page 161).

The Nobleman and the Servant—A Fable

Yeugenia Kochevrina
Electrical engineer, Moscow

There are many folk tales which mention traditional Russian dishes. One fable is this:

Once, a nobleman sat thinking about what the best thing and the worst thing in the world could be. He thought and thought, but he couldn't come up with the answer. So he called on his servant to help him. The nobleman ordered him to go to the marketplace and buy the worst thing in the whole world. The man left and soon returned.

"Well, did you buy it?" the nobleman asked.

"Yes, my lord," replied the servant, opening his basket. He took out an ox tongue. "What can be worse than an ox tongue? People use their tongues to slander and to deceive and to declare war. Wagging tongues are the cause of all arguments. There's nothing worse than a tongue!"

"You're right," agreed the nobleman. "Now go to the marketplace and buy me the best thing in the whole world."

Very soon the servant came back. He opened his basket and took out—another tongue. "Another tongue?" exclaimed the nobleman. "But you just brought me a tongue, saying it was the worst thing in the world."

"I know," said the servant, "but now look at it another way. Isn't it the tongue that speaks words of love and of gratitude? Isn't it the tongue that lets us sing? Could anything be more delicious than tongue in aspic?" The wise servant knew how his master loved food. And the nobleman agreed that there really was nothing better than a tongue.

⬚ Yazeek (Tongue in Aspic)

YEUGENIA KOCHEVRINA

1 fresh beef tongue (about 2 lbs)	1 carrot, cleaned and sliced in rounds
2 Tbs gelatin	1 cucumber, sliced in rounds
Parsley	1 lemon, sliced

Put tongue into a pot, cover with water and bring to a boil. Cover and cook over a low heat for 2 hours. Remove and cool tongue with cold water until you can handle it and remove outer skin. Chill.

Make a jelly from the stock: simmer the stock for 3–5 minutes. Add 2 Tbs of soaked and pressed gelatin. Bring back to a boil, stirring constantly until the gelatin has dissolved. Strain the stock.

Slice the tongue thinly. Put the slices in a dish and garnish with sprigs of parsley, sliced carrot and cucumber. Fix them in place with some of the jelly. Then pour an even layer of jelly over all and chill.

Serve with a sauce of horseradish and sour cream or substitute.

⬚ Lamb Moussaka

YEUGENIA ROMM

One of the most popular dishes in Moldavia, which shows its Greek influence, is moussaka. It contains largely vegetables (more than half its ingredients). All the ingredients are put in at the same time, then stewed. The popular meat is lamb, but veal can also be used.

1 lb lamb, cut into small pieces as for stew	1 Tbs chopped parsley
2 eggplants, sliced	3–4 bay leaves
2 tomatoes	1 entire head garlic, finely chopped
3–4 onions	2 Tbs sunflower oil
⅓ head cabbage, shredded	1½ cups sour cream or IMO
	Salt, pepper, garlic to taste

Preheat oven to 350°. Slice all the vegetables and shred the cabbage. Grease a heavy wide pan with butter or margarine and put a layer of sliced eggplant on the bottom, then a layer of onion, followed by layers of tomatoes, cabbage and finally the meat. Then repeat all the layers.

After each 2–3 layers, add the various seasonings. The meat layers and the top layer of vegetables should be particularly well seasoned.

Put sunflower oil and sour cream or IMO over the top and bake for one hour. Sprinkle the chopped parsley over the top. Eat hot in its own sauce.

184

 # Tongue with Tomato Sauce and Vegetables

ROSALIE SOGOLOW

My father refused to even taste this dish because he couldn't get past the idea of eating such a thing. It's a shame, because my family considers it a real treat. It's important to cook it long enough, so that the tongue is tender and peels easily.

1 beef tongue, about 3–4 lbs	1 small can mushrooms, sliced or caps
¼ cup minced onion	1 small can peas
1 Tbs seasoned salt	Sliced zucchini or carrots (optional)
1 can tomato soup	

Preheat oven to 350°. Put tongue into a roasting pan and cover with water. Add minced onion and seasoned salt. Cover tightly and bake for about 2½–3 hours. Remove from liquid and rinse with cool water.

When cool enough to handle, peel off outer skin. Trim away any fat or stringy parts. Slice and put into a baking dish. Spoon tomato soup between layers of meat. Put vegetables on top, cover and bake for another ½ hour.

Goes well with mashed potatoes or rice.

 # Pozharsky Rissoles (Chicken Cutlets)

YEUGENIA KOCHEVRINA

Rissoles are one of the most popular Russian dishes. People like them made with lamb, veal, minced beef, fish, cabbage or other kinds of fillings as well as chicken. They can be served with various vegetables and sauces. They are popular in every home. They are called Pozharsky rissoles because they were made famous by a man called Pozharsky who owned a restaurant in Torzhok, a small city near Moscow.

2 lbs ground chicken	Butter or oil, for frying
3–4 slices white bread, without crust	Salt and pepper to taste
½ cup milk or mocha mix	1 cup bread crumbs
2 Tbs butter, melted	

Preheat oven to 425°. Soak bread in milk or non-dairy creamer. Add bread to chicken, melted butter, salt and pepper. Mix thoroughly. Form mixture into small rissoles (oval patties) and coat with bread crumbs.

Drop the rissoles into a deep pan of butter or vegetable oil and fry for five minutes, until a light brown crust has formed.

Remove from stove and place in a hot oven for about 5 minutes.

Place on a dish and pour additional melted butter over the rissoles, if desired.

Rissoles are usually served with vegetables such as peas or beans and potatoes.

▦ Tabakah (Game Hens)

FAINA BELOGOLOVSKY

2 game hens (½ per person), split and opened up	Oil, for frying Salt and pepper to taste

Pound hens until flat. Sprinkle with salt and pepper.

Heat oil in fry pan. Place hens in oil, reduce heat and cover tightly. Cook 15–20 minutes over low heat. Turn and continue to cook for another 15 minutes, or until tender.

DRESSING

2–3 cloves garlic, peeled and mashed through a press Salt to taste	1 cup chicken stock or bouillon 1 tsp dill, for garnish

Mix ingredients and pour over hens after serving. Good served with fried potatoes or baked apples with plums.

▦ Chicken with White Sauce

RITA FAYNSHTEYN

1 chicken, skinned and quartered	2 Tbs flour
1 onion	2 Tbs butter or margarine
1 carrot	2 cups broth, strained
Parsley	1 tsp lemon juice
Fresh dill	Salt to taste

Place chicken in a large pot and add enough water to cover. Add the vegetables, cover the pot and cook until tender. Remove the chicken and cut into pieces. Strain and save broth for the white sauce. Place on a dish and cover with white sauce.

White Sauce

Melt butter or margarine and add flour, stirring until lightly browned. Don't burn. Add broth and continue to cook for 5–10 minutes, stirring constantly, until thickened and free of lumps. Add lemon juice and salt to taste. Stir well.

Serve with rice or potatoes.

◈ Braised Beef in a Pot

YEUGENIA KOCHEVRINA

Meat cooked in small pots was served many years ago, and is still popular today. Many families have a set of these special small earthenware pots that hold one serving each, but many cooks prefer larger ones for 4–6 portions.

1 lb beef, such as chuck, cut into medium pieces	1 bunch fresh parsley, chopped or 1 cup celery, chopped
2 lbs potatoes, peeled	2 cups beef stock
½ lb mushrooms, cleaned and sliced	¼ cup flour
2 carrots, peeled	4 Tbs butter or margarine
1 onion, peeled and sliced	Salt
Black peppercorns	Fresh parsley, chopped,
Oil, for browning	for garnish

Sprinkle salt on meat and brown until a golden crust has formed.

Slice the potatoes, mushrooms, carrots and onion. Sauté the vegetables in the oil and then divide them with the meat between 4 small pots, or put them into one pot which will hold 4 portions. If you don't have an earthenware pot, you can use any dish suitable for braising meat. Add some black peppercorns, a bunch of parsley or celery, pour over some stock and braise until tender—about 1½ hours.

Take out the parsley. Pour stock into a saucepan. Make a roux from butter or margarine and flour and add to the stock. Bring to a boil and simmer 5 minutes. Pour the sauce over the meat and vegetables, and bring back to a boil. Add some finely chopped parsley and serve in the pot.

Serve with boiled potatoes.

NOTE: There are other ways of making this dish. The meat can be braised in sour cream (or IMO, if desired) or kvass, for example. To use sour cream: Lightly pound the pieces of meat. Add salt, coat in flour and brown lightly. Add 1 cup sour cream and stew in the pot. When the meat is cooked, lay it out on a dish, season the sauce with lemon juice, salt and pepper. Add ½ cup wine and pour this sauce over the meat.

✳ Chicken Paprikas with Dumplings

KLARA DRIZO

4–5 lbs chicken, cut in pieces	1 tsp pepper
1 onion, chopped	2 Tbs salt
4 Tbs shortening	1 pt sour cream or IMO
1 Tbs paprika	1½ cups water

Brown onion in shortening. Add seasonings and chicken. Brown about 10 minutes. Add water. Cover and simmer slowly until chicken is tender. (About an hour.)

Remove chicken. Add sour cream or IMO to pan drippings and mix well.

DUMPLINGS

3 eggs, beaten	1 tsp salt
3 cups flour	½ cup water
3 Tbs sour cream or IMO	

Mix all ingredients together and beat with a spoon. Drop batter by teaspoonfuls into boiling salted water. Cook about 10 minutes. Drain and rinse with cold water. Add to Paprikas.

Escape!

ANN TOKAR
Stenographer, Lvov, Ukraine

It was at the time of that terrible war. Our small but very green and joyful town in the Ukraine (near Kiev) was being bombed. We took all precautions, glued the windows with paper and prepared water. A number of people had already been killed. We were waiting for our father's arrival, and we missed the last echelon. The town was empty. We had to hire a cart, and my mother, younger brother and I decided to try to go to my grandparents' town of Bazaar. But the cart broke down. It was very dangerous, and bullets were flying over our heads. We didn't see any way out. We didn't know what to do.

Suddenly, my uncle appeared out of nowhere. He came from the front, and was very worried. There was no time for talking. The Germans were very close. He told us not to take clothing or anything, but just run. People were being taken away and tortured, he said. We ran and made it to a passing truck, which was very crowded.

Only my grandparents refused to leave. They believed in G-d so deeply, they couldn't imagine how anything so bad could happen. They even thought the people who were leaving were foolish. Unfortunately, their faith couldn't save them. They were brutally tortured. Grandfather's beard was set on fire. Then they were killed. The local inhabitants of the shtetl told my father that awful story.

My First Date with the Arctic

REM MENSHIKOV
Office manager, St. Petersburg

It was the second year of Russia's war against fascism. I was seventeen years old when I went to fight. I was demobilized after being wounded and treated in the hospital. I took a job with a geological expedition of the Northern Seaway, on the coast of the Arctic Ocean.

My travels began at the city of Krasnoyarsk, through Yackutsk and Tiksy Bay to the coast of the northern ice ocean. In Yackutsk, the sun glistened brightly on the white snow. When I got off the plane, I immediately fell to the ground. I wasn't prepared for the shock to my eyes. I suffered from eye strain, and couldn't see anything for three weeks. In Tiksy, the winter temperature dropped to −40°C, with strong winds and severe snowstorms. There were no air fields, so the planes had to land on lakes of ice or on frozen river beds.

When we arrived at the Ice Ocean coast, it was in the middle of a big snowstorm. Visibility was zero, and we could see nothing in front of us. I don't know how the pilot landed his plane, but he did it, breaking only one ski. We had to wait for the drifting ice. The frozen river was 16–20 meters above the normal level. Traveling was impossible. It was June before we could go on foot to the place where the work was to be done.

Spring is a fine time in the Arctic. There are grasses, pygmy trees, berries of different rainbow colors, and glistening, small clear water lakes. There were also many birds, such as geese, ducks and swans. That was my first date with the Arctic.

I have since worked in Murmansk for the Arctic Shipping Line, on cargo ships and ice breakers, and served as chief of service of the seaport and coastal building. From my first experiences as a young man, I thought the Arctic had a wonderful beauty. I grew very fond of it then, and have loved it all my life.

Kartoffilnee Cutlyete (Potato Cutlets) with Mushroom Sauce

MINNA VAYSTIKH

1 lb potatoes, peeled and boiled
1 egg, beaten
1 Tbs flour
¾ lb ground beef
1 onion, finely chopped

1 Tbs oil
Salt and pepper to taste
½ cup oil
Sour cream or IMO for garnish

Mash potatoes and combine with egg and flour.
Sauté onions and ground beef together until beef is cooked.
Take spoonful of potato mixture. Flatten on a floured surface. Put one spoonful of meat mixture in center. Form potato around meat. Coat with flour and fry until brown.
Serve with sour cream or mushroom sauce (below).

Mushroom Sauce

YEUGENIA ROMM

1 onion, peeled and chopped
½ lb mushrooms, cleaned and chopped
1 Tbs flour
1 Tbs mayonnaise

1 Tbs sour cream or IMO
Salt and pepper to taste
Oil, for frying

Sauté onion until golden. Add chopped mushrooms and continue sautéing a few more minutes until mushrooms are soft. Mix in flour, salt and pepper. Add mayonnaise and sour cream and blend until smooth.
Good over any vegetable, meat or chicken dish.

Not quite right...

I like to cook, but my cooking doesn't always work out. One time I wanted to make some liver. So, I cut it into slices, rolled it in the flour and fried it. We began to eat our food and found that it tasted very strange. It was then I discovered that I had rolled the meat in baking soda instead of flour. I never made that mistake again!

—BENTSION PETRUSHANSKIY

Cousin Sarah's Sweet and Sour Meatballs

ROSALIE SOGLOW

This is good served with rice or mashed potatoes. This sauce is so delicious that you may want to reserve any that's left over to pour over chicken or beef later in the week.

SAUCE
1 onion, peeled and chopped
1 can tomato soup
½ tsp sour salt *

½ cup water
½ cup sugar (or equivalent of Equal)
Vegetable oil (enough to sauté onions)

*This comes in a bottle and sometimes looks like rock candy. You can probably find it at a kosher market, if your supermarket doesn't carry it.

MEATBALLS
1 lb ground beef (or ground turkey)
1 tsp salt

2 eggs
¼ cup matzo meal

Brown onions in a small amount of oil. Add water, tomato soup, sour salt and sugar. Bring to a boil. Shape meatballs and drop carefully into boiling sauce. Simmer about 15–20 minutes. Cool and skim fat from surface. Reheat before serving.

Second Chances

ISRAEL ABRAMZON
Engineer/economist, Leningrad

It was the beginning of World War II, June 22, 1941, twelve o'clock.

I was in Leningrad on the busy street, Nevsky Prospect. Suddenly I heard the minister for foreign affairs, Molotov, speaking on the radio. He announced that the Germans were attacking the USSR. Their planes had begun attacking along the border and had bombed Kiev, Minsk, Brest and the Baltic republics. After his speech, everyone was in shock. In minutes, the busy main street was completely empty. Everyone ran home. But all the young people went off to fight. I was among them. But when I tried to join in, they refused me because I was a student at the university. I insisted and said, "It's our war, and I must fight!"

In two days, I was taken to the front, 140 kilometers from Leningrad. We knew the Nazis had to be stopped there. They had to be kept out of the city.

Blockade

Oh, dear Loosky, place where they must be stopped,
Your people worked by night and day
With streams of sweat upon their faces,
That this place be strong by evening fires!

But they couldn't do it. The enemy was stronger than our army, and we had to leave. On September 8, their soldiers surrounded the city.

...And their bodies closed our native town!

After this, I was sent to study at a special school for radio communications. It was important to keep contact with the people trapped inside the city. When possible, drivers attempted to bring flour and some food to keep the people from starving.

Drivers, how many of you died upon this road?
...Those who survived will never forget your courage!

In 1942, when the ice had melted, the Germans attacked again. I was a radio operator on a ship at this time. One day, everyone was ordered to leave the ship. But I was asleep, and they forgot about me. Suddenly, in my dream, my father, who had died in 1930, woke me and said, "Israel! Get up!" I jumped up, but there was no one there. The ship was empty. I ran. When I had gone about fifty meters, a bomb hit the ship, and it sunk. I escaped with my life!

Later, while I was being treated for injuries in the hospital, an officer who was in shock tried to shoot me. Another man stepped in front of me, and the bullet that was coming towards me killed him. This was the second time I had escaped death. After these close calls, I thank G-d for my life. I have become a religious man!

Cholent—
The Twenty-Four-Hour Dish

R OSA Z AKS F ELDMAN
Teacher, Kirgezia, Russia

I have very little recollection of my childhood in Europe. One thing I do re-member vividly is the smell and taste of cholent. Cholent consists of potatoes, more potatoes and stewing meat with lots of *schmaltz* (fat). I asked my mother if she ever made cholent when she was living in Russia. "Meat was not avail-able in Siberia," she replied. "Nor in the little town of Marazee, Kirgezia, where you and your brother were born," she added.

My parents were nineteen years old when they left their little town of Pietrykow, Poland, after the first bombs exploded. The apartment building where my uncle lived was hit, and my mother, Gutcha Rosenstein, and father, Mayer Zaks, along with a dozen other young people, decided to flee from this dangerous place. They waved goodbye to their families as they boarded the train, knowing in their hearts that this might be the last time they would see them.

Like many of the young men and women traveling together, their jour-ney ended up in Siberia. Some joined the Russian army. My father was a tailor for the army from 1938–1945. As payment for making uniforms, he would re-ceive flour and other staples to feed his wife and surrogate families. During the war, the town they lived in was a very close-knit community. They all shared their food and their living space. When the American allies entered war-torn Europe, my parents went back to Poland with my brother and me to search for their families. But their beautiful town was devastated, and so we continued on by train to Landsberg, Germany.

I recall standing in line at the community outdoor oven with my mother by my side. She carried a big pot filled with meat and potatoes, wrapped with newspaper and tied with string. Waiting twenty-four hours for a pot of cholent to cook seemed forever to a three-year-old child. I could hardly wait for the next day to indulge in this incredible mouth-watering meal.

My mother often told me the story about the time my brother and I dis-appeared for hours. I was only three, and my brother, Heniek (Henry), four. My father was supposed to watch us while my mother went to visit someone in a neighboring town. When my mother came home, she became frantic when we were nowhere to be seen. "May-eh! Where are the children?" she shrieked. My father answered, a little bewildered, "Aren't they playing out-side?" Many hours later, my brother and I leisurely wandered back to town, faces streaked with dirt, our hands black as coal, holding a potato in each hand. My father was relieved to see us. My mother, on the other hand, was a nervous wreck because he was minding the sewing machine instead of us. I don't know if she made cholent that night with the potatoes we dug for all morning long.

Twenty-four hours is a long time to wait for a dish to cook, but I can tell you it was worth the wait for us. So now I will introduce you to:

Gutcha's Cholent

ROSA ZAKS FELDMAN

10 potatoes, peeled
2 lbs stewing meat or chuck roast
1 large onion, grated
1 clove garlic
1 Tbs salt

1 tsp pepper
1 tsp garlic powder
Dash of cayenne pepper (optional)
Water, enough to cover meat

Preheat oven to 250°. Place meat seasoned with salt, pepper and garlic into a large roasting pan.

Grate 6 potatoes and the onion finely and add to the pan. Cut remaining potatoes into quarters and place on top of the meat. Add water and cook, covered, for twenty-four hours.

NOTE: You can also use lima beans or barley for variety.

Cholent

According to religious doctrine, the truly observant do not do work of any kind on the Sabbath. So as not to violate this law, cholent could be prepared before sundown on Friday and placed in a slow-cooking oven for the next twenty-four hours. When it was time for Shabbos dinner, it was hot and ready to be served. Cholent was relished and served often for this reason.

Three Pilots

RITA GORLIN
Nuclear engineer, Moscow

For a long time after World War II, there was widespread anti-Semitic public opinion that Jews did not serve in the war. Supposedly, they all "hid" in Tashkent, in the middle of Asia. Not only was this not true, but many, many brave Jewish men and women were killed and wounded fighting in this war. As you can see by this photo taken in 1942, my husband and two other pilots were actively engaged in military operations—and all of them are Jews.

Gimelfarb, Granovsky and Gorlin (right), at the front, 1942. Courtesy Rita Gorlin

Kotlyete (Beef Patties)

IRINA MENSHIKOV

1 lb ground beef
3 slices white bread, moistened
Garlic, minced, to taste
1 onion, finely chopped
1 egg, beaten

¼ cup white bread crumbs, toasted
Ground pepper to taste
Salt to taste
2 Tbs margarine or oil

Add to ground meat: moistened white bread, salt, ground pepper, minced garlic and beaten egg. Mix the ground beef mixture well. Divide into 10 portions and form into oval patties. Coat with the toasted bread crumbs.

Add butter or oil to a medium-hot frying pan. Fry patties at medium temperature for 5 minutes on each side. They should be crispy on the outside and juicy on the inside.

Close Quarters

Malvina Alexandravskaya
Engineer, St. Petersburg

In my short story about my childhood, I told how my family lived in a village where the population consisted of Germans and Ukrainians. That's why there where only German and Ukrainian schools there. My parents entered me in the German school. The boys in the school were very mean to me. They teased me, threw stones at me and so on. At first, I bore this silently. I didn't tell anyone how I suffered. But after about two weeks of this, I went to my mother and cried and told her how bad things were. I asked her if she could send me to the Ukrainian school. But the other school was worse, and so, until I was eleven, I studied at home. Then it was decided that my parents would send me to school in Moscow, where my mother's brother lived with his family. They had moved to this city in 1922, after the devastation of World War I, and gotten a flat—which was a "communal apartment."

It looked like this: The five-story building was an hotel earlier, but not a comfortable hotel. On either side of the entrance were long hallways with ten (or more) doors opposite each other. After the Revolution, when many people flocked to Moscow, many different families constantly settled in this "apartment."

My uncle with his wife, three daughters and one son had two "apartments." The first had two normal rooms and one little room without a window. And opposite was the other "apartment"…with only one room. In these apartments there were only wash stands. At the end of the hallway, there were two toilets for all the tenants on that side of the hallway. There wasn't a bathroom or laundry or kitchen—nothing! For washing ourselves we had to go to the bath house. Our clothes we took to the laundry. Each family had their own number, which had to be on each thing, and we had to leave the clothes for two to three weeks!

This picture isn't typical. Later I saw other flats which were more comfortable for two to three families, with a bathroom and a kitchen. In the kitchen each owner of a room had a table, ordinarily with drawers for the dishes. Often each had a lamp for himself, and in the hallway or in the anteroom there were as many meters as there were families living there.

But I also saw buildings which were only barracks made from boards, with just one room for a family, and with the toilets outside. In these barracks, it was so cold in winter that water often froze in the rooms.

When I look at the place where I live now, it's hard to believe that I actually lived in close quarters like that with my uncle's family in those days. But many, many people lived like that. And, unfortunately, it's true that many people still share communal apartments in Russia today.

Khleba, Napeetki, Kasha

(Breads, Beverages, Kasha —and other good things)

No event in Russia's long history, other than the momentous birth of Communism following the 1917 Revolution, affected its people more profoundly than World War II. Russians from every walk of life suffered through this painful period. Besides the loss of millions of lives, starvation, and dislocation plagued the country. Bread, the traditional symbol of hospitality and always known as "the staff of life," took on an even more important significance.

BREADS, BEVERAGES, KASHA...

Two Pieces of Dry Black Bread

Alex Krasner
Surgeon, St. Petersburg

This happened a long time ago, during the days of World War II. I was seventeen years old when on Sunday, June 22, 1941, Hitler's army, without warning, attacked the Soviet Union and started the long and bloody war. The next day, Monday, I was taking my last examination of my freshman year in the medical institute when I saw the first tears of war. One of my friends, who was also majoring in medicine, got an order to go to a certain place on the front where her medical help was needed. She was crying when she said goodbye to us, as if she would never see us again. Unfortunately, her intuition was right, as we found out later that she had died on her way during the first days of the war.

The Red Army, which was then called "undefeated," suffered one loss after another. That was not surprising considering the fact that a short time before the war it had been beheaded. Most of the commanding staff had been shot because of some reasons that didn't make any sense. (These orders were from Stalin.) Only a few were saved. Taking advantage of these circumstances, Hitler's army very soon appeared near Leningrad (now St. Petersburg). The city was surrounded by a circle creating a blockade which lasted 900 days. During September 1941, the German air force bombed and burned the food storehouse. The horrible hunger began.

The daily bombing and firing on the city did not cause as many deaths as the cruel hunger in the unheated winter apartments. All the dogs and cats were already eaten, some even ate rats. Sometimes cases of cannibalism were discovered. Every day the slice of bread, which was the only food given out, was decreased until it reached a quarter of a pound per person per day. Yet that was not the bread that we enjoyed before the war. The bread that we received was made out of flour from the bones of animals, and the rest of it from unused scraps. It was black as coal and sticky as clay. And yet it was bread—the hopeful dream of the hungry ones. We ate anything, anything that in any way resembled food and made us feel like we were full, to satisfy our hunger. All the grasses and seeds that before the blockade were used to feed the cattle were now considered delicacies.

I remember one night when I was working in the hospital, my friend and colleague gave me a piece of dry glue, which was as hard as a rock. I held that little piece in my mouth and enjoyed it as if it was some kind of candy, and every swallow caused unbearable spasms of pain in my stomach. I was extremely hungry. All I could think about day and night was food. Sometimes I had hallucinations about it. I imagined a table covered with different kinds of foods that I liked, and in the middle of that table I saw a huge pile of delicious bread that looked so savory. And when I woke up with a smile on my face, the table disappeared, and I felt the tears rolling down my cheeks.

I lost a lot of weight, my legs swelled, and I could barely move from one place to another. I was a live skeleton, and even though I was only seventeen years old, I already looked like an emaciated old man. In that state I was evacuated from Leningrad on the "road of life," which was on ice through Lake Ladoznoye and the only road that connected the blockaded city with the rest of the "big land." I was seated with many people in the back of an open truck. From time to time, German planes appeared and tried to bomb us. One of their bombs fell behind our truck and created a huge hole in the ice into which the next truck that followed us fell and disappeared in the ice before we turned our necks.

On the other side of the lake, food was waiting for us. On the way to our destination, there were a couple of feeding points, where in the kitchens the army chefs cooked porridge and meat with a lot of fat on it. That food was used to feed the hungry people from Leningrad. And when it was time to move on, they gave us a couple of slices of bread for the road. In the heated tent where they tried to warm us up a little after the freezing wind on the lake we crossed, a soldier came up to talk to me. He was three or four years older than me and looked very tired. The following were his words: "I see that you are a starving one from the blockaded city. I am going to the front and I don't know if I'll stay alive or die, but I am very hungry. Can you please give me one slice of bread?" What he asked me was completely understandable considering the fact that the whole country suffered from the shortage of food. All the supplies that were sent from America went to the front where the soldiers received pork, bacon and other food. On the home front, however, the soldiers were really hungry. The soldier's request at first made me very angry. How could he even think of taking food from somebody that looked like a skeleton and to whom bread meant life? At the same time, another thought was drilling my brain. That soldier was hungry. He needed to eat. Not to give bread to him would have been a sin. I knew very well what it was like to experience hunger. I told him that I had only four slices, that I would give him two and the other two I would take with me for the road because it was long. "Don't worry," he said, "they are going to feed you on the way. You won't be hungry, but I must tell you something very important. I arrived from Siberia and saw that the whole road to your destination was full of dead bodies of people from Leningrad. They were so hungry that they ate without limit to satiate themselves and then died. Be careful. Don't eat everything that they give you. Try to restrain yourself."

I followed the soldier's advice. Everything he said was true. After the long starvation, people developed different physiological problems and changes in their digestion systems. The immune system was damaged, and even the right amount of food caused unbearable stomach pains from which many died. There was no medical help, since people were traveling west in the food wagons where there was no medicine. I felt horrible. To stay alive in starving and freezing Leningrad, to survive through the constant bombing of the city, to cross the lake safely, and step on the "big land," only to face the possibility of dying a preposterous death—from food! I was lucky to avoid that fate, thanks to the advice of that soldier.

Yet I remember how hard it was for me to withstand the temptations and not to fill my stomach till I could eat no more. On the road I tried to convince my traveling companions to be careful and eat less, to restrain themselves. Unfortunately, all my warnings were futile. Their hunger and greed took over their reasoning, and they jumped on food. The hunger deprived even intelligent people of their will power, and as a result they suffered horrible deaths.

More than fifty years have passed. I never again met that young man I gave the bread to. I don't know if he stayed alive or died like the millions of others. Yet, I owe him everything, because without knowing it, in exchange for two pieces of dry black bread, he saved my life!

▩ Challah

MICHAEL DUBROVSKI

1 pkg yeast	1 tsp salt
3 eggs, beaten	¼ cup oil
6 Tbs sugar	6–7 cups flour
1½–2 cups water	¼ cup poppy seeds

Dissolve the yeast in ½ cup warm water. Add 1 Tbs sugar and 1 Tbs flour. Cover and put in a warm place for 20–30 minutes. Using a large bowl, combine the yeast mixture with the remaining sugar and water; add and mix the salt, oil, beaten eggs and flour. Knead the dough. Coat a dish with oil and put in the dough. Cover with a towel and place in a warm place until the dough doubles in size (approximately 2 hours).

Preheat oven to 350°. Divide the dough into 2 portions for 2 large challahs (into 4 parts for 4 small challahs). Coat each part with oil and roll out like a sausage. Press the two ends of each piece together and twist. Coat a roasting pan with oil, put in the dough and cover with a soft moist cloth for 40 minutes to allow dough to rise again.

Brush the dough with beaten egg. Sprinkle with poppy seeds and bake for 40–60 minutes until the crust is brown.

A Kettle of Porridge

Moisey Kagan
Physician, St. Petersburg

It happened in the winter of 1942–43. Our ski unit had been secretly diverted to a new position. We had to deliver some food for our soldiers before dawn. A kettle of porridge was placed on a sleigh drawn by horses. The cook, Drygin, drove the horses, and I was sitting behind the kettle. We were moving along a narrow forest road. We were in a hurry, as the dawn was fast approaching. Suddenly, we heard a warning in Russian, saying that the Germans were near. We stopped and looked around, but we saw no one. Silently, we turned and headed back in the direction from which we came.

We soon discovered that if we had continued going straight ahead, we would have delivered the porridge directly into the hands of the German soldiers instead of our own. That whispered warning saved our lives. I am very thankful that I wasn't killed at the age of seventeen, for the sake of a kettle of porridge!

Kasha (Buckwheat Groats)

Nora Dreyzner

1 cup buckwheat groats	1 Tbs butter
3 cups water	salt, milk and butter to taste

Lightly fry the groats and then add to boiling water. Simmer the mixture until the water is absorbed.

Serve with milk and butter or serve as a side dish for meat.

Baked Kasha with Walnuts

Nadia Zaks

2 cups cooked kasha, or cracked wheat	½ tsp salt
1 medium onion, peeled and chopped	⅛ tsp pepper
3 Tbs butter or margarine	½ cup coarsely chopped walnuts

Preheat oven to 350°. Brown onion in butter over medium heat for about 10–12 minutes. Prepare kasha and add onion, salt, pepper and walnuts. Mix well. Put into a greased casserole and sprinkle with remaining butter. Cover and bake for 30 minutes. Serves 4.

Why Did G–d Get Angry?

RITA GORLIN
Nuclear engineer, Moscow

This story was told to me by my mother-in-law. Her parents lived in a shtetl near Minsk. Her father was an educated man. He was a rabbi, and wrote poetry about biblical subjects. But their family had a lot of children, and was so poor that they ate meat only on Saturday.

In spite of this, each Friday, when her mother cooked, she baked an extra, large loaf of bread for a beggar. She invited a passing beggar each week for Saturday dinner, and gave him the bread to take with him. If a beggar didn't pass her door, she became very upset and cried, "What did I do? Why did G–d get angry?" This was her custom, and she never failed to follow it.

Kasha Varnishkas (Kasha with Bows)

EDITH KRULAN, VIA R.S.

One of my mother's favorite dishes was kasha varnishkas. She often brought a generous casserole as her contribution to our family holiday dinners. It has a nice nutty flavor which complements the noodles. Serve as a change of pace from potatoes or rice.

1 cup medium- or coarse-grain kasha	2 Tbs finely chopped fresh parsley
1 egg, beaten	(optional)
1 large onion, finely chopped	1 pkg (1 lb) bow-shaped noodles
2–3 Tbs margarine or chicken fat	½ tsp salt
2 cups water or chicken broth	Pepper to taste

Sauté the chopped onions in margarine or chicken fat until golden. Remove from pan.

In a bowl, beat egg and stir in kasha. Make sure the grains are thoroughly coated. Put mixture into the fry pan, and cook until egg is dry and kasha is brown, stirring frequently.

Add water or broth and seasoning. Bring to a boil, add onions, cover and cook over low heat for about 20 minutes, or until liquid has been absorbed and kernels are tender. Stir in additional butter if mixture seems too dry, and 1 Tbs parsley.

Meanwhile, boil bows in salted water. Drain and add to cooked kasha. Put in casserole dish and sprinkle with remaining parsley, if desired.

Time Changes the Meaning of Happiness

MIKHAIL KINBERG
Otolaryngologist, Odessa

I was born and lived in the city of Odessa most of my life. Odessa has a lot of beaches, two seaports, a lot of universities and the best opera and ballet theatre in the country. When life was normal, there were many happy times there. It is very difficult to write about my childhood because of all the bad experiences, but some of the difficult years I remember very well. Those were 1921, 1932 and 1936. Those were the years of hunger and famine. Children died on the street, at school, near food stores and in the hospital. Between hunger and starvation there is a big difference. Starvation is a condition of depression and hyperactivity. Even in the movies, hungry children are difficult to portray. I didn't starve, but was very near to it. I saw children who didn't find their parents at home. People ask if I had a happy childhood. Sholom Aleichem wrote, "...Some want pearls for supper to be happy. Others want pearls on their necks." I understood early that happiness was coming home and finding everyone there. But everybody doesn't understand what such happiness is. That is because their happiness didn't come from *un*happiness. Time changes the meaning of happiness—and many other things.

❋ Kasha with Mushrooms

INNA EYDUS

1 oz dried wild mushrooms, such as porcini	1 cup whole kasha
	2 large onions, chopped
10 oz fresh white mushrooms, cleaned and sliced	Salt to taste
	1 cup sour cream or IMO
1 stick unsalted butter or margarine	½ cup chicken broth

Soak the dried mushrooms in 2 cups of warm water for 2 hours. Remove, pat dry and chop them. Strain the liquid through a coffee filter, put into a pan and bring to a boil. Reduce heat and simmer until kasha is ready.

Melt 2 Tbs butter or margarine in an oven-proof casserole over medium heat. Add the kasha and stir for 3–4 minutes. Add the simmering liquid and salt. Reduce heat and continue to heat until liquid is absorbed, about 15–20 minutes.

Melt another 4 Tbs butter or margarine in a large fry pan. Add the onions and sauté for 5 minutes. Add the fresh and wild mushrooms and sauté, stirring until nicely colored, about 15–20 minutes.

Preheat oven to 375°. Stir the mushroom and onion mixture into the kasha. Blend together the sour cream or IMO and broth and add to the kasha. Mix well and dot the top of the casserole with the remaining 2 Tbs butter or margarine. Bake until top is lightly browned, about 20 minutes. Serve warm.

Khleb ee Sol (Bread and Salt)

Bread and salt are ancient symbols of Slavic hospitality. Whether visiting a new home, or welcoming guests in one's own house, it is traditional to offer these symbolic foods. They are also a part of many rituals and ceremonies. Newly married couples in their first home are customarily installed with the same ritual offering, usually by the parents or relatives of the bride and groom. When guests arrive, they are greeted at the door with a platter of bread and some salt in which to dip it. This charming ritual means that the guests are welcome to share whatever there is. It is usually accompanied by a heartfelt *Dobra Pahzhalovet!* (Welcome!)

Tempura

Tamara Fayner
English teacher, Kharkov, Ukraine

Some students of the Moscow Institute of Oriental Languages (and I among them) were sent to southern Sakhalin, which belonged to Japan until World War II, to improve our Japanese. We couldn't get used to the queer Japanese food. For example, their common food was fish. But not fresh fish. They preferred it spoiled. There were some things I liked very much, though. Among them was tempura: slices of fish or meat mixed with dough and fried in a frying pan. It was a kind of thick pancake.

When I returned home after a long absence, I told my mother a lot of stories about exotic Japan, and couldn't help boasting that I'd learned to cook tempura. She smiled and said that she had been making this dish since her childhood, but instead of fish or meat she used thin slices of apples.

Many years have passed, but when I sometimes fry tempura, I always remember my unforgettable green years, my life in a Japanese Buddhist temple and certainly my dearest mother. You may not believe me, but I'm quite sure that my mother was the best cook in the world. I've never tasted such delicious food as she prepared.

 ## Japanese Tempura—Russian Oladee (Fritters)

Tamara Fayner

JAPANESE VERSION	RUSSIAN VERSION
½ cup sour cream	½ cup sour cream
1 cup flour	1 cup flour
1 egg	1 egg
¼ tsp salt	¼ tsp salt
¼ tsp baking powder	1 tsp vanilla
Some slices of meat or fish	1 Tbs sugar
Vegetable oil (for frying)	¼ tsp baking powder
	2 apples, peeled and thinly sliced
	Vegetable oil (for frying)

Japanese Tempura   Beat egg with sour cream. Add flour, salt and baking powder. Mix well. Dip pieces of meat or fish into batter. Heat enough oil in a pan to cover. Fry until crispy.

Russian Oladee   Beat egg with sugar. Add sour cream, vanilla, flour, salt and baking powder. Mix well. Cut peeled and cored apples into thin slices and dip into batter. Heat oil and fry until crisp and lightly browned. Serve with sour cream.

▦ Barley and Mushroom Casserole

INNA EYDUS

1 cup medium pearl barley	3 cups chicken or beef broth
4 Tbs butter or margarine	2 tsp salt
1 large yellow onion	¼ tsp pepper
1 cup coarsely chopped mushrooms	

Preheat oven to 350°. Stir-fry barley and 2 Tbs butter over medium heat for about 2 minutes until lightly browned. Put in an ungreased casserole dish.

Sauté onion with remaining butter for 5–6 minutes or until pale golden, add mushrooms and sauté 3–5 minutes longer. Add to casserole. Mix all the ingredients, cover and bake about 1¼ hours until barley is tender. Stir occasionally. Fluff with a fork and serve as a side dish instead of potatoes.

How Long Can a Man Go Without Sleep?

SOLOMON KUMKES

Editor of a geographical publishing house, Moscow

I'd like to tell about something that happened to me during the war in the summer of 1944 in the Ukraine. I served as a meteorologist at a meteorological station in an air bombing regiment. I worked every other twenty-four hours. I had to draft on the map information given to me by the radio operator. Every two hours, I had to process it and report to the staff regiment on the weather forecast in three parts: the weather on the aerodrome, the weather en route and the weather at the target. During the night, at the time of the operational flight, my chief or I had to be on duty on the aerodrome in the command post.

One day, another meteorologist and the chief of the station both became ill. I had to carry out all the work by myself. For three days and three nights, I couldn't close my eyes. Only on the morning of the fourth day did they send another meteorologist from the neighboring regiment. And then I could go home. As soon as I got to my house, I fell under a tree, unconscious, and slept without waking for a day, a night and another day!

Passover Bagels

ANN SOGOLOW VIA R.S.

2 cups matzo meal	1 Tbs sugar
½ cup chicken fat or vegetable oil	1 cup water
1 tsp salt	6 eggs

Preheat oven to 350°. Bring water, salt, sugar and fat or oil to a boil. Add matzo meal and mix well. Mix until it forms a ball and remove from heat. Add eggs, one at a time, and beat until well blended.

Grease a pan or cookie sheet. Wet hands and form the dough by rolling a ball of about 2" diameter and making a hole in the center with the finger after the ball has been placed on the pan.

Bake for about 30 minutes or until brown. Makes about 2 dozen bagels.

Compote of Dried Fruits

SOPHIE TARANTUR VIA R.S.

It was a standing joke at our Passover seders that we could never end the meal without a bowl of Grandma's famous compote to balance the effects of the matzo on our digestive systems. (Matzo is known to slow things down quite a bit.) My uncles would tease her without fail, "Okay, Ma…where's the compote?" "I'm sorry. I don't have any today," she would respond. "Well, I guess we'll just have to sit here till you make some then!" they shot back. At which point she always presented her sweet fruits with a flourish. It was always a fitting end to a side-splitting feast.

2 lbs mixed dried fruits*	2 slices lemon with 3 cloves
2 cups water	inserted in each
½–⅓ cup sugar	lemon juice to taste
	1 stick cinnamon

Can be made with prunes alone.

Put the fruit in a heavy saucepan with water, sugar, lemon slices with cloves and cinnamon. Simmer about 20 minutes or until tender.

After fruit is cooked, flavor with lemon juice and more sugar, if desired. Chill before serving. Best when made a day or two in advance.

One Day I Will Never Forget

MIKHAIL KINBERG
Otolaryngologist, Odessa

I was stationed in Germany. It was early morning on May 8, 1945. More wounded were brought to our hospital. We operated all day. The hospital was quiet after supper that night, so I left and went for a walk. The weather was very nice. Suddenly, shots were fired in the air from the direction of our soldiers. They had just heard of the Nazis' surrender. "Victory! The war has ended!" Together we cheered. At the hospital the doctors, nurses, the wounded and the rest of the staff were weeping from joy.

Our joy soon turned to grief after a group of Nazis attacked the hospital. One of the casualties was my friend. She was a surgeon. She was wonderful...a graceful woman. We liked each other. She was twenty-seven years old. She will be forever young. That was forty-nine years ago. She will always be in my heart.

Mikhail's Favorite Topping for Waffles

MIKHAIL KINBERG

2 cups nuts, chopped
1 cup honey

1 cup sugar
1 cup sweet butter

Chop up two cups of nuts. Put into a saucepan. Add one cup of honey and one cup of sugar. Put in one cup of sweet butter. Cook over a low heat for 15 minutes.

Prepare waffles. Pour mixture over waffles and serve.

Stawberry Kissel

SONYA SLUTSKER

Slavic tribes were making a kind of kissel as early as the tenth century, using grains instead of fruit. In Russia, kissel was usually made with strawberries, cranberries or loganberries. But other fruits, such as apricots or blueberries, can also be used.

1 lb strawberries, cored and sliced
2 Tbs sugar
Juice of ½ lemon
Finely grated peel of ¼ lemon

1 Tbs potato flour or cornstarch
2 cups water
Pinch of nutmeg

Pour just enough water into a pan to cover the bottom. Add strawberries and sugar and boil until soft and pulpy. Strain the mixture into another pan. Add lemon juice, lemon peel and nutmeg. Mix flour with remaining water and stir into the strawberry mixture. Bring to a boil and simmer for five minutes, stirring continuously.

Pour into 6 dessert dishes and cool before serving.

Hard Times

SONYA SLUTSKER
Engineer, Odessa

My father was born in 1885 in a small shtetl in Byelorussia, called Kostikovka. His father was a master cap maker, but the family was very poor because he did too good a job. He provided all the men in the town with caps, but they wore them for many years and very seldom bought new ones. Sometimes he also worked for a rich man and guarded his fruit orchard.

My grandmother worked very hard. She baked bread and rolls for all the people of the shtetl. When my father was only six years old, he had to get up very early in the morning and run to the customs office to sell the fresh bakery goods. In the summer, he and his sisters went to the forest to gather berries and mushrooms.

When my father turned ten, his parents gave him to a shoemaker to learn to make shoes. He was still very small, and the master had to put a board under his stool so he could reach the sewing machine. He lived at this man's house and worked from morning until night for two years. Then, he ran away.

Later, when there were pogroms, drunken bandits amused themselves by shooting at people, including my father. He fell to the ground. They took the ring from his finger and left. He stayed still for a long time before he understood that he wasn't dead. After that a Christian man hid him and his family in a damp cellar, where his wife fell ill and died.

After the Revolution, Father had a small business, but in 1930 hard times came again because the government took away all of his property. My sister and brother were expelled from college. My brother worked as a miner, but after a short time, there was a wreck at the mine, and my brother contracted tuberculosis. My sister, who was fourteen years old, went to a nearby small town and worked very hard. Our family overcame this hard time and all the children eventually received an education. The Second World War soon began. But that is another story.

▦ Verenya (Radishes in Honey)

FAINA BELOGOLOVSKY

This is a very old recipe that my grandmother liked to serve, especially for Passover. This delicious jam can be kept for a long time and served with tea or as a condiment.

2 lbs black radishes, peeled and grated (can use food processor)	½ cup chopped nuts
	½ cup sugar
2 cups honey	2 Tbs lemon juice

Cook grated radishes in boiling water 1½ hours. Drain through a strainer and squeeze out as much liquid as possible.

Heat honey until boiling. Add sugar, lemon juice and cooked radish.

Continue cooking over low heat until radish is brown. Stir often to prevent scorching. Add nuts, if desired.

▦ Kvass

SONYA SLUTSKER

This is a popular summer drink that is usually sold by street vendors, and can be served as a cool refreshment with meals. It can also be used as an ingredient for cold summer soups. Some prefer a more tart version, but more sugar can be added for a sweeter taste.

1 lb slightly stale black or dark rye bread	3 Tbs lukewarm water
3 qts boiling water	1 large sprig of mint
5 tsp (2 ¼-oz packets) active dry yeast	2 oz raisins
½–1 cup sugar	

Preheat the oven to 225° F. Place the bread in the oven for about 1½ hours, or until very dry. *Do not let it burn.* Crumble the bread into a bowl, and pour the boiling water over it. Cover with a towel, and leave for at least 8 hours.

Line a fine sieve with cheesecloth and strain the bread liquid through it into a large bowl, pressing the bread with a spoon to extract as much liquid as possible. Take out the bread.

Sprinkle the yeast and a large pinch of sugar over the lukewarm water, and stir to dissolve completely. Put in a warm spot for about 10 minutes, or until mixture is foamy or double in size. Stir the yeast mixture, the rest of the sugar, and the mint sprig into the bread water. Cover with a towel and let sit for another 8–12 hours.

Strain the liquid again, and pour into three sterilized one-quart bottles, until about ⅔ full. Then add 4–5 raisins to each bottle. Cover with plastic wrap, and secure with a rubber band.

Place the bottles in a cool, dark place for about three days, until the raisins have risen to the top and the sediment is on the bottom. Carefully pour off the clear liquid into a bowl, leaving the sediment behind. Remove the raisins, thoroughly clean the bottles, and funnel the liquid back into them. (There will be slightly less than before.) Cover tightly and refrigerate until ready to use. The kvass will keep for several weeks in the refrigerator.

Nezhin

YELENA BELYAVSKAYA
Architect, Moscow

In the Ukraine, the small town of Nezhin is the motherland of all my relatives. My grandparents were born and lived there. They were poor, but they worked very hard. One of my grandfathers was a tailor, and the other was a book binder. My father was born in 1889. His name was Aaron. When he was a little boy, he helped his father to make book covers, and from childhood he read many books. It was the beginning of his Russian education. His Jewish education he received in cheder (Hebrew school). Later he learned to repair clocks and became a clock maker.

After the Revolution, my father went to Moscow. My mother also came to Moscow to study at the university during this period. She became a doctor. They met there and fell in love. Her name was Anna. They had a great love affair during all of their lives. For many years, my father worked at the aviation factory. Once, he took part in the making of a plane for the most famous Soviet pilot, Chkalov.

I was born in this capital city of Russia, and lived there until we moved to America. But in my childhood, every summer vacation, I went to Nezhin to visit my dear grandmother. Nezhin was a beautiful, green town. Grandmother lived in a small house. In the yard, she planted vegetables, and there were fruit trees, also. Many Jews lived there at that time. My grandmother and her friends always spoke to each other in Yiddish. I was a listener, and little by little, I understood what they were saying. In Russia, there was always anti-Semitism. Jewish people didn't celebrate their holidays or speak their language openly. They were always ashamed of their nationality, and tried to become more "Russian." But it didn't put an end to their problem. Still, Grandmother was a happy woman. She often sang folk songs, and I liked that. She also cooked many different Jewish foods, and I liked that, too. I have many happy memories of Nezhin.

Sladkiye Blyuda

(Desserts; literally, "Sweet Dishes")

Many people in Russia today are unhappy with the new "democracy." The dream is fresh, but the optimism is gone. They didn't particularly like the old system either, but somehow they wish they could have their cake and eat it too!

No meal is complete without dessert—the perfect end to a satisfying repast...a sweet to accompany a nice cup of tea. Our grandparents sipped their tea from a glass, with the ever present lump of sugar. How nice it would be to hear the bubbling sound of a samovar supplying a comforting background to our nostalgic journey.

You may notice that there are more desserts than anything else. This is because Russians love their desserts, and our Russian babushkas are wonderful bakers. No respectable meal would seem complete without one of the many delectable sweets they are so good at preparing.

DESSERTS

My Grandmother's Napoleon

LILIYA KLEBOVICH
Nurse, Kirovgrad, Ukraine

It was July 4, 1945, after the war. My grandmother's birthday. My grandparents lived in a little town called Znamenka, in the Ukraine. Grandfather was a supervisor at a train station, and Grandmother worked on their farm nearby, and had a garden where she grew her own vegetables. Every holiday all the children came to celebrate with them. It was a tradition.

That day, a dog with a broken foot came to the door. Grandmother liked animals very much, and she felt sorry for the injured creature. She wrapped a bandage around its leg and put a big pillow on the floor in the kitchen for him to lie on. When the family arrived, they saw a big dog with very human-looking eyes. Everyone tried to think of names for the dog, but it didn't respond to any of them.

Grandmother had prepared a traditional Napoleon for her birthday celebration. It was also my birthday, and so it was my treat as well. On the table were herring, young potatoes, dill tomatoes, cucumbers, sour cabbage, fish, piroshki with meat, rice or mushrooms, and duck stuffed with apples—a feast! In Krakow, Poland, where she was from, Grandmother was recognized as a real beauty. Each of us gave a toast to this beautiful woman and wonderful hostess: "To the best and kindest grandmother in the world!"

Suddenly, we heard a crash from the kitchen. Grandmother cried, "The Napoleon!" We all ran into the kitchen. The Napoleon was on the floor, and the dog was licking his chops. He looked only at Grandmother with a guilty expression. Grandmother again cried, "My Napoleon!" The dog crept over to her and wagged his tail. From that time on, he only wagged his tail when he was called Napoleon. He had his new name! Napoleon lived with Grandmother for ten years. One day, he saw another dog and ran into the street in front of a car. It was a big tragedy for us because he had become a member of our family.

We bake the Napoleon very seldom now because it is very rich, but it's still a very beautiful and tasty dessert! It also brings back special memories of another time and the dog who inherited its name.

✳ Grandmother's Napoleon

LILYA KLEBOVICH

PASTRY
2 sticks (½ lb) butter
3½ cups flour
½ cup sour cream
1 large egg, beaten
½ cup water
½ tsp baking soda
1 Tbs vinegar

CREAM
6½ cups milk
4 large eggs, beaten
2 cups sugar
3 Tbs flour
½ stick butter, softened
1 tsp vanilla

Pastry

Preheat oven to 400°. Cut butter into small pieces. Combine with flour, sour cream, egg and water.

Mix baking soda and vinegar together. Add to butter–flour mixture. Blend until smooth and creamy. Divide the dough into six (6) segments. Refrigerate about 30 minutes.

On a floured surface, roll each segment into 8" rounds. Carefully slide each round onto a baking sheet. Before baking, pierce the dough with a fork (this will prevent bubbling). Bake for a few minutes until they are very lightly browned. Remove from oven and repeat baking the remaining rounds of dough.

NOTE: The 6th round must be slightly darker than the others. When cool, crumble into small pieces and set aside for use as a topping.

Cream

Combine ½ cup cold milk, eggs, flour and sugar. Mix until free of lumps.
Set aside.

In a saucepan, heat 6 cups milk; slowly add the milk–egg mixture, stirring constantly. Bring to boil and remove from heat. Add butter. Continue stirring. Cool and stir in vanilla.

Assembly

Place bottom pastry round on a round serving platter. Spread with cream and continue alternating with pastry crusts. Finish with a layer of cream on top, spreading it around the sides of the torte. Sprinkle the crumbs on top and sides as a finishing touch.

Make a day in advance and refrigerate until ready to serve.

▨ Rugelah

GISYA SHVARTS

½ lb butter or margarine, melted
1 cup sour cream (½ lb)
1½ Tbs dry yeast

2 eggs, beaten
4 cups flour
1 jar sour jam
(cherry, cranberry, apple, apricot—
not strawberry or other sweet
fruits)

Preheat oven to 350°. Prepare yeast as per instructions on package.

Bowl 1: Put sour cream, eggs and prepared yeast in a bowl.

Bowl 2: Combine butter and 3½ cups flour. Knead flour and butter until the mixture doesn't stick to your hand.

Combine the contents of Bowl 1 and Bowl 2. Knead well. If the mixture is too moist, gradually add the remaining ½ cup flour.

Divide the dough into five equal parts. Sprinkle some sugar on the worktable. Roll each piece of dough into an 8" diameter circle. Sugar should be on the underside only. Divide each round into 8 equal segments.

Starting ½" up from the 3" bottom edge of each segment, spoon 1 scant teaspoon of jam along that edge. Fold ½" of the bottom edge up over the jam, then fold the left and right sides and continue to roll up to seal.

Bake 20–25 minutes or until golden brown.

▨ Apple Cake

DAISY GELB

2 cups sour cream
2¼ cups flour
¼ tsp baking soda
4–5 tart apples,
    peeled and coarsely chopped

1 stick butter or margarine
1 cup sugar
2 eggs
1 tsp vanilla
Cinnamon

Preheat oven to 350°. Combine 1 cup sour cream, baking soda, margarine and 2 cups flour. Grease a cake pan and bake for 10 minutes. Remove from oven and cool.

Spread the chopped apples over the dough. Sprinkle with cinnamon.

Mix together sugar, eggs, vanilla, ¼ cup flour and 1 cup sour cream. Pour the mixture over the cake and apples and bake for an additional 40–45 minutes.

The Right Place at the Right Time

MIKHAIL KINBERG
Ophthalmologist, Odessa

When I was a student, I dreamt of becoming a radiologist. My plans were changed when the war began in 1941. I was drafted to serve as a surgeon in a military hospital. There were two professors in that hospital who taught me a lot. I tried my best to work hard and improve my skills. However, as you may know, it is not always enough to work hard to achieve success; luck is often very important as well! Sometimes it is necessary for an influential person to notice you.

After the end of the war, I continued working as a surgeon at a military hospital. I remember one day in particular when I had operated on an officer with a skull injury. Surgery lasted for about two hours. After checking on him and seeing that his condition had improved, I started to leave the hospital. As I began walking out of the building, I heard a woman scream, "The coin! The coin!" She was carrying a lifeless-looking child in her arms. Wasting no time, I carried the small, limp body to a nearby radiology room and removed the object from his throat with special forceps. After doing mouth-to-mouth resuscitation and heart massage, I was able to revive him. This whole procedure lasted less than four minutes—four minutes that led to a great change in my future professional life.

Following this incident, I was promoted to a higher military rank. I was also given an additional, unscheduled vacation and a free family trip to the best government resort. More importantly, I was given an opportunity to expand my knowledge in the area of otolaryngology (ENT). All these awards, recognition and future opportunities were given to me only because the child I had saved was the grandson of a high-level party boss.

Mazurka (Raisin–Nut Cake)

LARISA VILENSKAYA

2 large eggs, well beaten
1 cup sugar
½ tsp baking soda
1 tsp vinegar
1 cup flour
1 cup walnuts, chopped
1 cup raisins

Preheat oven to 350°. In a mixing bowl, cream eggs and sugar together. Combine baking soda and vinegar in small bowl. Then add to the egg mixture. Blend well. Gradually add flour and continue beating. Add walnuts and raisins.

Pour into greased 9¼" x 13" x 2" baking pan. Bake for 25–30 minutes.

Lekhah

LIBA RABKINA
Bookkeeper, Tallinn, Estonia

I was born in 1922 in the small Byelorussian town of Rechitza. My mother's parents lived there, too. The family was poor. My grandfather worked hard to support them. He was often abused by the village boys, who stole apples from the orchard which he guarded. He never forgot those boys and their treatment of him. My father was a good blacksmith, and rich people often hired him to make carriages (phaetons). Sometimes, he took the children for a ride. In our small town, most of the people were Jewish. They were shoemakers, tailors, blacksmiths and other craftsmen, and usually had a lot of children. They were friendly people, and respected each other.

I vividly remember how we observed our Jewish holidays. For Rosh Hashana (the New Year) and Yom Kippur, as well as Hanukkah, we baked delicious challah and lekhah with honey. Lekhahs were cut into small slices on the eve of Yom Kippur and brought to each family so that each person could have some. Walking on the street, people met their friends, wished them good health and happiness, and helped themselves to the lekhah. It was so solemn that it has remained in my memory ever since.

Now that my parents and grandparents are no longer living, my husband, our two sons and I continue the tradition of giving lekhah to our friends and relatives, as we wish them health and success.

Lekhah (Honey Cake)

LIBA RABKINA

1 cup honey	¼ tsp cinnamon
3 eggs	1 cup sugar
½ tsp baking powder	4 Tbs oil
2 cups strong tea	3 cups flour

Preheat oven to 350°. Mix eggs with sugar. Add baking powder, oil, cinnamon, tea, honey and flour. Mix well. Dough should be like thick sour cream. Pour dough in a greased cake pan.

Bake for 50–60 minutes.

Lekhah II

DORA GOUBERMAN

4 eggs, beaten
1 cup sugar
1 Tbs honey
½ cup strong tea

½ tsp baking soda
1 tsp vinegar
4 cups flour

Preheat oven to 350°. Combine the eggs and sugar and mix with all the remaining ingredients. Grease a cake pan and pour in the batter. Bake for 30–40 minutes or until brown.

Sharlotka (Sponge Cake)

GALINA SHAPIRO

1 cup flour
1 cup sugar
3 eggs, beaten

3 unpeeled baking apples, chopped
½ cup bread crumbs
½ tsp butter

Preheat oven to 400°. Beat the eggs. Gradually add the sugar and flour to an even consistency.

Melt butter in an 8" or 9" baking dish. Be sure the sides are also coated. Sprinkle enough bread crumbs to cover the bottom and sides of the dish. Distribute the chopped apples over the bread crumbs. Spoon the egg–flour mixture evenly over the apples. Bake for 30 minutes.

Sharlotka with Apples

EDIT MATOV

Sharlotka is particularly nice because it can be prepared very quickly.

5 eggs, separated
1 cup sugar
1 cup flour

Bread crumbs or matzo meal
4 (1 lb) baking apples, coarsely chopped
Butter

Preheat oven to 450°. Prepare baking pan with butter and sprinkle bottom with bread crumbs or matzo meal.

Beat egg yolks. Beat egg whites until stiff. Gradually add sugar, egg yolks and flour until well blended. Distribute chopped apples on the bottom of pan. Pour the batter over the apples.

Place pan on a baking sheet in the center of the oven. Reduce temperature to 400° and bake for 45 minutes.

Torte "Maximka"

LYUDMILA ORKIS
Customs office worker, Odessa

We had a very nice life in Odessa. We studied, loved, worked and had very devoted friends. My parents lived at the time of Nicholas II. They told us children many interesting things about their lives, but after the Bolsheviks took over, everything changed radically. They never lived in a small Jewish shtetl, but my family had a chance to live in one. It was after my husband's graduation from the university. The name of this small town was Balta. It was quite close to the place where members of my husband's family perished, first during the pogroms before the Revolution of 1917, and then during World War II when it was a Jewish ghetto. We often visited the cemetery and brought flowers to the symbolic tomb with the names of my husband's relatives.

My childhood was happy and cloudless until I was twelve. That was when the war against Hitler broke out, and we were evacuated to Alma-Alta, Kazakhstan. Our life there was miserable. We had nothing to eat, no clothes to wear, no decent home to live in. After the war, our family came back to Odessa, and we had to start life all over again. There were difficulties, and there were happy moments in our lives. Our family was large, and family celebrations occurred often. My mother always cooked a lot of delicious dishes of meat, fish and especially vegetables. But the main tradition in the family was the torte which Mother taught me to bake. She passed away many years ago, but her art of cooking and baking still lives in her children.

Here is the recipe of the torte. I call it "Maximka" because my grandson, Maxim, loves it so much.

▦ Torte "Maximka"

LYUDMILA ORKIS

DOUGH

1 cup honey
1½ sticks butter, melted
1 cup sugar
1 tsp vanilla
4 cups flour

3 cups walnuts
1 Tbs vinegar
½ tsp baking soda
(The vinegar should be
poured on the baking soda.)

Preheat oven to 350°. In a large bowl, mix all ingredients to make a soft dough, adding flour as needed.

Divide the dough into seven equal parts for seven layers. Bake layers individually in large round baking pans (or one at a time) for about 10–15 minutes each.

Allow to cool.

CREAM

1 large container sour cream (16 oz)
1¼ cups sugar
1 tsp vanilla

Combine all ingredients and beat for about 20 minutes with a whisk.

Assembly

Spread cream on six of the layers, arranging them on top of one another and using the most cream on the top layer. The seventh layer should be crushed into crumbs to cover the cream on the upper layer. Decorate with walnut halves. If desired, you can top with chocolate, powdered sugar or fruit.

▨ Prague's Torte

EDIT MATOV

MERINGUE	CAKE
2 egg whites	1 egg
⅓ cup sugar	1 cup sugar
	1 cup sour cream
CREAM	1 tsp baking powder
1 stick (4 oz) butter	4-oz can sweetened condensed milk
4-oz can sweetened condensed milk	1 Tbs cocoa
1 Tbs cocoa	1 cup flour

Meringue

Preheat oven to 350°. Beat 2 egg whites until stiff. Gradually add ⅓ cup sugar.

Butter a baking sheet and drop the egg white mixture by small teaspoons, approximately 2" apart, onto the baking sheet. Place the baking sheet in the center of the oven. Bake for 50 minutes. Turn off the oven, open the door and allow the meringues to cool slowly. When cold, remove from baking sheet and set aside.

Cake

Preheat oven to 350°. Prepare a baking pan. Beat egg, sugar and sour cream together. Continue beating and add baking powder, flour, ½ can (2 oz) of condensed sweetened milk and cocoa. Pour into prepared baking pan. Bake for 50 minutes.

Cream

Combine butter and ½ can (2 oz) condensed milk and cocoa.

Assembly

When the cake is cold to the touch, slice into 3 thin layers. Spread the cream between each of the layers and stack together. Apply the remaining cream to the top and sides of the cake. Then decorate the top with the small meringues.

The Line that Never Moved

GALINA SHAPIRO
Design engineer, Leningrad

Shopping was often a very frustrating experience. One time, I wanted to buy some meat for my birthday dinner. It was in Leningrad in 1991, and everybody had received ration cards for food, including meat. I went to the store and saw that the meat had a lot of bones. There was also a line where a lot of people were waiting for boneless meat. I decided, since this was a special occasion, I would wait in this line, too. After an hour of waiting, I went home and cleaned my rooms.

I returned to the store again and saw the same people waiting in line for the good meat. I left the line and went home a second time. I washed all my clothes, and went back to the store once again. The line still hadn't moved. I spent another hour, went home and and began to cook dinner, and then went back to the store one more time. The same line was still in the same place. The whole day was gone, and it was time to give up. I bought some meat with bones and went home.

A Hungry Child

Zoya Ozeryanskaya
Librarian, Donetsk, Ukraine

In 1918, when I was born, Vitebsk was a shtetl in Byelorussia. I was only three when my parents left it. When we moved from there to Vyatka, we were very poor. We walked barefoot, and I remember that, as a child, I was often very hungry. Our parents worked hard to support the family. There were five children, but we all received a good education. Though we sometimes had nothing to eat as we were growing up, we were still joyful. We took part in amateur art activities, sang in the choir, played tennis and volleyball and rode horses.

I lived among the Russian-speaking people, so I don't know Yiddish well. My parents had to speak Russian, too, and they only used their native language at home. I couldn't understand why it was a shame to be Jewish. On Passover, some people came to our house and baked matzo. We enjoyed it, but we weren't allowed to help our friends make it. The happiest holiday for us was Rosh Hashana—the Jewish New Year. We were given twenty kopeks each, and we ran to buy ice cream and candies. We were so excited! Our desires were very modest, and when my mother bought me my first shoes made of cloth and made my first satin dress, I was the happiest girl in the world.

I often remember the times in my life when I was so hungry. Maybe because of that, food has become a favorite hobby of mine. I love to bake, and I know many good recipes. I always try to learn new ones. When I lived in Russia, I liked to receive guests and prepare special dishes for them. I would like to entertain my new friends in America, too. I am thankful that my grandchildren will never be hungry, as I was.

◈ Megobrik (Honey–Nut Cake with Raisins)

ZOYA OZERYANSKAYA

2 cups flour	½ tsp vinegar
1 cup honey	1 cup walnuts, chopped
1 cup sugar	½ cup raisins
1 cup sour cream	½ tsp baking soda
5 eggs	1 tsp cloves
5 Tbs oil	1 Tbs cinnamon
1 Tbs butter, softened	1 Tbs vanilla (optional)

Preheat oven to 375°. Combine honey, sugar, sour cream, eggs, oil and butter. Mix vinegar and baking soda and add to the honey–sugar mixture. Slowly add flour and mix to form a soft consistency. Add walnuts, raisins, cloves and cinnamon.

Pour cake batter into a greased cake pan. Bake for 1 hour.

My Brave Friend

SONYA SLUTSKER
Engineer, Odessa

I was twelve years old when my friend, Pena, came to our class. She was named after a bird who was in a cage and died before she was born. Pena was tall, strong with short, light blond hair and rosy cheeks. She was very pretty and always smiled. She was very athletic and liked many kinds of sports like swimming, bicycling and running. Pena also had a good ear for music, and played the piano well. She always went walking with her big, clever sheep dog. Pena's mother was a director of a big school and was a very busy woman. Her grandmother took care of the house and of Pena, too. Pena studied well and graduated from school with a special gold medal. After school, she began to study at the medical institute.

In 1941, the Second World War began. Her family didn't evacuate. They decided to remain in Odessa. She was brave and began to work with the partisans. She did this until the Romanians entered the city and discovered her activities. She and her family went into hiding. They moved around frequently, but at last the fascists found her and put her in prison. When the Romanians left, she was released. The Russian army returned to Odessa and were suspicious of her. "Why didn't they kill you?" she was asked. Because the occupying Romanians had let her go, the Russians didn't trust her, and again she was arrested. It was a long time before they finally freed her. She was very sick when she got out of prison the second time. But she managed to finish her education and become a doctor. She married and had children, but she died very young. Her friends loved her very much. Her death was a big tragedy for all of us.

Strawberry Fantasy

RITA FAYNSHTEYN

CAKE
3 egg yolks
¾ cup sugar
2 sticks butter
2 cups flour

TOPPING
3 egg whites
¾ cup sugar
2 lbs fresh strawberries,
    washed and patted dry

Cake

Preheat oven to 350°. Cream sugar and butter together. Combine with flour and beaten egg yolks. Mix well. Pour batter into a greased sheet cake pan. Bake for about 30 minutes or until a toothpick inserted into the cake comes out clean. Cool but do not remove from pan.

Reset oven to 250°–300°. Arrange strawberries on top of the cake and proceed with topping.

Topping

Bring egg whites to room temperature. Beat until stiff then gradually add sugar to make a meringue. Carefully spread the meringue over the strawberries.

Bake the cake until the whites are dry. Cut the cake with a wet knife and serve.

Fruit Coffee Cake

SONYA SLUTSKER

4 apples (or other fruit), peeled and diced
Bread crumbs and oil to line pan
½ tsp baking soda
2 tsp vinegar
1 cup sugar

⅔ cup butter, melted
3–3½ cups flour
1 egg, beaten
1 cup sour cream
1 egg yolk, beaten, for glaze

Preheat oven to 350°. Mix together baking soda and vinegar and then add to flour, egg and sour cream. Add melted butter. The mixture should be firm but soft.

Oil an 8" baking pan and sprinkle with bread crumbs. Spread ¾ of the dough in the pan. Distribute the fruit over the dough. Sprinkle with sugar and cover with the remaining ¼ portion of dough.

Paint the crust with beaten raw egg yolk. Bake for about 45 minutes.

✳ Flaky Torte

SONYA SLUTSKER

CRUST
2½ cups flour
3 sticks (¾ lb) butter
1 egg
½ cup water

FILLING
3 eggs, beaten
½ cup sugar
1 cup milk
4 sticks (1 lb) butter, cut into pieces
½ tsp vanilla
Chopped nuts, optional

Makes 2 tortes.

Crust

Preheat oven to 325°. Knead together 1 cup flour and 3 sticks of butter. Chill. In another bowl, combine 1½ cups flour with egg and water. Chill.

After both mixtures are cold (approximately 1 hour) cut them together with a pastry cutter until they are the size of small peas. Form into nine balls and refrigerate for about 30 minutes. Roll out each portion into a thin layer.

Bake on buttered baking pans at 15 minutes or until lightly brown.

Filling

Heat eggs, sugar and milk stirring constantly. Don't allow the mixture to boil. Remove from heat and cool until it reaches room temperature. Using an electric mixer, gradually add the butter to the egg mixture. Add vanilla. Beat until the mixture is smooth.

Assembly

Each torte has four layers of pastry. Spread the bottom layer with butter cream filling. Chopped nuts may be scattered over the filling. Add second layer, filling and nuts. Repeat until four layers are prepared. Divide the last pastry layer in half. Crumble and sprinkle half on each torte as a topping.

Prepare one day in advance and refrigerate until ready to serve.

Hurrah for the Circus!

YEFIM LITVAK
Circus manager, Odessa

Adults and children alike all love the circus. It's a lot of fun. It is a tent city by itself. I think the Russian circus is the best in the world. Our show featured funny clowns, brave, skilled acrobats, jugglers and magicians.

But the main attraction was the animals. We also boasted a famous family of animal trainers called Zapashnee and Durov and the renowned woman lion tamer, Boogreemova. There were lions, tigers, bears, seals, monkeys, horses, trained dogs and cats, birds and, of course, the elephants. These animals came in all shapes and sizes, and all of them had different personalities.

Usually, circus artists came from circus families. Their skills were passed down from generation to generation. The troupe traveled from town to town with their tents. They lived in inns and hostels in each town from two to six months at a time. The children attended school wherever they happened to be, but at other times, they studied their art. Youngsters began to study their circus skills from the age of six.

The animals were trained from one month of age. They were generally well cared for and rewarded with love and sweets. In fact, these valuable creatures were often fed better than the children.

Once, the door to the tiger's cage was accidentally left unlocked. The tiger got out, and the whole town panicked. Tigers are dangerous animals. The entire staff, the zoo officials, the local police and fire department all went looking for him. He appeared in different places. People were so nervous, it seemed to everyone that this scary beast was lurking behind every door. They finally found him in the forest two days later. He was very hungry, and tamely followed his trainer back to his home.

Animals have excellent memories, especially elephants. They never forget offenses. I remember an occasion when one of the new assistants was cruel to one of the elephants because it had broken a table. The elephant didn't understand that it had done something wrong. Shortly afterwards, the assistant was sent away for a month's vacation. When he returned after his several weeks' absence, the elephant immediately picked him up with its trunk and began swinging him around. The trainer had to rescue him. Circus life is never dull. It's a happy place, and people never stop wanting to see all the wonderful sights.

From Shtetl to Cinema

SOFIA LEVIN
Pediatrician, St. Petersburg

The city of Ekaterinoslav, in the Ukraine, was where I was born and grew up. My mother also grew up in this city, in a prosperous family. I think this city is now called Dnepropetrovsk. My childhood was happy.

My father's life was very interesting. He was the youngest child in a big family. They lived in a Ukrainian shtetl, and were very poor. When he was fourteen, he came to Ekaterinoslav. He was barefoot. He got a job in a movie theater that belonged to his older sister and her husband. In his free time, he studied and studied. After the Revolution, he quickly moved up to more important jobs. He became one of the leading workers in the movie industry.

A Painful Reminder

MOISEY VINETSKY
Engineer, Kharkov, Ukraine

When my son graduated from the institute, he had the right to choose the place of his permanent job after graduation. But he was refused at all the plants, though they accepted others. I asked the director of the plant where I worked to give my son a job. But he told me outright that there was a directive from our ministry forbidding them from admitting any Jews, or allowing them to advance in their posts. In addition, they were not to "hinder their dismissal." All that, in spite of the fact that leaving one's job was very difficult. My son had to work in a job outside of his profession. Only here in America did he find employment in the profession for which he was educated. So that was how we were painfully reminded that we were not "equal" to others in the Family of Peoples.

▓ Mandelbreit (Almond Slices)

SOFIA LEVIN

1 cup sugar	½ tsp vinegar
2 eggs, beaten	¼ tsp baking soda
2½ cups flour	¼ cup nuts, chopped
2 sticks butter, melted	¼ cup raisins

Preheat oven to 350°. Beat eggs and sugar together until light, stir in butter, vinegar mixed with baking soda, and flour. Mix until a dough is formed. Add nuts and raisins. Form dough into long rolls about 3" wide and 1" thick. Bake in an ungreased baking pan for about 30 minutes until the top is a light brown.

Remove from oven. Slice, while still warm, into ½" slices. On the same baking sheet, arrange each piece cut side up and return to the top shelf of the oven to brown on both sides, approximately 15 minutes more.

▓ Cousin Sarah's Mandel Bread (Almond Slices)

ANN SOGOLOW VIA R.S.

Cousin Sarah Millman was always such a good cook. If it was one of her recipes, we always knew it had to be good!

4 cups flour	¼ cup orange juice
3 eggs	1 tsp baking powder
1½ sticks melted margarine	⅔ cup slivered almonds
2 tsp vanilla	¼ cup Bisquick (my addition)

Preheat oven to 350°. In a large bowl beat eggs, and then add sugar, vanilla, orange juice and melted margarine. To this add flour, baking powder, almonds and Bisquick. Mix well first with fork and then with hands until formed. (If necessary, sprinkle additional flour until dough is no longer sticky). Shape dough into six long loaves, about 2"–3" wide and about ¾" thick.

Place on two ungreased cookie sheets and bake about 20 minutes, or until tops of loaves are lightly browned. Remove from oven and slice on a slight diagonal, making slices about ½" wide. Turn slices on their sides and return to oven for approximately 20 minutes longer, or until browned on both sides. (Turn pans about halfway through for more uniform browning.)

◪ Chocolate Torte

TIRCA GINZBERG

TORTE

7 eggs, separated
⅔ cup semi-sweet chocolate chips
¾ cup sugar
½ cup hot water
¾ cup almonds, finely ground
1 Tbs bread crumbs
¼ cup sweet butter or margarine, melted

CHOCOLATE GLAZE

¼ cup semi-sweet chocolate chips
2 Tbs milk
¼ cup sweet butter or margarine, melted

Torte

Preheat oven to 350°. In a mixer, beat egg whites until fluffy. Gradually add sugar and egg yolks. Melt chocolate in hot water and stir until smooth. Cool and add to egg–sugar mixture.

Stir almonds and bread crumbs into melted butter. Add to the egg–chocolate mixture. Mix well. Turn into a greased and floured 9" springform pan. Bake for 45 minutes. Cool and unmold onto platter before glazing.

Chocolate Glaze

Melt chocolate in milk and add melted butter. Spoon over cooled torte. Let icing drip down sides.

NOTE: Our tester pointed out that this could easily be adapted for Passover, since there is no flour.

Mother, Ida Lerner Blumenthal (back row, far right), grandparents Dvorah and Itzak, and aunts and uncles, Kiev, Ukraine, c. 1900.
Courtesy Ann Sogolow.

Lemony Apple Meringue Cake

FEYGA GOLDMAN

CAKE
2½ cups flour
3 egg yolks
1 small container sour cream
¼ cup sugar
1 Tbs vinegar
½ tsp baking soda
1 stick margarine (softened)

FILLING
3 large apples, peeled and
 coarsely grated
3 egg whites, whipped
½ cup sugar
1 lemon, grated

Chopped walnuts or shaved chocolate (optional)

Cake

Preheat oven to 350°. Beat egg yolks, and add sour cream, sugar, baking soda and vinegar mixture, softened margarine and flour to make dough. Divide into two sections and bake the two layers for about 25 minutes. Remove from oven and cool.

Filling

Coarsely grate peeled apples and lemon. Whip egg whites and ½ cup sugar. Spread grated apples and lemon over the layers and cover top layer with whipped egg whites. Bake for an additional 10 minutes, or until meringue is lightly browned.

Top with chopped walnuts or chocolate (optional).

Cranberry Fruit Roll

MARIA KHASIN

5 large eggs
1 cup sugar

¾ cup flour
1 can cranberry sauce
 (jellied or whole)

Preheat oven to 350°. Blend eggs and sugar in an electric mixer. Add flour and mix until batter is smooth. Cut parchment paper to fit the bottom of a jelly roll pan. Oil the paper and pour the batter evenly over all. Bake for 15–20 minutes until lightly browned.

While still warm, remove from pan and spread the cranberry sauce over the cake. Roll the cake lengthwise. This must be done while warm so it will roll easily and set.

Before serving, slice into 1" slices and arrange on platter.

The City of Heroes

Sonya Slutsker
Engineer, Odessa

It was the time of the Second World War. Odessa was a very beautiful city—a health resort on the Black Sea. It was an industrial and cultural center with many institutes and universities. When the war began, nobody thought that it would last so long or be so cruel and bloody. Before the war our government told us, "If the war begins, we will be fighting on the enemy's territory." We believed this and were assured of it. From the first night, the planes flew over Odessa, and our anti-aircraft guns fired at them. After a month they began to drop bombs. At first, we didn't understand that we needed to hide from the bombs. Our family lived in a big stone house on the fourth floor. When the bombs began to fall, we and our neighbors hid under the stairs. We didn't understand that if a bomb fell, we would be trapped under a ruined house.

The Fascists moved quickly, and it was almost impossible to leave the city because there wasn't enough transportation. On the streets we saw many refugees traveling with wagons pulled by horses and filled with old people and little children. Many people walked with heavy bags on their backs. They looked tired and very sad. We didn't know that in a short time we would be like them. Many of them were killed before going very far, because the Fascists went around and cut them off. When the enemy entered the city, Jews were killed immediately. So it was with our neighbors. We found out about it after the war, when we came back to Odessa. They also bombed the trains that carried many fleeing refugees. Such was the fate of the family of our close friends.

Our family left on a ship. On the way, our ship was bombed, too, but G-d helped us, and the bomb narrowly missed its mark. Meanwhile, the Fascists surrounded the city. Our soldiers and civilians continued their heroic resistance. For two and a half months, the city defended itself without assistance. Because of their brave fight, the city of Odessa was the first to get the honorary title "City of Heroes." During the war there were many cities that received this name, but the city of Odessa was the first.

▦ Black and White Sour Cream Torte

Etya Nudelman

2 cups sugar	½ tsp vinegar
4 Tbs butter	2 cups flour
3 cups sour cream	⅓ cup milk
½ tsp baking soda	4 Tbs cocoa

Torte

Preheat oven to 350°. Mix together 2 Tbs butter, 1 cup sour cream and 1 cup sugar. Combine baking soda and vinegar and add to the mixture. Add flour and mix well.

Divide the dough into two equal parts. To only one part, add 2 Tbs cocoa.

Divide the two pieces of dough again, so that you have four parts: two dark and two light. Put these four pieces of dough into the refrigerator for 5–6 hours. Remove and bake the layers separately in cake pans for 8–10 minutes.

Cream

Whip 2 cups sour cream and ½ cup sugar, using a mixer.

Cover three of the four layers with the cream.

Place the layers on top of one another, alternating dark and light layers, so that the bottom layer is dark.

Icing

Add 2 Tbs of butter to ½ cup sugar, ⅓ cup milk and 2 Tbs cocoa and mix well.

Cook the mixture for about 25 minutes on very low heat, and while still hot, quickly spread the icing on the top layer.

IMPORTANT: This torte should be prepared 2–3 days before serving so that the layers can absorb the cream.

Aeroflot

ZALMAN KHASIN
Electrical Engineer, St. Petersburg

Until 1993, Aeroflot was a government organization ruled by the Department of the Civil Airfleet. There was no competition between companies. There was only one company. There were often series of planes that were defective. Planes were manufactured and repaired exclusively in government-owned factories, and only after a string of accidents were the defects corrected. And Aeroflot had a high percentage of accidents. Of course, the people were never told about these. Things like that were not reported in the newspapers or on TV as they are here. People trusted that they would arrive safely, and never knew about the dangerous conditions.

Planes were not able to fly in bad weather, such as rain, snow or fog. As a means of fast transportation, air travel was unreliable. In bad weather, people could spend many days waiting at the airport in uncomfortable waiting rooms, never knowing when they would be allowed to take off. And service in the airports and on the airplanes was a joke. For shorter trips, the train was the best bet. In spite of all this, in the summertime when more people liked to travel, tickets were always difficult to get. (Of course, this was partly because of the limited number of flights available.)

Then in 1993, Aeroflot fell apart. Private airplane companies came into being, and only some companies belonged to the government. Airplanes from other countries began to appear on the runways. Maybe, now there will be competition to make the service and performance better—and safer, too.

The city of St. Petersburg (formerly Leningrad) is like a wonderful dessert—a great splurge. The city Peter the Great created features balconies, columns, pilasters and porticoes. In creating such masterpieces as the huge Winter Palace (the Hermitage), he borrowed from the elaborate baroque architecture of Western Europe and the classic temple architecture of Greece and Rome. In spite of the fact that more than 600,000 people died in the 900-day siege of Leningrad during World War II, this elegant city miraculously escaped destruction.

▦ Pteetchnya Moloko (Bird Milk Torte)

MARIA KHASIN

CAKE
1 cup sugar
1 stick butter or margarine
3 eggs
1 cup flour
1 tsp baking soda
1 Tbs vinegar
2 Tbs cocoa

CREAM FILLING (BIRD MILK)
2 cups milk
2 Tbs Cream of Wheat
1½ sticks butter, unsalted
1 cup sugar

CHOCOLATE CREAM FROSTING
2 Tbs sugar
¼ stick butter, unsalted
2 Tbs cocoa
3 Tbs water or milk
Walnuts, finely chopped (optional, for garnish)

Preheat oven to 350°. Combine baking soda and vinegar in a small bowl.

Cream sugar and butter together. Add eggs, flour, baking soda–vinegar mixture and mix until dough is smooth. Divide in half. Pour one half into a cake pan. Add cocoa to the other half and pour into another cake pan. Bake for 15–20 minutes or until a toothpick inserted into the center comes out clean. Remove from pans and cool. When cold, slice each layer in half. You will now have four thin layers, 2 white and 2 black.

Bird-milk filling
Cook Cream of Wheat and milk and allow to cool. In a mixer, cream sugar and butter together. Add cold Cream of Wheat. Beat until well blended.

Assembly
The prepared white and black cakes will be stacked alternately. Spread the Bird-milk filling on top of each layer.

Chocolate cream frosting
Heat all ingredients together, mixing well. Immediately pour over the torte. Sprinkle walnuts on cake, if desired.

▨ Hvorvest (Bows)

Lilya Klebovich

5 egg yolks	Powdered sugar
1 cup flour	2 cups corn oil
1 Tbs cognac	

In a large bowl, combine ¾ cup flour, egg yolks and cognac. Mix until smooth.

Divide the dough into 3 portions. On a floured surface, roll out each portion into a thin layer. Cut into 2" squares. Make a 1" diagonal slash in the middle of each square. Insert a corner of the square through the slash.

Heat corn oil. Drop bows into the oil a few at a time until each is golden brown. Don't crowd. Using a slotted spoon, remove the bows and drain on a paper towel. Sprinkle with powdered sugar and serve immediately.

The Orphan and the Medal

Roman Rakhaylov
Engineer, Kharkov, Ukraine

When I was thirteen years old, I was a mechanic on the children's railway in a park in Kharkov. It was about five miles long. I was very happy with this job. I put on a railway uniform, and loved it when everyone looked at me in it. I studied about railroads in the Palace for Children, where others studied music, art, aviation and other interests. Before the revolution, it was a club for wealthy people. I was very proud to go there.

During World War II, the boys who learned about the railway worked in the factories where the trains were repaired after being at the front. Once, a train arrived with an orphan on board. He was about fourteen years old. He was wearing a medal, and I asked him why he had it. The boy said that he had it because he had been at the front. I wanted a medal, too. So I told him that I could take care of the trains, and I was an orphan, too, although I really wasn't. I tried to go back with him to the front. But my parents got worried when I didn't come home on time, and they came looking for me. The military brought me back to my family. I was only thirteen then. When I turned fifteen, I finally joined the army, became a captain and spent thirteen years as a soldier. There were many medals during my military career. But when I received my very first one, I thought of that boy on the railway car and how wonderful his had seemed to me. I had earned my own medal, and I knew what an honor that was.

A Face I'll Never Forget

BERTA SHAPIRO
Bookkeeper, Odessa

In 1900, my grandparents lived in Moldavia. There were seven children in their family—five boys and two girls. My grandfather was arrested as a political prisoner, and sent to Siberia. He walked all the way, wearing shackles on his hands and feet. The whole family followed behind him in an open horse-drawn sled.

When my mother was eighteen years old, her parents died, and she became the head of the family with five brothers and one sister to care for. My aunt and uncle tried to help her with money as much as possible. So, my mother had a very difficult childhood. She met my father and married when she was twenty-two. He helped her to raise her brothers and sister until they were grown.

On June 21, 1941, the Germans attacked the USSR. My father went to fight in the Second World War. At the beginning of the war, they bombed Odessa. My mother, brother and I were evacuated on July 20th. We left with a horse and a cart. There was bombing everywhere. We hid in the corn. A German pilot flew his plane over us and shot at the corn. He was so close, I could see his face. My brother and I clung to our mother and cried. Afterwards, we got on a train. The Germans bombed the train. We hid in the woods. We finally arrived in Uzbekistan and stayed there until the end of the war.

My father came back in 1944, and we returned to Odessa. I was only a young girl during that war, but the face of that pilot is etched in my mind forever.

Kartoshka (No-Bake Chocolate Cookies)

ROSA KINBERG

1½ lbs (1 box) arrowroot cookies
2 cups sugar
½ lb (2 sticks) butter

3 Tbs cognac
3 Tbs cocoa

Pulverize the cookies. Add sugar, butter and cognac. Mix well. Form into potato-size balls and roll in powdered cocoa. Refrigerate until ready to serve.

▦ Rozachki ("Roses"—Cream Puffs)

BERTA SHAPIRO

4 large eggs, separated	2 cups sugar
1 tsp baking soda	1 cup sour cream
½ Tbs vinegar	½ tsp salt
3½ cups flour	½ tsp vanilla
½ lb (2 sticks) margarine or butter, softened	1 cup nuts, chopped

Preheat oven to 350°. In one bowl, bring egg whites to room temperature and beat until stiff peaks form. Gradually add 1 cup sugar. In another bowl, combine baking soda and vinegar. In a large mixing bowl, combine flour, baking soda and vinegar mixture, egg yolks, margarine, sour cream, salt and vanilla. Knead the mixture until a soft dough is formed. Divide into 4 equal portions.

On a floured surface, roll out 1 portion of dough into a rectangle approximately ⅛" thick. Spread ¼ of the the egg white mixture over this rectangle. Sprinkle with ¼ cup chopped nuts. Starting at the narrow end of the rectangle, roll up the dough, jellyroll-fashion. Using a sharp knife, cut a 2" thick slice off the end of the roll. Squeeze or pinch one side of this slice. The unpinched side will open up and look like a rose. Spoon some of the egg whites into the center of each rose. Continue slicing 2" strips. Pinch the bottom of each rose.

On a well-greased baking pan or parchment paper, carefully place the roses pinched side down. Bake until the roses are lightly brown, approximately 45 minutes. Remove from oven.

Makes about 24 roses.

▦ Fruit and Nut Cake

ANNA YAROSLAVSKY

1 cup sugar	1 cup nuts, chopped
2 eggs, beaten	1 cup raisins
1 cup flour	1 cup dried apricots, sliced
¼ tsp baking soda	

Preheat oven to 350°. Beat eggs and sugar. Add baking soda and flour. Mix until the batter thickens. Combine nuts, raisins and apricots and stir into batter.

Butter the bottom of a 1½" high baking pan and line with waxed paper. Pour the mixture into the pan.

Bake for 25–30 minutes. When cool, remove the cake from the pan. Remove the waxed paper. Sprinkle with granulated sugar while warm, if desired. Slice and serve.

Nuga

KLARA DRIZO
Physician, Odessa

I was born in Odessa in 1926. My parents were barbers. During the war, I worked in a military hospital. I was wounded and left Odessa with the last transport. I was evacuated to Buhara, where I joined my relatives and my brother. My husband and I met and married while he was still in the army. After the war, he returned and we moved to his home in East Byelorussia (formerly Poland). In 1989, our children and grandchildren came to America, and we followed in 1992. My mother came with us. At that time, she was ninety years old. She got to live in America only three days before she died.

This recipe of "Nuga" was given to me by a patient of mine many years ago. It is easy to prepare. It is tasty and can be made very quickly.

Nuga (Nut Cake)

KLARA DRIZO

1 cup sugar
½ cup butter
1 cup flour
2 eggs, beaten
1 cup raisins

1 cup walnuts, chopped
½ tsp baking soda
½ tsp vinegar
Graham cracker crumbs

Preheat oven to 350°. Combine vinegar and baking soda.

Cream butter and sugar until smooth. Add eggs, flour, raisins, walnuts and baking soda mixture. Mix well.

Grease a baking pan and cover the bottom with graham cracker crumbs. Add the batter and bake until firm and lightly browned, about 25–30 minutes. Do not over-bake.

Allow the cake to cool. Cut in ¾" squares and arrange on a large platter. Dust with powdered sugar and serve.

Forty Years is a Long Time

Dora Gouberman
Hatmaker, Moscow

I was born in 1913 in a small shtetl in the Ukraine called Kamenetsk-Podolsk. In 1917, when I was four years old, there was a pogrom by the bandits of Petlura. They threatened to kill my father and me, but my father gave them money, and they let us go. My brother ran out to join the partisans, and I didn't see or hear from him for many years.

In 1932, at nineteen, I got married and moved to Moscow, where I worked in a factory making ladies' and men's hats. My husband and I both worked. There was no one to care for our daughter, so when she was four, we sent her to stay with my parents. During the Second World War, my daughter, my parents and many relatives were still in the Ukraine, and they were all killed by the Germans.

Then, in 1957, a tourist came from America to see me. It was my brother! Forty years had passed since the day he left our house. I could hardly believe it was him. A lot had happened in my life in those forty years. The synagogue in Moscow had a program trying to locate relatives in the United States via radio. He somehow heard this appeal, and decided to come all the way from New York to find me. Now I, too, live in America with my other two daughters. My son will soon come from Russia to join us. I am happy that all my children and their children will live in a free and independent country and won't suffer as I did.

Torte Annetchka (3 layers)

MILA PASTERNAK

CAKE
2½ cups flour
1 stick butter
1 cup sugar
1 egg
½ cup honey

1 Tbs vinegar
½ tsp baking soda
½ tsp vanilla
2 Tbs sour cream

CREAM
¾ lb sour cream
½ cup sugar
½ tsp nuts
½ tsp vanilla

ICING
½ cup sugar
3 tsp cocoa
5 Tbs milk

Preheat oven to 350°. In small bowl combine baking soda and vinegar. In mixing bowl, cream butter and sugar. Add flour. Mix well. Add remaining ingredients. Continue mixing. Pour into 3 lightly buttered and floured cake pans. Bake for 15 minutes or until each layer springs back when lightly pressed. Cool.

Cream

Combine sour cream and sugar. Mix. Add nuts and vanilla.

Icing

Combine all ingredients. Cook over low heat. Stir continuously until thickened, approximately 15 minutes.

Assembly

Spread cream over the bottom layer. Place another cake layer on top and cover with some cream. Place the last layer on top of cake. Cover the top and sides with the hot chocolate icing.

To America—and Back!

LYUDMILA PASTERNAK
Engineer, Odessa

I was born in the Ukraine, in the city of Odessa on the Black Sea. I had a good childhood. But I often wonder what my life would've been like if things had happened differently. My mother's parents emigrated to America in 1890. My mother was born there in 1897. But the climate didn't agree with my grandfather, and when my mother was three years old, he fell ill and they decided to return to Odessa.

My father's family was very poor. He couldn't study at the university because few Jews were accepted, and also, because he had to support his family after his father died. When he met my mother, she was working in a drug store. They fell in love and decided to get married. There were many happy celebrations and good memories from my youth. I especially remember my twentieth birthday. It was raining heavily, and I was so worried that nobody would come. But, in spite of the bad weather, everybody came. They brought me roses, which are my favorite flower. We played the piano, sang and danced, and my mother prepared a lot of delicious food. We had a good time.

My husband and I, our sons and their families and my parents have all lived in Odessa for a very long time. Not all my memories are happy ones. The war was terrible, and life was very difficult sometimes. There were a lot of hardships during our lives. I'll never know how different things *might* have been. It's almost ninety years since my mother's family came to America, and then made the fateful decision to return to their old, troubled country. For good or for bad, they made their choice. Now, my family has come again. I know that this time, there will be no "going back." This time, we are here to stay!

Buttermilk Cake

FREDERIKA RAKHAYLOVA

1 cup sugar	1 egg, beaten
1 stick butter (4 oz)	½ tsp baking soda
2 cups flour	1 Tbs vinegar
1 cup buttermilk	½ cup raisins

Preheat oven to 300°. In a small bowl, mix vinegar and baking soda.

Cream butter, sugar, and egg. Add flour alternately with buttermilk. Add baking soda–vinegar mixture. Beat until smooth. Add raisins.

Bake for 30 minutes. Before serving, sprinkle with powdered sugar.

✳ Lemon Pastry

MANYA REYZIS

1 pkg yeast
¼ cup milk, warm
1 Tbs sugar
1 Tbs flour
½ lb butter or margarine
1 egg, beaten
1½–2 cups flour

FILLING
1 lemon, grated
1 cup sugar

Mix yeast, milk, sugar and 1 Tbs flour. Place in a warm place for 1 hour and allow to rise.

Beat butter, egg and flour and add to yeast mixture. On a lightly floured board, knead dough until smooth. Place in a greased bowl. Put in a warm place for 1 hour and allow to rise again.

Filling

Preheat oven to 350°. Combine grated lemon and sugar. Divide the dough into 2 parts. Lightly roll each part into a 9" square. Place in a lightly greased baking pan. Spread the lemon mixture over the bottom layer. Cover with the remaining layer.

Bake for about 25 minutes or until golden brown. Cool slightly and turn out of pan. Dust with powdered sugar and cut into squares.

The Blessings of Life

ITA BLEKH
Factory worker, Odessa

I was born in Odessa, in the Ukraine, in 1921. My mother's parents lived in Odessa, too. There were seven children in their family. My grandfather had a Jewish school for ten children. In this school he taught only boys until the age of thirteen. He charged 1 ruble for each child. My father's parents also lived in Odessa. They had seven children, too. My grandfather had twenty cows. He was able to travel to America to buy the animals for his farm and ship them back to Russia. He and my father worked together. Until 1917, they lived well. Then the new government took everything away.

My husband's parents lived in a shtetl called Mostovoy. His father was the rabbi of Mostovoy. He had eleven children. But his children could not go to public school because their father was a rabbi. So they were educated at home by their father until 1934, when the family moved to Odessa, and the children started working.

My childhood was not a carefree one. In 1933, when I was twelve years old, my father died. We were poor and hungry. Three years later, I went to work in a factory as an accountant. When World War II came, life was very difficult. My mother and I were put into a German concentration camp near Odessa. My mother died there. I worked in the camp until April 28, 1944, when the Red Army freed me.

After the war, I worked in a factory, sewing buttons on shirts. My husband worked in a factory, too. We came to America in 1992. Now our lives are much different. Our children's lives have been easier than their parents' and grandparents', and our grandchildren live well in America and look forward to a promising future. I am thankful for the blessings of life.

⊠ Strudel

MINA PETRUSHANSKAYA

DOUGH

1 stick margarine, softened
1 Tbs sugar
3 Tbs oil
½ cup sour cream
2 eggs, beaten

¼ tsp baking soda
¼ tsp vinegar (combine with baking soda)
½ tsp salt
6–7 cups flour,
 enough to make a firm dough

FILLING

1 cup jam
½ lb raisins
1 cup nuts, chopped

3 apples, chopped
1 tsp cinnamon

Preheat oven to 250°. Combine all ingredients for dough. Knead well until smooth and divide into 3 pieces. Roll out each piece to a thin dough. Coat each piece with oil.

Mix all the ingredients together. Divide into 3 portions. Spread each layer of dough with ⅓ of the fruit mixture. Roll each into a log. Bake about 30 minutes or until light brown. Cut while warm.

Grandma's Strudel

ROSALIE SOGOLOW

My grandmother's strudel was a family favorite from the old country, but it was a full day's work. Because it was such an effort, this tasty dessert was made only for special occasions and in large quantities. Grandma used to wrap pans of it and hide it around the house. At various intervals, she would pull out a small amount for the family's pleasure. Of course, the longer it sat, the harder it became. And the harder it got, the more it was savored!

DOUGH

5+ cups flour	⅓ cup sugar
2 eggs	⅛ tsp salt
⅔ cup peanut oil	1½ cups water

Knead ingredients well and shape into round loaves. Let stand covered for at least an hour or overnight in the refrigerator.

FILLING

1½ lemons	1½ tsp cinnamon
2 cups sugar	2½ cups shelled, chopped walnuts
1½ boxes of golden raisins	

BREAD CRUMB MIXTURE

1½ grated lemon (rinds only)	⅔ cup sugar
⅔ cup bread crumbs	⅔ Tbs cinnamon

Preheat oven to 350°. Flour table lightly. Divide dough into 3 or 4 equal rounds. Roll very thin one section at a time. Stretch dough as you roll out. Oil rolled piece, spreading evenly with hand. Sprinkle bread crumb mixture over oiled surface.

Make a chain of filling across the top of the dough and roll dough over filling. Continue down, using ½ of the section. Cut off the finished roll and place on oiled cookie sheet. Flatten and pinch ends to seal edges.

Before putting in oven, spread oil over tops of finished rolls.

Cut before baking (but not all the way through). Bake for about 1 hour or until golden brown.

After removing from oven, cool and then dampen top of baked strudel with water. (Use your hand or a cloth.) Sprinkle sugar on top, if desired.

Makes about 10 dozen pieces.

The Whim of Fate

ASYA CHERNOMORDIK
Engineer, St. Petersburg

I lived in the town of Nevel from 1923 until 1930. It's a rather small town. There were about 30,000 people there. I went to the Russian school, though there was also a Jewish one. When I was in the fourth grade, a boy came to our class from another town. I thought he was rather nice and very clever. He was the top student in the class. We became friends, and later our friendship turned into love. We married in 1938, and our son, David, was born the following year. My husband graduated from the polytechnic institute, and I graduated from the railway institute. But we worked for only a year. Then fortune decided otherwise.

In 1939, my husband went into the army and was sent to the Far East. I became ill at this time, and had to go to a sanatorium. My son was with my parents for the summer. So, all three of us were in different places when the war began. Nevel was bombed, and many left. Knowing that my son's safety was in their hands, my parents left also. They walked for eleven days and nights, until they came to a small railway station in Kirov district. They stayed there until the war ended.

When I returned home, no one was there. I didn't know where to find my family. I ended up in the blockade around Leningrad. There was no food, no light, no warmth, no water, no sewerage, no transportation. We received 250 grams of bread, though nobody could understand made of what, half a kilogram of sugar (which I never got), half a kilogram of smoked cheese, no vegetables or fruit at all. In 1941, a bomb hit our yard. All the windows were broken, and then covered with plywood. It was very cold, and the temperature was the same both inside and out. I slept in my warmest clothes, and went to work in the same suit.

But, finally, the blockade was lifted, and little by little, it got better. Thank G-d, we were alive. But only my mother-in-law, father-in-law and me. My husband was killed in the battle. It wasn't until 1946, that my parents finally returned to Leningrad with my son. He was already seven years old! He is the treasure of my life.

▦ Cookies with Condensed Milk

RITA FAYNSHTEYN

I make these cookies very often because my grandson loves them so much.

4 cups flour	1 can sweetened condensed milk
¾ cup milk	Powdered sugar (optional)
½ lb butter	Chopped walnuts (optional)

Melt butter. Add milk and flour. Divide dough into two portions and freeze for 1–2 hours.

Preheat oven to 350°. Coarsely grate each portion of dough and spread on a greased cookie sheet. Bake until golden in color (about 15 minutes.) Turn into a bowl to cool.

While crumbs are baking, place *unopened* can of condensed milk in a pot of hot water. Bring to a boil, reduce to a low heat, and continue cooking gently for 1 hour. (This will change the consistency of the milk and make it thicker.) Pour out hot water, and let can cool in cold water until cool enough to handle. Open can and combine condensed milk with cookie pieces. Mix gently.

Moisten a tray or large baking pan. Spread mixture evenly over bottom. Press down very firmly. Refrigerate. Sprinkle powdered sugar and chopped walnuts on top if desired. Cut into squares and serve.

▦ Russian Pastry Bites

RITA GORLIN

This tasty dessert can be served plain or with a fruit filling.

2 sticks butter or margarine	½ tsp baking soda
1 cup sour cream	1 Tbs vinegar
3 cups flour	2 cups sugar

Cut the butter or margarine into little cubes. Add sour cream and flour. Mix baking soda with the vinegar and add to the mixture. Beat well and refrigerate for at least ½ hour.

Preheat oven to 350°. Divide dough into two pieces. Roll out each piece as thin as possible. Sprinkle all surfaces with some of the sugar. Fold in half and sprinkle with sugar again. Fold once more and sprinkle once again. Cut into triangles or squares. Bake until bottoms are light brown. Turn and bake for an additional 3–5 minutes.

Lilichka's Cake

MALVINA ALEXANDRAVSKAYA

DOUGH
½ lb butter, chilled
1 egg
2 Tbs sour cream
2½ cups flour
½ tsp baking soda
1 Tbs vinegar

CREAM
Sour cream (rest of a 16-oz container)
⅓ cup sugar
¼ tsp vanilla
⅓ cups walnuts, chopped

CHOCOLATE ICING
4 Tbs cocoa
⅓ cup sugar
⅔ cup milk
2 Tbs butter

Preheat oven to 350°. Grate butter. Mix baking soda and vinegar and mix with other ingredients to form dough. Divide dough into three parts. Roll out and bake on 3 cookie sheets or oblong cake pans for about 30 minutes or until brown.

Whip sour cream, sugar and vanilla together for cream. Add walnuts and spread on the layers. Stack on top of one another.

For chocolate icing, mix cocoa, sugar and milk in a saucepan and bring to a low boil. Simmer for 20 minutes, stirring often. Remove from heat and add 2 Tbs butter. Cover the top layer of the cake with icing, pouring quickly to cover all surfaces.

Cool and serve.

"Oogashayteez, pazhaloosta!" "Please, help yourself!"

▦ Cherry Meringue Pie

GALYA ROZENBLYUM

CRUST
½ stick (4 oz) butter
1½ cups sugar
2–2½ cups flour
1 cup sour cream
5 egg yolks
½ tsp baking soda
2 tsp vinegar

FILLING
3 cups cherries, pitted and drained
2 tsp sugar
1 tsp cornstarch

MERINGUE
5 egg whites, room temperature
1 cup sugar

Crust

Preheat oven to 375°. In a small bowl, combine baking soda and vinegar. In a mixing bowl, cream together the butter and sugar. Slowly add the flour, sour cream, egg yolks and baking soda–vinegar mixture. Knead the dough until smooth.

Set aside ⅓ of the kneaded dough to use for the top crust. On waxed paper, roll out to ⅛" thick.

On waxed paper, roll out the remaining ⅔ dough to ⅛" thick. Transfer to a deep-dish pie pan.

Filling

Combine the drained cherries with sugar and cornstarch. Spread the filling over the bottom crust and cover with the top crust.

Bake for 40–50 minutes. Remove from oven and cool for 10 minutes.

Meringue

Beat egg whites and gradually add sugar until stiff. Do not overbeat.
Spoon the meringue over the pie and bake another 10 minutes.

Veterans

MARK SMOLYANITSKY
Engineer, Odessa

Translation by Victor Eydus and Rosalie Sogolow

We stood up for Stalingrad and succeeded,
We didn't choke with the waves in the Crimea;
But as a sniper, hidden in the ambush,
Death picked us up—one by one.

As long as we had bullets in our cartridges,
As the old hearts kept up the beat,
"Go around, make a circle and defend!
Fight, Veterans...to the end!"

The projectiles are falling very close by now,
The shell-splinters whistle overhead;
But, dear friends, we have to keep holding on
To this, the last front line we tread!

When the ground was shaking as though alive,
When the ice was melting from our blood;
Our frontier friendship helped us carry on,
That friendship is still to us a bond.

We burned together in the flame of battle,
We weren't used to a fight halfway;
But if we overcame such a struggle,
We'll overcome our old age today.

Some Reflections on My Eighty-Fourth Birthday

ESFIR DYNKINA
Technical designer, St. Petersburg

I have had a long life, and I have met many different people. They were bad and good. But such sympathetic, patient, kind and independent people as our volunteers, I met only in America. Thank you! I'm upset that I don't speak well. I get nervous and forget much that I have to tell.

After the Second World War, the Russian people said that Jews weren't in the War. That is a lie. All Jewish families had someone in the military. In my family, there were three. My brother, my brother-in-law, and my husband. They all died long ago. I am a veteran. I worked in a munitions factory during the blockade of Leningrad and received a medal for the defense of my city.

In the 1950s many Jews were dismissed from their jobs. Thirty people were fired at the same time as I was, and only two of them were Russians. Those two found new work in a short time. I went around to fifty places where work was advertised. None of them would take me. One said that they needed an unskilled worker, and another said they needed a more skilled worker. They also laughed at my name. A Russian friend of my husband worked at a plant where the manager's wife was a Jewish woman. He gave me a job. It wasn't in my profession, but I was very happy, nevertheless.

During the time of Khrushchev, it was a little better. Repressed people were "rehabilitated." Cooperative houses were built, and some were able to buy them. Before Khruschev, everyone had a percentage taken from their salaries every month, for the state. It was called a "state loan," but I think it was like a tax. At the end of the year, we received a bond for this amount. After he came to power, this practice was canceled. We didn't have to pay this anymore. One would think that things would improve. But, once again, anti-Semitism reared its head. I lived in an apartment with four rooms. In each room was a family with two, three or four people. After the death of my husband, I lived alone. The others were all Russian. They told me that I looked Jewish, but not so much. They thought that was a compliment. Afterwards, one woman told me that she heard in the garden that Jewish people murdered children. She said that she had seen someone photograph them in the street, and if anything happened to her grandson, I would be in trouble. What could I say to her? And when another young neighbor read in the newspaper about a crime, he said that all crimes were done by Jews, but they had changed their names!

All that really happened. It is impossible to forget about it, but I don't want to remember that. Today, I am here in America. My family is with me, and all is good. I can study English and write little poems. I am glad.

Reminiscences of Emigration from the USSR

ESFIR DYNKINA, OCTOBER 1990

I wish to remind you, my friends, of how we came here;
We fought for it in every way—and, at last, we won.
But, of course, it was a hard and a long way;
For ten years most of us were refused,
With the help of the well known OVIR.*
And then, like in a fairy tale, we got it!
But, again, problems....
How to get the tickets? Never without problems!
There were tickets only for:
"Come forward!" "Keep quiet!" "Shut up!" "Don't push!"
Though our blood was boiling,
We had to obey.

And then the custom houses came along;
"What you can..." and "What you can't...."
Our family heirlooms had to stay.
So we left things which were simply "a burden" for us—
And so "valuable" for the USSR!
The small packages that Mothers gave, as well as
canned food and medical supplies;
All these things the custom officer took away.
And so he does even with the baby's doll—
Nowhere is the baggage checked this way!
All the suitcases and bags were shaken,
So that everything should remain there.
And then, all our torment was over...
And we flew away!

Vienna met us with friendship.
All you need there is a birth certificate—
to prove your name.
In Italy, we rented apartments for a million,
and spent very little for food.
HIAS† helped us get along,
encouraging us to spend a few months,
bathing in the sea and admiring nature.

So we lived there trembling,
Waiting for the consul to call and say
we had the right to come to the USA—
There were so many problems and delays;
Though we sold our things for next to nothing,
We had so much to do and see;
At last, permission was finally granted,
Our dream came true...and we were free!

But people are used to always being dissatisfied with something:
No trains...no subway...no rapid transit,
So many products, and kinds of food,
vegetables and fruit for every mood....
But, also, no lines to wait in at all!
It's difficult to find a job,
No material possessions (Thanks to Gorbachev!)
and the language is different, the people despair;
We must start again, though we don't know where.
But we thank G–d we are now on the way
to a better life and a happier day!

*OVIR—Dept. of Visa and Registration
†HIAS—Hebrew Immigrant Aid Society

Translation by Yeugenia Romm and Rosalie Sogolow

*Esfir Dynkina (left) and
Inna Eydus.*

Afterword:
Journey's End

With halting steps, Russia's fledgling democracy treads gingerly into a nebulous tomorrow. The country stands with one foot in the new world and one in the old. The once-regimented machinery is broken, and no one is quite sure how to fix it. Products which were virtually impossible to obtain only a short time ago are now readily available—but at an exhorbitant price. With staggering inflation and a mistrust of government, where banks containing life savings can close without warning and large-denomination bills can suddenly be declared worthless, it seems understandably prudent to plunk down precious rubles for automobiles, VCRs and TVs and let tomorrow take care of itself. Who will be in power next year? People shrug their shoulders and say, *"Pazhevyom oo-veedim!"* ("We will live and we will see!").

The new revolution does not enjoy unanimous support, any more than the first unprecedented revolution of 1917. Despite seventy-five years of Communist domination, the country has not forgotten its history. There are many who would like to return to the old ways. At least, they feel, there was order and not so much crime or hunger. Anxieties increase as a new breed of criminal rules the streets. And with less restriction and more discomfort, there are always those that look for someone to blame. While an undercurrent of anti-Semitism has been present throughout Russian history, there is a great fear that it is, once again, returning with greater force. Jews enjoy more religious freedom today, but still look over their shoulders and worry about what the future will bring.

During these times of political, social, cultural and economic upheaval, the present and the past are still intimately linked. A country that boasts of modern accomplishments, like sending men into space, still finds peasants living in places that look no different today than they did a century ago. They still have no running water or any modern conveniences. They never understood the old "system," and are equally unfazed by the new one. For them it's as though time has stood still.

But for our modern-day emigrés, time has not stood still, except in the recesses of their own minds. They've made their journey that began in the shtetl and now brings them apprehensively to a new home in "the Golden Land." Looking back and remembering means seeing both the good and the bad. But all of these images are part of our heritage, a precious reminder that the past still lives on. It is our legacy, and one that we proudly pass to the next generation. Our memories of the *Rodina*...the Motherland...the place that was home.

Contributors

	Occupation	From	Birthplace or Family Origin (if different)
Abramzon, Israel	Engineer/Economist	Leningrad	Uhoviche, Byelorussia
Alexandravskaya, Malvina	Engineer	St. Petersburg	Orechev, Ukraine
Altshuller, Boris	Plant Manager	Vilnius, Lithuania	Ukraine
Belogolovsky, Faina	Engineer/Economist	Moscow	
Belyavskaya, Yelena	Architect	Moscow	Kursk, Nezhin
Bezymenskaia, Mira	Surgeon	Moscow	Bobrusk, Byelorussia
Blekh, Ita	Factory Worker	Odessa	
Chernomordik, Asya	Engineer	St. Petersburg	Litsevo, Byelorussia
Dolberg, Gusta	Engineer/Economist	St. Petersburg	Ghmerinka, Ukraine
Dreyzner, Nora	Building Engineer	Moscow	
Drizo, Klara	Physician	Odessa	
Dubrovski, Michael	Contruction Engineer	St. Petersburg	
Dynkina, Esfir	Technical Designer	St. Petersburg	Dvinsk, Latvia
Eydus, Inna	Oncologist	Leningrad	Ukraine
Fayner, Tamara	English Teacher	Kharkov, Ukraine	Ostrog, Ukraine
Faynshteyn, Rita	Metallurgical Engineer	Odessa	Ochakov, Ukraine
Feldman, Rosa Zaks	Teacher	Kirgezia, Russia	Pietrykow, Poland
Fiterman, Meri	Pediatrician	Kiev	
Gelb, Daisy	Computer Operator	Tallinn, Estonia	
Gelb, Judith	Pediatrician	Tallinn, Estonia	
Ginzberg, Tirca		Belgrade, Yugoslavia	
Goldman, Feyga	Barber	Minsk	
Goldshteyn, Rosa	Gastroenterologist	Moscow	Kamentsk-Podolsk, Ukr.
Gorlin, Rita	Nuclear Engineer	Moscow	Izaslvl, Ukraine
Gouberman, Dora	Hat Maker	Moscow	Kamentsk-Podolsk, Ukr.
Gurfinkel, Juliya	Chemical Engineer	Kiev	Odessa
Gutman, Stalina	Engineer	Kiev	
Herman, Vivian	Yiddish Teacher	New Hampshire	Slavuta/Suslav, Ukraine
Kagan, Moisey	Physician	St. Petersburg	Nevel, Russia
Kantorovich, Genia	Car Parts Worker	Riga, Latvia	
Kashlinsky, Isaac	Electrical Engineer	Kharkov, Ukraine	
Kashlinsky, Lucy	Economist	Kursk, Russia	
Khasin, Maria	Electrical Engineer	St. Petersburg	Vitebsk, Byelorussia
Khasin, Zalman	Electrical Engineer	St. Petersburg	Veliky Looky, Russia
Khodosh, Victor	Mechanic	Minsk	Bobruysk, Byelorussia
Khorol-Sharal, Jenny	Radio Engineer	St. Petersburg	Cherniga, Ukraine/Odessa
Kinberg, Mikhail	Otolaryngologist	Odessa	Kiev/Odessa
Kinberg, Rosa	Ophthalmologist	Odessa	Ukraine
Khlebovich, Lilya	Nurse	Kirovgrad, Ukraine	Znamenka, Ukraine
Kochevrina, Yeugenia	Electrical Engineer	Moscow	
Kogan, Victor	Builder	Odessa	Bershad, Ukraine/Moldavia
Kouchnir, Matvei	Railroad Worker	Tashkent, Ukraine	Mahknovka
Krasner, Alex	Surgeon	St. Petersburg	
Krol, Maria	Teacher	Kharkov, Ukraine	
Kruker, Ides	Accountant	Odessa	
Kumkes, Solomon	Editor	Moscow	Slutsk, Belarus
Kutikov, Arkady	Design Engineer	Kiev	Buda Koshelev, Byelorussia
Levin, Sofia	Pediatrician	St. Petersburg	Ekaterinoslav, Ukraine
Litserman, Maria	Engineer	Moscow	
Litvak, Yefim	Circus Manager	Odessa	Ribnitsa, Moldavia
Lurye, Rachel	Engineer	Tallinn, Estonia	
Markman, Patricia	Teacher	New Jersey	Bessarabia/Ukraine
Mass, Basya	Economist	Moscow	
Matov, Edit	Shipbuilding Engineer	Moscow	
Matov, Ilya	Shipbuilding Engineer	Moscow	Ekaterinoslav, Ukraine

Melitseva, Liya	Teacher	Riga, Latvia	
Menshikov, Irina	Speech Therapist	St. Petersburg	Zaporozhe, Ukraine
Menshikov, Rem	Ship Pilot	St. Petersburg	
Menshikov, Irina	Speech Therapist	St. Petersburg	
Moyzhes, Boris	Professor, Physics	St. Petersburg	
Neyman, Maina	Radio Engineer	St. Petersburg	
Nudelman, Etya	Pediatrician	Kiev	
Nudelman, Semyon	Mechanic	Kiev	
Okin, Anna	Economist	Moscow	
Orkis, Lyudmila	Customs Office Worker	Odessa	
Osipova, Vera	Professor of Physics	Baku, Azerbaijan	Piatygorsk, Caucasus
Ozeryanskaya, Zoya	Librarian	Donetsk, Ukraine	Vitebsk, Byelorussia
Pasternak, Mila	Engineer	Odessa	
Petrushanskaya, Mina	Economist/Engineer	Kazan, Tatarstan	
Petrushanskiy, Bentsion	Design Engineer	Kazan, Tatarstan	
Polovets, Juliya	Physician	St. Petersburg	Mogilev, Byelorussia
Popova, Liliya	Tour Guide	St. Petersburg	
Rabkina, Liba	Bookkeeper	Tallinn, Estonia	Rechitza, Byeorussia
Rakhaylov, Roman	Engineer	Kharkov, Ukraine	
Rakhaylova, Frederika	Contruction Engineer	Kharkov, Ukraine	
Reyzis, Manya	Pediatrician	Odessa	
Romm, Yeugenia	Teacher	Odessa	
Rozenblyum, Galya	Teacher	Minsk	Gomel, Byelorussia
Segal, Leonid	Mechanical Engineer	St. Petersburg	Moscow
Shapiro, Berta	Bookkeeper	Odessa	Moldavia
Shapiro, Galina	Design Engineer	Leningrad	
Sheer, Riva	Dept. Store Manager	Tallinn, Estonia	Rujew, Latvia
Shulman, Mila	Construction Planner	Moscow	
Shur, Iosef	Engineer	Riga, Latvia	Kadino, Mogilev dist.
Shvarts, Gisya	Bookkeeper	St. Petersburg	Krementchung, Ukraine
Slutsker, Sonya	Engineer	Odessa	
Smolyanitsky, Mark	Engineer	Odessa	
Sogolow, Rosalie	Teacher	Chicago, Illinois	Dubrovitsa/Laudizhinka
Sverdlov, Leah	Pediatrician	St. Petersburg	
Tokar, Ann	Stenographer	Luvov, Ukraine	
Trilesnik, Berta	Engineer	Moscow	Klichev, Byelorussia
Tsesina, Marina	Engineer	Kiev	
Tsynman, Elena	Music Teacher	St. Petersburg	Petrograd
Vaystikh, Minna	Physician	Voronezh	
Venetskaya, Tsilya	Economist	Kharkov, Ukraine	
Vilenskaya, Larisa	Engineer	Tbilisi, Georgia	Poltava, Latvia
Vinetsky, Moisey	Engineer	Kharkov, Ukraine	
Volkhover, Raisa	Editor	Leningrad	Dvinsk, Latvia
Yaroshevskaya, Yevgenia	Teacher	Tashkent, Uzbekistan	
Yaroslavsky, Anna	Otolaryngologist	Moscow	
Zaks, Nadia		Ukraine	
Zaltsman, Samuel	Radiologist	Tallinn, Estonia	

A Brief History

The following chronology is not intended to be all-inclusive, but merely a synopsis of people and events comprising the multi-layered character that is known as "Russian."

A.D. 500–700 Displaced indigenous Baltic and Finnish tribes migrated from central Europe into the great forests north of the Russian steppe. Known as the East Slavs, they evolved into three separate groups: the westerners, known as Byelorussians; the southerners, or Ukrainians; and the easterners, sometimes known as Great Russians. The Khazar dynasty took the unusual course of adopting Judaism in about 740 A.D., and Jewish refugees from Christian Constantinople helped create a golden age of trade and learning on the Black Sea.

862 The probable founders of the first Russian state were a rugged breed of Viking traders known as the Rus. They established their rule in Novogorod. By the 10th century, when Kiev became their major center, the Rus were being assimilated by their Slavic subjects.

988–989 Kiev became a major point of contact with the Byzantine empire. The Rus prince, Vladimir, began mass conversion of his people to Orthodox Christianity. With religion, writing came to Russia in the form of the Cyrillic alphabet.

1237 The Mongols, led by Batu Khan, grandson of the infamous Ghengis Khan, plundered their way through Kievian Russia, including the young river fort of Moscow. For more than two centuries the grand princes of a fragmented Russia endured humbling vassalage to the Tatar Khanate of the Golden Horde.

1462–1505 The Tatar yoke loosened and fell. Grand Prince Ivan III of Moscow, often called "Ivan the Great," expanded Muscovite Russia by annexing neighboring princedoms.

1533–1584 The first Russian to be crowned tsar, Ivan IV, earned the sobriquet "the Terrible" during a long reign of tyranny and reform. By opening the door to Siberia, he launched Russia on its path as a multi-ethnic empire.

1613 Mikhail Romanov, father of a dynasty that would rule Russia for three centuries, succeeded to the throne.

1682 Six-foot-eight Peter the Great, an intelligent and charismatic man, almost single-handedly pulled Russia into the European community. Obsessed with his vision of a great sea power, Peter built Russia's first navy and secured access to the Baltic Sea. He then built St. Petersburg, his "window on the West." He made it his capital in 1712.

1762–1796 Catherine II, "The Great," presided over a period of cultural and territorial growth. During her reign, Russian sovereignty extended west to absorb much of the Polish and Lithuanian commonwealth. Huge numbers of Russian peasants and German immigrants were settled in the Ukraine and along the Volga and the Black Sea. A large influx of Jews suddenly found themselves living in Russia.

1812 Napoleon invaded with a French force of more than half a million, including large numbers of Poles anxious to regain independence. Only one major battle was fought. The enemies occupied a burning and deserted Moscow. With the onset of an early winter, the French retreated across the Russian plain, pursued all the way to Paris by the Russian Army. More than ninety percent of the French forces perished along the way. In Moscow, the Triumphal Arch commemorates the year—also celebrated by Tchaikovsky's *1812 Overture*.

1812–1855 The militaristic Nicholas I helped free Greece from Turkish rule, but died during his army's stalemated battle with the Turks in the Crimean War.

1820–1900 Russian literature of the nineteenth century produced remarkable talents, able to mirror the distinctive qualities of Russian life: Aleksandr Pushkin, Nikolay Gogol, Anton Chekhov, Fyodor Dostoevsky and Leo Tolstoy, to name a few, became beloved spokesmen for their times.

1861 Tsar Alexander II signed an historic proclamation emancipating the serfs, who by then totaled more than a third of the Russian population. A wave of radical terrorism arose, sustained by socialist members of the upper classes.

1881 Tsar Alexander II was assassinated, after which a series of disturbances began that made the world familiar with the chilling word "pogrom."

1881–1923 Jews began leaving in large numbers. Over two million people left Russia for America between 1881 and 1923, fleeing the persecution of organized massacres and looking for a better life.

This history brings us up to the period during which many of our writers and their parents lived.

1905–1917 Filled with resentment against Nicholas II and humiliated by defeats in the Russo–Japanese War, Russia was ripe for rebellion. Revolution swept through the streets of St. Petersburg and Moscow. In the confusion following abdication of the tsar, Vladimir Ilyich Lenin, a Marxist who had been living abroad, used the Bolshevik Party to seize power from the provisional government. Nicholas II, his family and servants were arrested and later murdered.

1921–1924 A bloody civil war raged until 1921. The following year, the Union of Soviet Socialist Republics was formed, with Russia the largest of its republics. Lenin, as head of that regime, remained dedicated to Communist World Revolution until his death in 1924.

1922–1953 Groomed for leadership by Lenin, Joseph Stalin assumed control of the Communist party from 1922 to 1953. The native Georgian pushed aside all rivals, and by the late 1920s was the unchallenged dictator with unlimited power. Part of his scheme to transform the country involved forced collectivization of agriculture. It was government policy during his regime to forbid Jews access to universities or advancement in their jobs. His reign of terror cost at least twenty million lives.

1941–1944 Germany's invasion of Russia in June 1941 caught Stalin by surprise. Hitler had promised non-aggression and trade in the 1939 German–Soviet Pact. The German army was eventually turned back—but at a cost of about twenty-five million Soviet lives. There wasn't a person alive in Russia who was not affected by that war, including Russian Jews. Nearly every family experienced the loss of relatives and friends.

1980–1991 After years of economic stagnation, Mikhail Gorbachev emerged in 1985 advocating glasnost (openness) and perestroika (restructuring.) These policies, plus the reduction of global tensions, won him the Nobel Peace Prize in 1990. But these same policies also had the effect of resurrecting long dormant feelings of ethnic pride and led to a rebirth of nationalism. They spelled the beginning of the end for the seventy-five-year reign of communism.

1991 Following the overthrow of the old communist regime, Boris Yeltsin assumed control of the "new democracy." As the first democratically elected president of the Commonwealth of Independent States, he faces the challenge of steering the country on a bold new course. At this writing, there is much doubt as to the longevity of his tenure or the future of a country struggling with its awakening into the modern world. As the Russian proverb states: *"Pazhevyom...oo-veedim"* —"We will live...and we will see."

Metric/U.S. Equivalents

Weights

5 gr	=	1 tsp
28.35 gr	=	1 oz
50 gr	=	1¾ oz
100 gr	=	3½ oz
200 gr	=	7 oz
227 gr	=	8 oz
500 gr	=	1 lb, 1 oz
1 kg	=	2 lb, 3¾ oz (2.2 pounds)
4 oz	=	¼ lb
8 oz	=	½ lb
16 oz	=	1 lb (453.59 grams, 45 kg)

Fluid Measures

1 deciliter	=	6 Tbs plus 2 tsp
1/4 liter	=	1 cup plus 2¼ tsp
1/2 liter	=	1 pint plus 4½ tsp
1 liter	=	1 qt plus 4 Tbs
4 liters	=	1 gallon plus 1 cup
10 liters	=	2½ gallons plus 2½ cups (approx)

OTHER EQUIVALENTS TO REMEMBER

4 sticks of butter equals 1 cup	8 Tbs of butter equals 1 stick
1 stick of butter equals ½ cup melted	2 sticks of butter equals 1 cup melted

Pinch or dash	=	less than ⅛ tsp
3 tsp	=	1 Tbs
2 Tbs	=	1 fluid oz
4 Tbs	=	¼ cup
5 Tbs	=	⅓ cup plus 1 tsp
12 Tbs	=	¾ cup
16 Tbs	=	1 cup

1 cups	=	8 oz (approx. 1 "Russian glass")
2 cups	=	1 pint, or 16 fluid oz, or 236.6 ml
2 pints	=	1 quart
1 quart	=	32 oz, or 4 cups, or 1.06 liters
4 quarts	=	1 gallon, or 3.79 liters

Glossary

Following are some cooking terms as well as some Russian, Hebrew and Yiddish (Jewish) words or expressions which may seem unfamiliar. We have also included a few historical references which may have been used in the book. ([R] denotes Russian, [Y] denotes Yiddish and [H] Hebrew.)

Adjust To taste before serving and add seasoning as needed.

Ahfakomen [H] The hidden matzo during the Passover seder—a favorite part of the evening for the children. The one who finds the hidden treasure is rewarded with a special treat.

Aspic A preparation made with a liquid to which gelatin has been added.

Aubergine The French word for "eggplant."

Bahnya [R] Bath or bath house.

Bake To cook by dry oven heat.

Bar Mitzvah [H] Religious ceremony where a thirteen-year-old boy becomes an "adult" member of the religious community, according to tradition.

Baste To brush liquid or drippings over food as it cooks to prevent drying.

Bat Mitzvah [H] Similar religious ceremony for girls, adopted in the US in the Reform movement.

Bind To use a sauce, such as mayonnaise or cream, to hold other ingredients together.

Blend To mix various ingredients together until smooth.

Blini [R] A thin crepe-like pancake. Can be served with or without filling.

Blintz/Blinchiky [Y/R] A crepe-like pancake, usually filled with cheese, fruit, caviar or meat.

Blyudo [R] Course or dish. (plural: Blyuda)

Boil To heat liquid until bubbles break the surface (212°F/100°C).

Bolsheviks Under Lenin's leadership they stressed a more extremist revolutionary Marxism. In 1919, the Bolshevik party was renamed the Communist Party.

Boodtye Zdarovi! [R] Toast meaning "Be healthy!"

Borscht A Russian soup, usually of beets or cabbage but can contain other ingredients.

Braise To brown in fat and then cook covered on top of the stove or in the oven in some liquid.

Brown To cook at high heat, usually on top of the stove or under broiler until touched with brown color.

Butterfly To split food down the center, almost but not quite all the way through so that the two halves can be opened flat.

Cantonists Soldiers of the tsar's army.

Caviar Roe or fish eggs. Can be black, red or yellow, depending on the fish.

Chai [R] Tea.

Challah [Y] A braided egg bread, traditionally served on holidays or the Sabbath.

Cheder [Y] Hebrew or Jewish school.

Cholent [Y] A slow-cooked dish of meat and potatoes, and sometimes beans.

Chop To cut into small pieces with a knife or chopper. More coarse than "minced."

Chremsel [Y] Deep fried fritter, made from matzo meal and served at Passover.

Chuppa [H] Canopy under which the traditional Jewish wedding ceremony is performed. Symbolizes the home, or sanctuary.

Coat To dip in flour, crumbs or other dry ingredient. Also to cover with sauce or aspic. **Coating** with flour helps meats brown more quickly while sealing in the juices.

Combine To mix together two or more ingredients.

Compote Stewed dried fruits.

Cossacks (R) One of the war-like pastoral people of the Russian steppes, skillful as horsemen and used as cavalry troops.

Cream To beat butter or fat either alone or with sugar or other ingredient until smooth and creamy.

Crumble To break up into little pieces with the fingers.

Dacha [R] Country home.

Dilute To weaken or thin by adding liquid.

Dissolve To melt or liquefy. To pass a solid into solution, as sugar or salt into water.

Dobra Pazhalovet! [R] Welcome with good will.

Dosvidanya [R] Goodbye (Until we see each other again.)

Dot To distribute some bits (usually butter) over surface of food.

Dust To coat very lightly in flour, sugar or other powdery mixture.

Entree The main course of a meal.

Fillet A boneless piece of meat, chicken or fish.

Filter To strain through several thicknesses of cloth.

Flake To break into small pieces with a fork.

Flute To make a decorative edge on pies or pastries.

Fold or Fold In To mix a light ingredient into a heavier one. As adding beaten egg whites to a batter.

Fry To cook in a skillet with some butter or fat, usually over a medium or high heat.

Galushki [R] Dumplings.

Garneer [R] Side dish.

Garnish To add something to a dish as a final decorating touch.

Gebairnya [R] Old term meaning province or region (as in Kiev Gebairnya).

Gefilte [Y] Stuffed, as in gefilte fish.

Gelatin All fresh bones of meat, fish or poultry contain some natural gelatin which is released when cooked in liquid. This causes some soups or stews to become firm or "jelly-like." In American markets it usually comes as a powder that is dissolved in liquid.

Giblets The heart, liver and gizzard of fowl or small game.

Glaze To cover food with a glossy coating, such as syrup or aspic. Also to brush pastry with milk or beaten egg to make it shiny.

Gorilka [R] Ukrainian vodka.

Grate To cut food into small particles by using a grater.

Grease To rub with butter or shortening to keep food from sticking to the pan while baking.

Grebbinis [Y] Fried cracklings from chicken fat.

Grind To turn into fine particles by putting through a grinder or food processor. Russians often use the term "mince" to mean the same thing.

Hors d'oeuvre A French word meaning appetizer. In Russian, "Zakooski."

Kasha [R] Cracked buckwheat groats, or wheat or other grain.

Kashas [H] Questions. During the Passover seder, the youngest child traditionally asks the "four kashas." ("Why is this night different from all other nights?"etc.)

Kazakhs [R] See *Cossacks*.

Khleb [R] Bread.

Knaidlach [Y] Matzo balls.

Knead To work with the hands, usually dough, until smooth.

Knishes [Y] Strudel or pastry dough wrapped around cheese, rice, meat or potato filling and baked.

Komsomol Communist youth league.

Kosher Food prepared or processed according to Jewish ritual law.

Kotlyete [R] Generally refers to chicken or meat patty. Also called a "chop" or "cutlet."

Kreplach [Y] Filled pasta-type dumplings. Similar to Russian pelmeni.

Kugel [Y] A baked pudding or casserole, usually of noodles, potatoes, bread or vegetable. Not to be confused with a custard-type pudding.

Latke [Y] Pancake, usually potato.

Leaven To lighten the texture and increase the volume of breads, cakes and cookies by using baking powder, soda or yeast.

Lekhah [R] Honey cake.

Lokshen [Y] Noodles.

Lox Smoked salmon.

"Luft Menschen" [Y] Refers to men who in the shtetl had no trade and lived as if "by air," usually existing from hand to mouth.

Mamaloshen [Y] The Yiddish language. Literally "mother tongue."

Marinate To steep in a spicy liquid for several hours or until food absorbs the flavoring. The steeping ingredients are called "marinade."

Matzo Flat unleavened bread, traditionally eaten by Jews during Passover.

Matzo meal Flour made from matzo.

Melamed [H] Teacher.

Mikvah [H] Ritual bath.

Mince To cut into fine pieces. More finely cut than "chopped."

Minyan [H] The ten men required in order for any official Jewish religious service to take place.

Mir [R] Peace.
Mishpocha [Y] The entire extended family.
Mix To stir together.
Mogen David [H] Star of David.

Napeetki [R] Beverages.

October Revolution The uprising which toppled the rule of the Tsar and led to the birth of Communism in October 1917. All private property was nationalized at this time.

Pale of Settlement Area in the Ukraine where majority of Jews were segregated in small towns before the Revolution in 1917.
Pare To cut the peeling from fruits or vegetables.
Pazhaloosta [R] Please. Also, "You're welcome."
Peel To remove the peeling from fruits or vegetables by pulling off rather than cutting away.
Pelmeni [R] Filled pasta-type dumplings.
Petlura's Gang Roving band of Ukrainian nationalists who terrorized Jews.
Pirog [R] Pie.
Piroshki [R] Small pies.
Poach To cook submerged in simmering liquid.
Pogrom Organized massacre of helpless people.
Preahtnova Appeteéta! Good appetite!
Preheat To bring oven to desired temperature before adding food.
Prick To pierce with a fork to keep pastry from shrinking or to free juices during baking.
Puree To grind to paste by putting through a blender or food processor.
Pushkin Beloved Russian poet. Also a town near St. Petersburg named for him.

Ragout A hearty brown stew.
Red Army Soldiers of the Revolutionary forces. Also Soviet Army.
Render To cook foods so that they give up their fat.
Rissole [R] A filled sweet or savory deep-fat fried pie or turnove₁.
Roast To cook uncovered in the oven by dry heat.
Roe Fish eggs.
Roux A butter and flour paste, used as thickener for soups and stews.

Samovar Literally "self boiler." Used in Russia to make tea.
Sauté To cook small portions of meats, poultry, fish or vegetables in a small amount of oil or fat until done. Usually done over a low heat.
Score To make shallow cuts over the surface of food in a crisscross pattern.
Seder [H] Traditional meal during Jewish holiday of Passover.
Shabbos [Y] The Sabbath, Saturday. (Hebrew: Shabbat)
Shmaltz [Y] Animal fat.
Shoychet [Y] Person who slaughters chickens in the prescribed kosher way.
Shutt-arein (Y) Age-old form of measurement. By the eye; literally, "throw in."

Shtetl Small Jewish village or town.

Simmer To cook food in liquid over low heat.

Skewer To thread chunks of food on long metal or wooden pins.

Skim To scoop fat, froth or other material from the surface of a liquid with a spoon.

Sliver To cut in fine, thin pieces.

Smetana [R] Russian sour cream.

Sol [R] Salt.

Spaceeba [R] Thank you.

Steam To cook, covered over a small amount of boiling liquid so that the steam does the cooking.

Steep To let tea leaves, coffee grounds, herbs or spices stand in hot liquid until their flavor is extracted.

Steppe Vast tract of seemingly endless land, generally level and without forests.

Stock The broth strained from stewed or boiled meats, seafood, poultry or vegetables.

Strain To separate fluids from solids by passing through a sieve.

Tanta [Y] Aunt.

Tenderize To make tender, especially meats, usually by pounding with a mallet. Also by adding acidic marinade to soften the tissues.

Torah [H] Jewish holy scriptures.

Tsar (also czar). Emperor. Ruler of Russia before the Revolution of 1917. The last Russian tsar was Nicholas II, who was murdered along with his family and servants.

Tsimmis [Y] Sweetened baked vegetables and meat, often with dried fruits. Also idiomatically, "a big deal!" "A gantsa tsimmis."

Tsouris [Y] Trouble.

Varnishkas [Y] Pasta shaped like bows.

Whip To beat until stiff.

White Army Soldiers supporting the tsar.

White nights The long daylight hours experienced in the northern cities during the summer nights, where darkness barely comes.

Yiddish The Jewish language.

Zakooski [R] Appetizers. Literally, "little bites."

Zest The colored part of citrus rind used as a flavoring. Also the oil pressed from it.

Bibliography

The background material found in this book came from a variety of sources. Among them:

Dimont, Max I. *Jews, God and History.* Signet Books, N.Y., 1962.

Edwards, Mike, "Mother Russia." *National Geographic,* Washington, D.C., Feb. 1991.

Edwards, Mike, "Pushkin." *National Geographic,* Washington, D.C., Sept. 1992.

Howe, Irving, *World of Our Fathers.* Simon and Schuster, N.Y., 1976.

Howe, Irving and Libo, Kenneth, *How We Lived.* New American Library, N.Y., 1979.

Nelan, Bruce; Kohan, John; Aikman, Otto Friedrich, "Soviet Disunion." *Time Magazine,* N.Y., Mar. 12, 1990.

Vadrot, Claude-Marie; Ivleva, Victoria, *Russia Today.* Atomium Books, Inc., Wilmington, Delaware, 1988.

Yarmolinsky, Avrahm. *Pushkin, Poems, Prose & Plays.* Random House, Inc., N.Y., 1936.

Index of Recipes